Classic Motorcycling

A Guide for the 21st Century

Rex Bunn

*With a Foreword by
Hugh Anderson*

Panther Publishing

Published by Panther Publishing Ltd in 2007
Panther Publishing Ltd
10 Lime Avenue
High Wycombe
Buckinghamshire HP11 1DP, UK

© Rex Bunn

The rights of the author have been asserted in accordance with the Copyright, Designs and Patents Act 1988.

Dedication

To Jenny for creating the writing space for me; to Elsie and Lyle and also to Tony Parker my surgeon-mentor, who taught me to analyse and question. I never forgot.

Acknowledgments

Many riders' ideas and advice shaped these pages, not least Rollo who had he not been publisher, may have become co-author. Peter Thoeming wisely reviewed the concept stage. Members of the BSA Club of NSW, especially Trevor and Stuart assisted more than they knew. Peter and other BSA club members contributed advice and photos. Simon, John, Chas and other Rotorua Classic Motorcycle Club members assisted with New Zealand and technical advice at crucial points. Hills Ulysses Club members provided part of the template for chapters 5 and 11. Rob Cochrane of BSAOCNZ deserves special thanks for his dual BSA and VMX advice and photos of the Kiwi scene. Dale and Greg at MAW Sydney helped with technical resources for chapter eight. Tim of British Spares gave sage advice whenever I called. Darren of Southern Spares encouraged the project and introduced author and publisher. The VMCC, LTNZ, StatsNZ, ABS, BTS and state bodies, StatCan, VJMC, DVLA, DETR, DFT, ONS, and RTA all assisted with the interminable statistical enquiries for chapters 11 and 12. Vital First Aid contributed ideas and proofed the First Aid section. Thanks to Hugh Anderson, for agreeing to write the foreword, when the project was at an early stage. In a non-fiction work, there will be errors and omissions, despite repeated proof-reading. All brickbats should be directed at me. People in the anecdotes and stories are real, but names are changed among the anecdotes, to assure anonymity. Only the story-teller, can associate his name with his story, and assess any licence I took.

Rex Bunn, Sydney, 19 November 2006.

Cover photographs: Image of number 87 on the cover by Stephen Piper of SP Photographics. Triumph engine is a mid 60s Bonneville, photo by R Turner.

ISBN 97809547912 8 5

Contents

Foreword   v
1 Why Are Classic Bikes So Popular?   **1**
2 Choosing The Right Classic Bike   **4**
Classic Scooters   4
Harley-Davidson   4
Royal Enfield   6
Hinckley Triumph   6
Modern or Classic?   7
Classic Availability   7
Recency   8
Costs   8
Budgeting   9
Classic Advertising Channels   10
Restore or Ride Away?   11
Ergonomics   12
Of Legs and Seats   13
Image and Riding Style   15
Matching Classics to Rides   15
Road Traffic Conditions   16
Brakes and Suspension   17
Originality   18
Completeness   19
Security   19
Recognition   19
Reliability   20
Ease of Starting   20
Kick starting for duffers   21
3 Where And How To Buy Your
First Classic Bike   **24**
Classic Motorcycle Shops   24
Newspapers   25
Magazines   26
Auctions   27
EBay   29
Fossicking   30
Motorcycle Swap-Meets   31
Classic Motorcycle Clubs   32
What Defines a Classic Motorcycle?   33
How to Assess a Classic bike?   34
Assessing a bike in fifteen minutes   34
Completing the Purchase   43
Classic Bike Negotiation   43
4 Licencing, Registration And Insurance   **45**
UK Classic Registration System   45
USA Classic Registration System   46

Australian Classic Registration System   46
New Zealand Classic Registration System   47
Rider Licensing   49
The duffers guide to passing your
motorcycle test   50
Classic Motorcycle Insurance   53
Breakdown and Salvage   54
International Aspects of Licensing,
Registration and Insurance   55
Reciprocal Motoring Association
Membership   55
Shipping your Bike Overseas and
International Documentation   56
5 Bonding With Your Bike   **57**
6 Global Resources For Classic
Motorcycles   **70**
EBay   70
Other Electronic Channels   71
Autojumbles, Swap-meets and Auctions   71
Guide to swap-meet etiquette   72
Pattern Parts, NOS Parts and Used Parts   74
Tricks of the Retail Parts Trade for
Canny Buyers   78
Australian Motorcycling Resources   80
New Zealand Resources   86
United Kingdom Resources   88
North American Resources   90
7 Riding, Survival And Shibboleths   **92**
Who Rides Classic Bikes?   92
Do classic riders take riding training?   94
Motorcycle Training and Accident Risk   94
Classic Riders and Accident Risk   98
Are Classic Riders Put at Risk by
Today's Rider Training?   100
Throttle friction control   101
Braking techniques   102
Cornering lines   102
Signalling   103
Top Tips for Classic Riding Survival   104
Do Crash Helmets Cause, as Well
as Prevent Injuries?   106
Classic Near Misses   111
Classic Riding Ergonomics   113
Change Blindness and the
Visual Scratchpad   115
Trout fishing and classic road craft   116

First Aid 116
   First aid kit 119

8 From Waders To Kevlar **120**
Motorcycle Clothing of Yesteryear ... 120
   Waders 120
   Riding coats 120
   The Brando jacket 121
   Services clothing 121
   Leggings and chaps 121
   Waterproof overpants 122
Classic Riding Clothing for Today 122
Clothing Technologies 123
Shopping Channels 124
What to wear 126
   Leathers 126
   Jackets 127
   Leather vests 128
   Gloves 128
   Trousers 129
   Helmets 130
   Neckwear 132
   Boots 132
   Rainwear 132
   Prostheses 133
There's Leather and There's Leather ... 135

9 Maintenance At Home And
On The Road **137**
Maintenance Information 137
The Garage Toolkit 139
The Bike Toolkit 144
Top Tasks for Classic Bikes 145
   Gapping the tappets 146
   Adjusting the clutch 148
   Wheel alignment and balancing 151
   Carburettor care 154
   Monobloc and Concentric issues ... 158
   Tuning an Amal Carburettor 159
   Troubleshooting a persistent carburettor
     problem 160
   Fuel additives and valve seat recession ... 161
   What fuel to run in classic bikes? ... 162
   Oil filtering 162
   Air and fuel filtering 163
   Keeping nuts and bolts in place 164
   Cable care 165
   Tyres 167
   Classic oils, greases and fluids 167
On Breaking Down 170
   Five break down steps 170
   It's up to you, Doctor! 170
   Electrical system breakdowns 171

   Fuel system breakdowns 172
   Mechanical system breakdowns 173
   Tyre breakdowns 173
Listening to The Engine 174
   Tappets 174
   Knocks and Noises 175

10 Wherever Your Classic Bike
Takes You **179**
The Classic Club Scene 180
Solo Riding 181
Rallies 182
Concours 184
Offroad Riding and the VMX Scene ... 186
Circuit and Road Racing 2006
   A classic racing season downunder ... 190
Street Racing 194
Very Long Distance Riding 199
International Riding 202

11 Classic Motorcycle Survival **205**
United Kingdom Survivors 205
Australian Survivors 208
New Zealand Survivors 210
World Conservation 215
Classic Bikes in Other Countries 217
Basket Cases 220
A Note on Scrappage 221
A DIY Guide for Classic Bikes
   in Any Country 223
Methodology Used in the Classic Bike
   Survival Model 225

12 The Bonnie Index: Consumer
Price Index For Classic Bikes **236**
The British Bonnie Index 237
The Australian Bonnie Index 248
Methodology Used in the Bonnie
   Index Model 255

13 Improving Perfection: Projects
For Any Classic **258**
Theft: Protecting Classic Motorcycles
   from Villains. 259
Mudflaps, Oilflaps and Chainflaps 261
Improving Engine Breathing and
   the Bunn Breather 263
Wet Sumping and Staying Dry without
   Stripping the Engine 268
Electrical Shockers - Preventing
   Electrical Problems 270
Vibration 271
Engine Feedback: Adding Sensors
   to Your Engine 275

14 Some Thoughts For The Road **277**

Foreword

The Classic Movement

Opportunities in later life to revisit the most pleasant periods of our youth are rare indeed. Happily, via the Classic Motorcycle movement many thousands worldwide have had this pleasure.

Back to the Begining...

During the 1939-40 period, government agents throughout Australasia commandeered virtually every motorcycle that could be found for military use. (Some were hurriedly dismantled and hidden by their canny owners). From early 1945 these machines were being offered to the public by tender: the local station-master, an avid enthusiast purchased eight of them. I grew up on a farm with a well-equipped workshop which had become a gathering place for local young men. Many, like my older brother, had recently been demobbed from various services but all of them it seemed had a similar interest, motorcycling.

On a day I clearly remember, a truck arrived at the farm loaded with the station-master's purchases. The hoist was raised and the precious cargo gently lowered to the ground. All the bikes still had their original factory finish. All pre-war of course, and in reasonable condition. There was a bronze head Rudge Ulster, a CSI Norton, purchased by my brother, an Ariel, Velocette, New Imperial, BSA, Douglas and a Francis Barnett Cruiser.

That evening excited potential buyers and admirers arrived. The bikes hadn't run for several years: two were hurriedly serviced. The first tried refused to fire a shot, the shed became very quiet. The second started first kick, and a cheer went up. Mother came out to enjoy the atmosphere but she too became caught up in the moment and was soon taking orders for tea and coffee. Mum was a motoring enthusiast, well informed and prudent in purchase: her Chevrolet always immaculate. During the coffee break, prices were negotiated. Everyone seemed to be in a highly animated state, all talking at once. Deals were done and within a few days all eight bikes were sold. More shipments followed.

Copies of The Motorcycle and other motorcycling magazines were eagerly sought and read from cover to cover. These magazines sold motorcycling in all its forms to the world in a most exciting and well-informed way. Readers felt they were very much part of a fast growing international movement. Similar groups were being formed throughout Australasia and beyond. After so many years of doom and gloom, motorcycling seemed so refreshing. What a way to kickstart a future - quite different from any that could have been envisaged a few months earlier. This was the beginning of an era when youth gained skills, earned high wages and made their own decisions. The time had come to break away from Victorian restrictions and dogma: the very air they breathed was sweetly scented with freedom. This was a time when country folk, even when on holiday, would never lock their homes for the very simple reason that a passing motorist might have mechanical bother and need to use the phone. A time when the safest place for the car key was in the ignition switch, that way it couldn't be lost

The Classic period of motorcycling was born within this social structure of trust and helpfulness. Clubs were established based on the British example, and membership grew rapidly. Maintenance, as per the instruction manuals, was carried out with care and enthusiasm and tool kits carefully packed to include those spares and tools for road side repairs. The excitement when preparing for a weekend away - the joy of you and your machine cruising the countryside, discovering what was around the next corner, beyond the next hill. In those days a rider never passed a stationary motorcyclist but always stopped to offer assistance ranging from a tow to a bed for the night. Sometimes all that was required was perhaps just a chat, a cigarette, some shared experiences and possibly to ride on together for company. Such was the trust and camaraderie.

In a very short time, trials, grass track and road race events were held. Supported by community leaders, large crowds, and the local and national press, motorcycling became ever more 'this new and exciting activity'. On a Friday evening dealers showrooms became a meeting place. Handsome, glittering, gorgeous new models arrived weekly. Technical specifications were studied: makes, models, and prices considered, endless discussion entered into. Courtship too was part of the scene. Handsome young women were attracted to this mildly rebellious, leather-clad, Brylcream-coiffured, animated, restless group.

World economies developed rapidly. By the late fifties if you didn't own a car you weren't climbing the materialistic ladder and society began to frown on us motorcyclists. We responded readily, more noise, speed and Brylcream. The hair styles and dress of rebellious American youth were adopted, and the Cafe Racer and 'Milkbar Cowboy' era began, based on powerful motorcycles, high speed and the latest rock and roll music. We had fun, developed a unique sense of humour and bugger stuffy convention. However, that age passed all too quickly and by the mid sixties demand for British motorcycles was fading away, the rockers were marrying and the bikes were seen as old fashioned and troublesome.

Revival

From the mid-Sixties on, the imaginative marketing by the Japanese factories steadily raised the profile of motorcycling worldwide. Their products were proving reliable, innovative, and fast. This had the forty and fifty year olds becoming a little restless, memories of their adventurous, independent, carefree, freedom-loving youth came flooding back. A ride on a model similar to that owned so many years before confirmed most riders weren't too old, certainly not 'past it'. The children had moved on, the mortgage was under control, so why not join in? A suitable bike was found and the restoration began.

In no time groups were formed, friendships of yesteryear renewed and Classic Clubs set up. The early to mid seventies were exciting. Classic bikes and parts were cheap and plentiful. A strong unity or bond existed within the Classic scene. Selflessness encouraged a sharing of knowledge, skills and time; no problem seemed so great that it couldn't be easily overcome by a helpful club friend. Meanwhile your own project was coming together nicely. How handsome it was, up on its stand, its shape constantly changing as finished parts were added. Now there was so much of you, the owner, painter, electrician, engineer built into it that it become a part of you. Entering the workshop each evening gave pleasure, and with more parts fitted daily the completion date grew ever nearer. Finally finished and ready to run, a group of Club members and their wives arrive to share the joy and celebrate the first start-up.

You nervously turn on the fuel tap. Have I put oil in the gearbox? Did I tighten the crankshaft nut? Will it be noisy? Will it vibrate? Will the generator charge? Would it even start? A long swinging kick, it kicks back, that's good, retard the spark a little, another kick - please go this time old girl - and it fires up, a puff of smoke, it settles down firing evenly, wow! I've done it! Your heart is pumping, hands trembling; Club friends offer their congratulations on a job well done, what a wonderful moment, those months of work but a memory. Your family now understands why you have shown such commitment, perhaps now they will see more of you. The first ride, not too far from home just in case, and then with some fine adjustments made, it gets ever better. So much more pleasure felt than ever expected. The sense of satisfaction and joy, difficult to describe but sufficient to have you starting and restarting it, taking it for an early morning run before work, and again in the evening. It runs superbly and it takes me back, I am a teenager again. Who ever would have imagined this could be, what luck, what pleasure!

By the mid nineteen sixties Japanese manufacturers dominated the World Championship Grand Prix scene in the smaller 50cc, 125cc and 250cc classes. With new technology and expense no object, they created fabulous high revving, exotic race bikes. Each factory set up a race team: competition was fierce with world market share resting on race results. Vast crowds of up to 250,000 people were drawn to the race tracks and an excited world market was created. Who wasn't impressed by the availability of these high performance multi-cylinder machines? Five and six speed gearboxes were the norm, self starters that worked and electrics that gave no bother. Quality off-road bikes became available, creating the sport of trail riding. The ability to explore hills, valleys, gold mining and historic logging sites, using long abandoned roads and tracks became a world-wide weekend hobby.

A new era, quite like that post-war period where the young and not so young were enjoying independence and new experiences. By the late nineteen eighties, as the latest models became ever more sophisticated, bigger, heavier, faster and more expensive, an enthusiasm developed for those earlier, simpler, raw motorcycles of the seventies. The Japanese classic period had begun,

We now have a world wide network of very capable clubs supported by several quality international magazines and a plethora of websites dedicated solely to historic motorcycle activities, sales and services world wide. Against this background, Rex Bunn's new book, Classic Motorcycling: A Guide for the 21st Century, shows just how much there is still to learn about our favourite pastime. I gained a great deal from it, and expect every other reader will gain likewise. Somewhere in the classic motorcycling mix, you will find your place and like myself, relive the most pleasant times of your life.

Hugh Anderson MBE,
World Champion 1963, 1964, 1965.
Hamilton, New Zealand, 2007

(Above) Hugh Anderson aboard the legendary Britten at speed. (Below) Hugh Anderson winning the Mike Hailwood Memorial Trophy at Brands Hatch in 1990. Hugh's 'knee-down' riding style was criticised by officials in the 1960s as a brash, ugly way to sit on a race bike. Look where it lead!

1 *Why Are Classic Bikes So Popular?*

"Men are said to read with a certain degree of possessiveness and a certain degree of authority. Their reading tends to confirm what they already know to be true..."
Richard Nile

Motorcycling is enjoying a resurgence everywhere. In Australia and New Zealand motorcycle sales have grown strongly since 2001. In Australia, the 2005 sales growth of 14.3% included growth of 20% in road bikes and 30% for scooters. This continues in 2006. The growth rate for road bikes as this book goes to press is 31.5% per annum. That means road bike numbers are doubling every 2.5 years. This surge has displaced off-road bikes from their leading position in Australia and New Zealand. The boom in scooters reflects population congestion in cities. Cruisers outsell sports bikes, reflecting the boom in the numbers of older riders and recreational riding. Other factors responsible for this growth include the strong economy and currency, retirees returning to riding, the 'sea and tree change' population shifts to coastal and inland towns, better roads and high fuel prices. These demographic and economic factors also exist in the UK, USA, Canada and NZ, and are driving the growth in bike demand there as well.

Reports from Australian licensing and insurance sources show demand for classic bikes is also growing at about 15% per year. As Hugh Anderson notes, this is driven by the same demographics that drive the motorcycling mainstream. Such growth in classic bikes cannot be growth in the usual sense, for most of the manufacturers are now closed. Market growth occurs via supply from restorations, imports of bikes, manufacture of replicas, the break-up of classic bike collections, museum leakages, the assembly of 'new-old' machines from parts, and supplies of 'brand new' classics from Royal Enfield for example. North America acts as a global warehouse for classic bikes and parts, reversing its imports that supported British plants into the 1970s. Of course, bikes also exit the market via 'parting out' (breaking for spares) and accidents; for example the recent tsunamis have reduced the number of classics in Asian countries. In market segments with high attrition like racing, replica manufacturing is likely to ensure the supply of bikes through this century. Meantime, the continuing availability of New Old Stock (NOS) and pattern parts for later British classics continues to support a healthy market.

It's almost a case of the customers taking over the factory. The demographics of this 'rider takeover' are interesting. It is said that today's classic riders are those who rode the bikes in their youth. Whilst undoubtedly correct for many, a look around motorcycle clubs shows this doesn't explain the resurgence in classic motorcycles entirely - especially for British machines from the 1940-1980 period. Many riders attracted to these machines were born *after* the British industry collapsed in the early sixties, and even after many classic Japanese machines had gone out of production. However, the post-WWII generation is instrumental in this market. They rode mainly British motorcycles in their youth but then gave up bikes whilst they pursued wealth, marriage, parenting and careers. Now, cashed up, and with hippy idealism they're returning to motorcycling, recapturing that 1960's zeitgeist, and once again innovating.

It's more than coincidence that the vehicles and values associated with classic (and for that matter today's) motorcycling, come from the 1960s and from the UK. The 1960s cultural decade is recorded as lasting from 1958 to 1974. These are important motorcycling dates. 1958 in the UK saw motorcycle-friendly changes in employment, income, credit, insurance and tax, working hours, new open speed-limit motorways, and helmets optional. These factors underlay the record 'Summer of '59', when 331,806 new motorcycles and scooters were sold in the UK, a record that still stands. The 1960s decade ended in 1974 with the demise of the BSA-Triumph group, and the end of innocence in Vietnam.

That period of intense social and cultural change established many values for motorcyclists. These include individual freedom, rebelling against authority, a sense of anger, a youth culture, revolution, dropping out, and sex, drugs and rock and roll. It's no surprise it was British motorcycles and pop music that characterised the 1960s counter-culture. As Marwick says in his seminal book *The Sixties (Arthur Marwick, the Sixties: Cultural Revolution in Britain, France, Italy and the United States, 1998)* the UK became the crucible of the 1960s because of it's open, secular society when compared to the USA. It also had the right motorcycles to appeal to the booming working-class pop culture. That zeitgeist continues to drive motorcycling, attracting all riders to it's potent core values.

Forty years later and in another century, we are entering a time when no one living will remember the British motorcycle industry in its heyday. It is not surprising therefore that a new classic guide is required: something akin to a motorcycling version of Old Moore's Almanac. A guide to choosing, buying, restoring, maintaining, conserving and enjoying these 'mobile works of art' into their second century. Riders need information on today's road and traffic conditions and how they affect older motorcycles. They need information on licensing and registration, parts and service; updates on classic clothing and health and safety issues, and maintenance data for the 21st century. As bike supply tightens, information on classic bike survival round the world will be vital so that we know where to look for the classic bikes of our choice. It's time to look on classic motorcycling as a global industry and market. There have been considerable swings and variations in classic bike prices since the 1970s and it would be useful to have a 'Price Index' to track sales prices. We could then make forecasts to gauge the future prices of our bikes. This book covers each of these topics, and also includes core work on ownership and technical matters for the 21st century classic rider and especially the first time owner.

The first (and really the last) book published on these topics was by Holmes and Smith in 1986 (*Collecting, Restoring and Riding Classic Motorcycles*). That's still an excellent read, though classic motorcycling has changed a lot since then. A decade later Clew and Porter published their *Classic Bike Service Guide*. This contains advice on maintenance in logbook form as well as a general service guide, with a short buying and selling section. Later Westworth published his *Classic Bike Guide*. This is again an excellent read, but two thirds of it covers marque histories. None of these books cover today's issues in classic motorcycling.

The current boom in motorcycling spills over into classic bikes, where the 'fun and freedom' aspects are intensified by greater rider involvement. The simplicity and heritage nature of classic motorcycles are special attractions. These bikes provide a masculine frame of reference in a world where many men feel displaced. A classic bike responds to male logic. The classic club provides a network of friends, qualified by a common passion. For men without a workplace focus, a classic bike may even provide a reason for living. It can make you a more 'interesting' person (a major benefit to your spouse and family!). It changes your life in unexpected ways. It's a grand adventure.

2 *Choosing The Right Classic Bike*

"The Velocette muffler is an example of 1911 Brooklands muffler design, named for the Brooklands track where riders found a muffler ten times engine capacity reduced noise without power loss. The fishtail further reduced noise." B.Buzzelli

Only a small percentage of riders ride motorcycles throughout their lives: more people daydream about a motorcycle, 'one day, when I retire...'. This book explores classic British bikes built from 1946-1980. Yet it's worth mentioning some of today's classic bikes. Makers like Harley-Davidson and Triumph make retro-models to appeal to classic riders. Royal Enfield are still building classic British singles in India with their Bullet range, and are now complianced for sale in Western countries. A growing number of classic bikers are becoming COBBERs, or 'Cross-Over Bikers' who criss-cross between modern and classic bikes and often own both together. They're often found among the BABs, or 'Born Again Bikers' who have come back to motorcycling after a period without a bike. For this group especially, it's worth browsing the modern classics before choosing a used classic British bike.

Classic Scooters

For today's 'Mods', the Vespa and Lambretta scooters that swept the world in the 1950s and 1960s are still produced. Scooter sales are booming as fuel prices inflate and cities become congested. Brisbane has recorded a 20% annual growth in scooters for some years now. China has 50% of global motorcycle production, and exports cheap scooters and lightweights much as Japan did in the 1960s. Chinese, Indian, Indonesian and Thai scooters and motorcycles dominate world production, creating a potential tipping-point for the conventional Western traffic makeup. Its conceivable many Western cities will soon resemble Italian cities, with a primary role once more for two-wheeled transport.

Harley-Davidson

These iconic bikes are low, long and twice the weight of a British classic. They can be manoeuvred easily, except on slow turns where they fall-in alarmingly on the front brake. Riders who can't lift heavy weights or have back trouble may want like Fagin, to 'review the situation'. Harley-Davidson make a wide product range with a small number of engines and frames. The range is positioned for niche markets with an 800 page catalogue of customising accessories. If that's not enough, Zodiac supply a further 800 pages of pattern accessories.

The Harley-Davidson range includes one bona fide classic - the Sportster. It's design goes back fifty years to the time Royal Enfield set up in India. In 1957 the Sportster 883cc owed it's odd capacity to a US tax concession on sub-900cc bikes. Whilst there's no truth in the rumour Phil Irving designed it by cobbling two BSA B44 engines together, it is true the famous 'peanut tank' was inspired by the BSA Bantam tank, after Harley produced a DKW/Bantam clone, the Hummer. In another less known BSA connection, Harley-Davidson reportedly purchased BSA B50 technology to develop a single for the US army.

The Sportster is positioned for classic value-shoppers. They are keenly priced to attract new riders into the brand. The design and build quality for post-2004 models is a quantum jump ahead of older Sportsters. The Sportster is still a heavyweight at 260kgs (575lbs). It cruises all day at 2,400rpm and 60mph (100kmh) without vibrating, and returns 25-30km/litre or 70mpg: a typical figure for British classics with engines half the size. The Sportster engine develops maximum torque at 3,000rpm, it's modest power matching many British classics. That engine is going to last a very long time, especially with it's extraordinarily thick barrel liner that allows over-boring by as much as an extra 300cc.

Illus. 2.1 The author's Sportster setting off on the return leg round Australia. Harley-Davidsons are favoured downunder for their long-distance reliability

Royal Enfield

The other modern-day classic bike is the Royal Enfield 500cc Bullet. I road-tested one for a week recently and, at two-thirds the Sportster price a test-ride is recommended. The Royal Enfield motorcycle plant in India was a turnkey production line transferred from the UK parent to supply bikes to the Indian army. The plant survived the UK industry demise and still makes authentic Royal Enfield bikes for export around the world. Production numbers now dwarf the parent factory's original output.

Illus. 2.2 A nice Royal Enfield Bullet visiting a BSA Rally in Australia.

The new 500cc Enfield Electra, with it's roller big end, steel conrod and high-flow oil pump is an attractive package if you care for a thumping new single at the price of a used 1960's twin. All recent road tests of the new Enfields are now positive, after a factory development program that overcame earlier criticisms on quality. The UK Bullet design offers five speeds, electric start and electronic ignition, while retaining a kick-start and even a valve lifter. It starts easily by kick or button. There's little vibration, compared to say a BSA single. It cruises at 75 mph (120kmh) and there's plenty of power for traffic-light take-offs. Friends say they are fine two-up, cruising at 60mph (100 kph). It's the nearest thing to travelling back into the 1950s and riding a new British motorcycle, straight out of a British factory.

Hinckley Triumph

The Hinckley Triumphs are developing their classic credentials with the reintroduction of the Bonneville range at Sportster prices. The Sportster, Bullet and Bonneville offer satisfying choices for many riders seeking a warranty and dealer support, along with their classic bike.

Modern Or Classic?

Choosing between modern bikes and classics, is really about one's involvement with the bike. Riders of modern bikes are insulated from their bikes by distributors, complicated service regimes and often unhelpful owner and workshop manuals. In the Ulysses club (a large Australian motorcycle club for older riders of mainly modern machines), looking at the Japanese, American, German and Italian bikes, I asked the club President which members to talk to about maintenance. He stunned me, quipping that few riders would change their oil, let alone work on the engine. So if you're looking for something you set aside in the 1960s; if you want to bond with your bike, to work on your bike and learn as you go; if you want passion, vibration, fear and breakdown - these are definitely Classic signs.

Holmes and Smith nicely caught the fascination with classic bikes twenty years ago. Their book covers the early years to 1986. History records the Classic Period started with the 1978 publication of the magazine *Classic Bike*. Just about everything has changed since then except the fascination, but Holmes's description has lasted well...

> *"...the fun of owning an old motorcycle reaches into the library and museum, the garage and workshop, the clubroom...the conscience, ...into history and into the highways and byways, both at home and abroad. It will bring untold frustration, embarrassing breakdowns, unlooked for acts of kindness by complete strangers, the inimitable satisfaction of a job well done, and the unique experience of getting about on your own machine..."*

Classic Availability

There aren't enough classic bikes coming on the market to allow great choice, particularly in the smaller marques. This prompts some riders to wait months or years, or to venture overseas to find exactly what they are looking for. Prior to this book, there really was no source of information on the international availability of classics. As a result, some classic riders may feel forced to buy in haste.

In Table 2.1, classic marques are grouped into purchasing categories by their international availability. In Chapter 12, there is further analysis of international differences in classic marque availability and prices. It is easy to see how first time buyers gravitate to the marques on the right of the table. Collectors may wait years to add a bike from marques to the left of the table. Collectors can lionise a marque in a country, and even create a shortage. In Australia, for Vincents and Velocettes up to 10% of the marque population exists in just a few individual's collections. Museums also act in this way, and the number of museum bikes is growing. In the long run, this is in the public interest, but in the short run, it can impact on buyers' choice.

Table 2.1   International Classic Availability by Marque

Category 1 Hens Teeth	Category 2 Fairly Rare	Category 3 Available	Category 4 Some Choice	Category 5 Lot of choice
Brough	Bultaco	Ariel	AJS	Triumph
Coventry	Douglas	Laverda	BMW	BSA
OK	Francis-Barnett	Moto-Guzzi	Ducati	Honda
Excelsior	Gilera	Sunbeam	Royal Enfield	Norton
Indian	Greeves	Velocette	Harley-Davidson	
Levis	James		Kawasaki	
New Imperial	Jawa		Matchless	
Norman	Panther		Suzuki	
Rudge	Rickman		Yamaha	
Scott	Triton			
Veterans	Vincent			
Pioneers	Vintage			
	Post-Vintage			

Recency

There's a dimension to marque availability, termed 'recency'. Many British marques have celebrated centenaries in the last decade, and not surprisingly more of their later models survive. Younger classics generally have better parts and technical information available. It's also worth looking for bikes towards the end of a model production series. British makers did a lot of their development work after they'd introduced a model! This makes recency a useful predictor of overall satisfaction for first-time buyers and others who prefer the ready availability of parts and expertise.

Costs

There's a classic bike to suit every rider's budget. At the entry end of the market the cost of makes and bikes differ by country. Looking at complete bikes in original running condition, in the UK the cheapest bikes are East European (CZ and MZ), early Indian Enfield models, less favoured British two-strokes (Villiers models), and selected Honda models (CB/CX for example). In Australia, the cheapest bikes are all Japanese and from the 1970's, including Hondas (CT/CB) and Yamahas (YZ/MX). Minimum prices downunder start from £100-200 (AUD $2.5=£1). The cheapest British bikes are BSA Bantams with asking prices of £600-£800. Any British four-stroke from the 1950-1960's is asking £1,200 and up. The most expensive bikes are Vincents, Harleys and Indians asking £8,000-£12,000 or more. In New Zealand, classic bikes generally have similar prices to those in Australia but can be more or less expensive allowing for the exchange rate. An entry-level Suzuki (ST/K10) or Kawasaki (KZ) may cost £200 up; a Yamaha (XS/TX) or Honda (CL/XL) £300-£400 or more. British four-strokes in New Zealand are comparably priced to Australia, with some makes and models in better supply.

Budgeting

If you are going to buy a classic, and especially if you are a first time buyer then it's vital to include a cost estimate for not just the initial purchase of the bike, but also the costs of running a classic bike. Over the first two years these include clothing, registration and operating costs, repairs and maintenance, plus a budget for restoration. (Those with a classic already in the garage can ignore additional clothing costs etc.) A pro-forma cost budget for Australia is shown in Table 2.2 below. Numbers can be dropped in for any country.

Table 2.2	A First Classic Bike Budget			
	Example is a BSA 1960's Single			
Item	**Description**	**Cost Min**	**Cost Max**	**Notes**
Purchase	1968-1970 B44	£1200	£2000	a good bike
Clothing	Helmet, gloves, jacket, pants, boots	£250	£400	basic kit
Operating Costs	Licence, insurance, fuel, oil, club plates, registration	£100	£200	a provision only
Maintenance	Tools, gaskets, plugs.	£200	£400	a minimum
Restoration	Replace missing parts	£200	£800+	how far do you go?
TOTAL Cost	**Year One**	**£2000**	**£3800**	
Note	*£1 = AUD $2.5 = US$1.8 approx*			

Several noteworthy points arise from this table. Firstly, the price break between a run-of- the-mill example and a good restored, licensed bike can be 60-100%. Secondly, the on-costs (everything other than that initial purchase) doubles the cost of the bike. Thirdly, saving on the budget by buying a ratty bike only ramps up restoration costs and the final cost will be much the same - possibly considerably higher, except for a black hole that's swallowed 500 plus hours of leisure along with the family goodwill! Fortunately, after the peak expenditure in the first year, restoration and maintenance spending normally tapers off for some years.

TIP: By splitting a bike's total cost into the up-front capital cost and later operating costs, it's much easier to sell one's partner on the idea.

Classic Advertising Channels

For readers wishing to go more deeply into classic bike pricing, say as collectibles, then the commercial collectors' guides provide further useful reading e.g. *Glass Guides* (now out of print but can give some guidance if you can find one on the second hand market), *Millers Classic Motorcycles Yearbook and Price Guide*, auction guides etc. It helps researching classic bike prices that there are only a few channels for classic bike ads in each country. These are summarised in Table 2.3 below, and discussed further in Chapter 3.

Table 2.3   Classic Bike Advertising Channels

Country	Channels	Published	Notes
UK	Old Bike Mart	Monthly	Good source in print and web.
	Classic Bike	Monthly	Top end bikes & surveys.
	Classic Motorcycle	Monthly	Top end bikes and surveys
	Classic Bike Guide	Monthly	Top end bikes and surveys
	Real Classic	Monthly	Good source for all bikes
	EBay		Becoming a major pathway
Australia	Trading Post	Weekly	Top source, on web and print.
	Just Bikes	Monthly	New and old bikes
	Motorcycle Trader	Monthly	New and old bikes
	EBay		Becoming a major pathway
New Zealand	Motoring Marketplace	Monthly	Top source, on web and print.
	Trade Me		Similar to EBay in Aus. and UK

Within most countries, the above media allow vendors in each country to set selling prices with a fair knowledge of other asking prices, albeit with little knowledge of actual selling prices. There are regional differences, e.g. city vs country prices. Naturally, the bargains are at the margins where this market knowledge breaks down. The budget table above, plus the statistics on Classic Motorcycle Survival rates (Chapter 11) and the Bonnie Index (Chapter 12) will enable makes and models of bikes to be selected and their availability gauged. The country sales channels above will (eventually) turn up the available bikes and their asking prices. Good Hunting!

Restore Or Ride Away?

First-time classic bike buyers are often counseled to avoid basket cases, i.e. bikes that are stripped down into several boxes of parts, or bikes that aren't running or that are clearly in a poor condition. It's tempting to settle on a tatty '70s Triumph Bonneville that goes smokily and 'just needs a bit of a tune-up' rather than a nicely presented, but unsexy BSA B31 when both are offered for a similar price. This could be a costly mistake. Every bike looks good in a photo, unless it's missing the fuel tank or seat. Human perception being what it is, the eye and the heart gloss over defects that are immediately obvious the second time you visit a bike - or immediately you get it home if you don't make that all important second visit. Instead, you generally form a first impression of a nice, complete motorcycle, even when it ain't.

Buying a first classic bike is meant to be a fun time, out riding with new clubmates. Buying a basket case means six months of effort and £800 to £1600 (Aus $2,000-$4,000) minimum expenditure, working on possibly unfamiliar technology, often lacking information, in cramped shed space, with inadequate tools and outside a support network. For some this is exactly what they seek, but many new classic riders are turned off by it and leave the scene, never getting to ride their bike. That's why there are so many basket cases offered and re-offered for sale. How did they become basket cases in the first place? Humpty-Dumpty stripped them down, and couldn't put them back together again. The reasons include lack of time and know-how; cost blow-outs; objections by spouse; ill health; a sudden love of lawn bowls; moved house; couldn't get parts; needed the cash etc. Probably 80% of basket cases remain so for these reasons, sometimes for a generation or more. Yet it's not as if classic bike restoration is impossible for first-timers. Many British bikes were designed simply, so riders could strip and reassemble them in the typical 8' by 6' English garden shed.

It's also important our spouses see us having a good time out of the household expenditure on the bike. She needs to see us well, *riding* the bike for a start. Many spouses fail to understand how their partners can spend so many hours a day in the shed, without food and drink, and return filthy, smelly, bleeding and depressed, and yet claim to be having tremendous fun for the third straight month. Spouses inevitably come to interpret this as personal rejection - there be dragons down that path! Anyway, you don't want the whole exercise to transform you into a Walter Matthau style grumpy old man. Plenty of time for that later!

Ergonomics Or How Much Should A Bike Weigh?

A classic bike's dimensions need to suit its rider rather like a bespoke suit. With classic bikes there are no longer any helpful distributors to fit us onto our bikes, so it's all up to us. This question brings us into the field of ergonomics, or the engineering aspects of how we fit in, on and around our bike, and it to us.

As a rule, the lighter the bike the easier it is to handle. This is pronounced at low speeds, when parking, when stopping on inclines, in traffic, or on soft verges. Many heavy bike accidents occur when manoeuvering it inside the garage: when working on the bike, or when lifting it on and off its stand for example. Once up and running the natural gyroscopic effect of the wheels coupled with rider input through the bars, helps keep it upright. Harley-Davidsons are renowned for having light steering, despite their weight. This reflects their weight distribution with two thirds of it over their rear wheel. A Harley and a British classic half it's weight and size can feel identical on the handlebars at speed.

The weight range for today's modern bikes is from 114 kgs (250 lbs) up to 363 kgs (800 lbs) for a Goldwing. There's another 30 kgs (65 lbs) for fuel, options, saddlebags, screen, fittings and tools. That's a weight range of some 300%. For many riders, shoving almost 400 kgs of metal around the garage isn't much fun, and that's a good argument to get a classic British bike where weights are less. Classic bikes start at 102 kgs (225 lbs) for a BSA Bantam and go to 220 kgs (480 lbs) for an Ariel Square Four. That's half the weight of a big Harley (and no, we haven't forgotten the formidable 356 kgs (783 lbs) 1932 Brough-Austin). British bikes fall into four weight categories as in Table 2.4 below

Table 2.4	Classic Bike Weight Selector	
Weight Category	**Weight Range***	**Look for these Bikes**
Lightweights	80-100 kgs	Triumph Cubs, Bantams, James etc
Middleweights	101-150 kgs	250-500cc BSA/Triumph singles
Heavyweights	151-200 kgs	500-650cc Twins, Pre-unit Singles
Really Heavy!	220 kgs plus	Ariel Square 4, Harleys, Indians
* *Gross, dry weight.*		

Using this table it's easy to check for a preferred weight class by finding friends or club members with a BSA Bantam, a 650cc British Twin or 1950s-1960s 350/500cc Single, a Unit BSA/Triumph single, and a Harley. While many riders don't welcome test-riding, nearly all are happy for us to sit on their pride and joy, and feel its weight and balance. And now about that inside leg measurement sir...

Of Legs And Seats

Perhaps because people are taller and bigger now than in classic times, many punters assume any classic bike will suit any rider today. Not so. Today's riders find some classics more comfortable than others due to their different seat heights. It's important to choose a bike that suits your anatomy, one you can comfortably straddle at rest. One ideally where your legs can reach the ground on both sides. One where you can safely swing the kick-starter without toppling over…. I don't know how our shorter fathers managed some of the bikes their generation manufactured. My father at 5'6" was the tallest of his four brothers. His legs wouldn't reach the ground on a 1971 Triumph twin. This is a real issue for today's classic riders on congested roads. When riders cannot reach the ground properly, they are forced to start their bikes on the centre stand which is fine, but what do they do on soft ground? These riders can be restricted to mounting and dismounting their bikes over a kerb or other raised bit of street furniture, where they can get sufficient height to handle the bike. If required to stop, say at a driveway entrance, or on a road surface with a significant dip or camber, they can and do drop their bikes. Taking off on inclines in a shopping centre carpark or the high street, becomes a risky matter. Where's the fun in this, when the bike is so plainly mismatched to it's rider?

A simple way to avoid later disappointment is to take an inside leg measurement, preferably in riding boots and heavy riding socks. The best measure is from the ground up to the left testicle…the one that hangs a bit lower. This gives a comfort margin in leathers, versus measuring up to the perineum that ex-airforce readers will recall as the 'Fintab', and I decline to set out the ditty going with that one. If the inside leg is 30-31 inches plus, then riders will feel comfortable on anything short of a penny-farthing. If it's less than 30", riders might consider the table of seat heights below. Of course inside legs can be boosted. Riders can follow in John Wayne's footsteps with built-up boots. Motorcycle boots with cowboy or stockman's heels also give a lift. It's also simple to pack up the inner sole using liners if there is space in the boots; the lambswool ones are good, as they also keep the feet warm in Winter.

In Table 2.5, British bikes are sorted by their seat heights which varied considerably over the decades. British makers raised their seat heights approximately every decade throughout the Vintage and Classic periods. I cannot find any published evidence to explain this, but you can assess the trend by taking Roy Bacon's excellent marque guides and following seat heights over time. Clearly the major factors would have been the change from side-valve to taller, overhead valve engines; the shift from saddles to dual seats; the introduction of rear suspension, and the larger frames needed as engine capacities, speeds and power all increased. The trend to increasing height in the rider population arising from better diet and health care, may have also encouraged classic designers to ramp up seat heights.

It's nice to imagine the great designers such as Turner, when trying to fit larger engines into existing frames, striding around his Meriden plant with a tape measure taking inside leg measurements from startled workers!

Table 2.5	Classic Bike Seat Height Selector	
Inside Leg*	**Seat Heights**	**Bikes you can easily Straddle**
Less than 25"	approx 26"	Looks like a Harley for you then?
25-27"	up to 28"	Typical 1930s British makes & models
27-28"	up to 29"	Typical 1940s British makes & models
28-29"	up to 30"	Typical 1950s British makes & models
29-30"	up to 31"	Typical 1960s makes & '70s Triumphs
30-31"	up to 32"	Typical 1970s BSA Twins, Unit Singles, most Vincents
Current Bikes		
Harleys*	26"	
Hondas	31"	
Triumphs	31"	

* The minimum Harley seat height of 26" is designed so a rider of 5'4" can comfortably sit on a Harley, with both feet flat on the ground.

The trend to increased seat height peaked around the end of the 1960s and the beginning of the 1970s, when BSA reached 33" with their twins and triples. This milestone seemingly wasn't celebrated. The wet-frame A65s and Unit Singles were castigated in the motorcycle press for seat heights reaching 32". This was a bit unfair as they were actually lower than earlier Vincent seats. Admittedly Vincent seat height was adjustable, but mainly in the upward direction via its braces. The hinging architecture of the Vincent frame would have brought heavier riders a bit closer to ground. Triumph used their tape measure more wisely, allowing the Bonneville seat to peak at just 31" before reducing it to 29" in 1973, thus maximising their potential rider market. This also maximised rider safety through a better fit to shorter riders' legs. Harley-Davidson never forgot those basic lessons.

In Table 2.5 above, some of today's marques have been added for comparison. Seat heights have been maintained by Honda and Triumph at the 1960's elevation of 31", despite the significant population height increase over the past 40 years. Harley has kept their average seat height down to a Vintage height of just 26", clearly appealing to the shorter rider and to female riders. This discussion would lead older and shorter riders to seek classic bikes from the 1930-1950s when seats were low, bikes more stable, and riders well, lower! "shorter legs go for older bikes or Harleys." seems the Golden Rule.

Image And Riding Style

Despite the underlying rebellion involved with motorcycle riding, many riders are concerned with the motorcycling image they project. This derives from the kind of bike, how it's equipped and ridden, it's exhaust (muffler) note and how the rider dresses. It's fun to explore this dress impact by, for example wearing long white socks with the tops turned down over the boots. Accusations of 'Rocker' or 'Cafe Racer' are soon made. Younger riders ask, seriously, what it means.

Riding into town with a white open face helmet and a high visibility vest causes drivers to suddenly notice the bike. They become reluctant to pass and even hang back a few lengths. Once they work out its not an 'official' rider of some sort, they tear past and cut in as usual. That's one riding style that leads to survival. Younger, modern bike riders take styling to extremes with branded, colour-matched bikes, luggage, leathers and helmet.

The style issue for classic bike buyers is a lot simpler. Riding a classic positions the rider within the biking world. It implies the rider is technically competent in ways modern bikers cannot know. Secret men's business, if you like. You hold secret knowledge about the pre-history of bikes ridden by the rest. You are respected for conserving heritage machines. You are pitied because of the presumed unreliability and messiness of classic bikes. You are deemed approachable at any time, by any passer-by, for a rundown on the bike and its marque. Old gaffers spin memories around the bike and bygone days. You become a sort of lightning rod for people. At times, it causes you to forget your start-up sequence, flood the bike, look like a dill, and hope they'll go away!

Matching Classics To Rides

It's useful to match the bike to its riding tasks, as well as to its rider. For many classics bikes in Australia and New Zealand that are under Conditional or Concessional Registration, Club Plates etc. these tasks include:-

- Club runs, typically weekly or monthly rides of 100-200 miles (200-400kms)
- Short solo rides for tuning and show-off calls on family and friends.
- Annual rides to Rallies and Field Days,
- Occasional short rides in parades, events, charity functions etc.
- Marque rallies 300-600 miles (500-1,000kms) away where the bike may be trailered part way.
- Starting it up just to hear that magic sound, and for a quick run round the block.

Many riders have only a foggy notion about where their first bike purchase will lead. Often, the rider's motorcycle licence has lapsed and memories of earlier riding days are of little help. Even so, it comes down to choosing one bike.

Here are some rather general guidelines for the first time buyer of a classic bike, assuming little mechanical knowledge.

- If you want to join longer club rides over 300kms, forget bikes under 350cc, and look at 450-500cc or more.

- Look for recent bikes, with 12 volt electrics, alternator, and a Boyer transistor ignition. A bike from the 1960s-1970s say, which are generally likely to start easily and go well without any special skills.

  Pick the most popular Triumph, BSA or Norton brands for which parts and knowledge are readily available.

- Pick a clean, complete bike, that passes two inspections, including one from a friend with classic bike know-how.

TIP: It's better to look at what not to buy, and by excluding some types of bike, the choice becomes clearer.

Road Traffic Conditions

Imagine riding a classic 'time-travelling' motorcycle back in time, starting at the end of the Classic period in 1979, and riding back through the Classic, Vintage, Veteran and Pioneer times, and on back into the 19th century. What would we see ahead over the handlebars?

Firstly, the roads would become narrower, closing in on the front wheel; the traffic slowly thins out; vehicles become smaller and shortened; buses, trucks, lorries, semi-trailers and long articulated trucks slowly vanish from the road in front of us; the traffic stream slows down; the road deteriorates; we have to slow down; a cloud of dust hangs in front of us, the tar finishes; what's that?...it's a horse, and it's on the road! Ruts, dung, stones and huge potholes make an obstacle-course under the wheels; suspensions bounce and bottom; there is a metallic taste in our nose; suddenly we shoot up off the saddle, the front wheel slides off in a rut, and we're unseated - surely our grandfathers didn't ride in conditions like these?

And yet they did, and if they could ride their bikes forward up the same 'time stream' towards us, what would they see? Such smooth, wide roads; no dung! Potholes and ruts vanish; street lights pick out the night; bewildering huge vehicles, traveling at unthinkable speeds in silence like wraiths; all traffic halts; it's as crowded as the Thames at Henley Regatta time; all traffic go, hard on the brakes; I can't keep up, horns behind me; how dare they come so close, can't they see me? Bugger! Why is this road surface burning my skin so?

For motorcyclists, while roads have improved since the Vintage period, traffic conditions have deteriorated. Regulatory authorities are consistent in their disrespect for motorcyclists. They exclude them from their road planning then, paradoxically encourage classic motorcycles onto the roads with subsidised plating and licensing schemes. The physical road hazards of yesteryear are exchanged for a cloak of invisibility, making us more vulnerable in traffic.

Brakes And Suspension

Modern suspensions are superior to girder forks, but for club riding on tar the suspension hardly ever bottoms, compared with metal roads (graded dirt roads with no tarmac). For club runs, girders are fine. The success of the Harley Springer, with girder suspension demonstrates its continuing practicality. The Springer suspension travel is comparable with fork travel on other Harleys and works well on tarmac roads.

Brakes are a different matter. On older classic bikes, brakes can be a real safety issue. There are two key things to look at - the brake diameter and the wheel diameter:

- The larger the brake diameter, the better the braking.
- As wheel diameter goes up, braking goes down.

Older classic and vintage bikes featured 21" or greater wheels to handle the poor roads. Small diameter brake drums were in use because speeds were limited by the metal roads. This combination on today's roads can be very unsafe, as illustrated in Table 2.6 below:

Table 2.6	Classic Bike Braking Comparison				
Year	**Bike**	**Wheel Dia.**	**Brake Dia.**	**Ratio Brake:Wheel**	**+/-**
1951	BSA C11	20"	5.5"	0.275	
1971	BSA B50	18"	8"	0.444	+62%

The B50 has 62% more braking than the C11. If the 20" C11 wheel is swapped to the B50, it's braking effect drops by 10%. The brake shoe area on the B50 is 80% more than the C11. It's no surprise Moto GP riders experimented with smaller front wheels during 2006. (The braking formula is given at the end of this chapter see page 20).

Classic bikes with 18" wheels and 7" or 8" brakes appear desirable, especially with TLS (twin leading shoes), but friction and pressure are also important. The TLS front brake on later Triumph and BSA twins and singles is often criticized even though it's an 8" brake with 10% more area than the 7" brake it replaced. The combination of short levers and poor pressure on the rear shoe is the reason. As shown in Illus 2.3 below, the cure is to extend the levers. The extenders are available at The Muttz Nutz (see http://www.themuttznutz.com/)

Illus. 2.3
A twin leading shoe (TLS) 8″
Triumph/BSA brake from
1971-2, with some 12.0 sq.in.
of brake-shoe area. Note the
shorter levers with extenders
installed.

Extenders

Illus 2.4
A TLS 7″ BSA brake from
1970, with approx 10.9 sq.in.
of brake shoe area.

Originality

This is confusingly used in two different contexts in classic motorcycling. An 'original bike', is often advertising code for an unrestored bike. It can mean the bike is due or overdue for a lot of work before any serious riding or registration can occur. It is not necessarily a good thing and is often used very loosely.

The second common usage is for a bike that is in or close to, it's original ex-factory build state, as compared to another that's been chopped or equipped with say the front end from another make, sourced from the wreckers.

Completeness

This term is also commonly applied to classic bikes in advertisements. Its usage overlaps that of 'originality' and the two are often found in the same sentence, i.e. 'a complete and original bike'. It means that all components on the bike are present, and perhaps in their correct place. It does not necessarily mean that all components are 'original'. Indeed, it's a rare classic bike that is 100% complete and original. This is due to two main reasons. Firstly, over the course of 30-40 years and multiple owners, non-standard and pattern or substitute parts find their way onto most bikes. Secondly, British manufacturers did not always follow their own specifications. There was no ISO6000 certification for BSA and Triumph then. Parts and components migrated backward or forward a model year or even two, according to stock availability on the production line. This makes it practically impossible now to state categorically whether any bike is totally complete and original.

Security

In short-listing a classic bike for purchase, security considerations ought to be considered. Motorcycles by their size and weight are portable. Being essentially an assembly held together with 100 bolts, they are quickly carried away and stripped down. Often, the bike is worth more as a collection of parts than as an intact bike. Some rare makes and models are targets for thieves. Thus, it's prudent to plan ahead for bike storage in secure quarters - ideally, a locked shed or garage, where it can be parked up and worked on. Classic bike insurers may also insist on further security measures. These typically comprise an approved heavy-duty floor mount, usually dyna-bolted into a concrete slab, with the bike attached to the mount by a heavy wire rope or chain.

Perhaps the outstanding example of such a facility was created by a US friend. He retired and with a mate, built a reproduction classic motorcycle shop. It includes workbenches, bike lifts, compressor, proper lighting, radio, tea and coffee making facilities, indeed all the usual equipment, even a Bundy employee time clock. His best mate and he spend their retirement 'working' on their bikes in their own 'Classic Bike Shop', downtown in a Western city. There's only one thing missing - Joe Public.

Recognition

When choosing a classic bike, one question always comes up - how to go about recognising an outstanding example of a particular make and model, without looking at dozens of the same model and when few of the model are ever on the market at the same time? The first approach is to co-opt a friend onto the bike-search team. The next practical alternative is to join a classic club. Often good classic bikes circulate within club circles, and at fair prices to members. Marque guide books are also invaluable. Roy Bacon's guides dominate this area. They are still available new from many specialist bookshops and classic bike dealers round the world. Used copies are on EBay continuously, and local libraries often have his works on their shelves. One of his *Illustrated Guides* is useful for any BSA or Triumph. These give excellent colour photos and summary data on the complete range of that marque.

More comprehensive information on models and ranges within a marque is found in Bacon's *Restoration Guides*. These enable the restorer to 'drill down' to the paint finishes at the nut and bolt level for any particular bike or model series. Such works generally contain the breakdown of frame and engine numbers, which are vital in correctly identifying a classic bike within its model and production year. These production data are also available through classic marque clubs. A Parts Manual is another early purchase to aid recognition of chosen makes and models. These are cheap and readily available as original copies. They contain exploded diagrams of every bike part and its assemblies, and their part numbers. Classic parts suppliers stick to the original factory parts numbering schema, so parts recognition and ordering is straightforward.

Reliability

If there's one issue dividing classic and modern bikers, it's the perceived unreliability of classic bikes. We're told today's riders don't want to work on their bikes for three weekends, so they can ride on the fourth. Is this deserved criticism? Today's riders rely on dealer service and their service intervals and warranties are extended. Many riders do no work on their bikes. That perhaps forms their view that classics require frequent work and are thus unreliable. It completely misses the point that classic riders want to get involved with their bike maintenance. It's true classic runs often include a salvage vehicle, but so do runs for contemporary motorcycles, for example HOG (Harley Owners Group) rallies include salvage vehicles and mechanics. Riding around Australia last year, one group took three salvage trucks and the lot broke down, whilst every bike made it home. A well maintained classic bike is as reliable as a modern bike over the 1-200 miles (200-400kms) a day running we ask of them. When one does break down, they're also far easier to get going again.

Ease Of Starting

Electric starts on classic bikes are limited to Enfields, Triumphs, Sportsters and Nortons. The art of kick-starting, especially a big single with it's heavy flywheels, inertia and big piston, remains a mystery to many riders. On any club run one sees a variety of sequences and rituals. Part of the problem today lies with the brevity of the British manuals. Writers treated the subject as if it was common knowledge, and perhaps it was in those days. A difficulty lies in the evolving language; today's usage is different to English in classic times. Standards of technical copywriting are also different. In fact a Triumph or BSA Owners or Workshop Manual compared to today's Harley-Davidson or Japanese manual holds up extremely well.

Easy starting is the sign of a well-maintained classic bike. It should be simple, but it frequently isn't. In vintage days bikes were mostly single cylinder, requiring the rider to know about the art of kick starting. Twin cylinder engines made starting easier, due to the smaller cylinders and double the chance of getting one to fire. It's still true British twins start easily, even if the engine's in bad shape.

Much that was written in British manuals about starting is misleading. It's in the form of biblical parables. It's almost as if the workshop manuals relied on a larger body of knowledge, available to riders from some other place. Wasn't it Einstein who said, "...a thing should be simplified as far as possible, and no further..."

Kick Starting Singles For Duffers

The secret to first-kick starting is only this... 'finding the POINT where you start the downward KICK'. To describe kick-starting a big single, this step-by-step approach breaks starting down into two phases:

One: Four Steps to TDC

1. Sit on the bike, with ignition off and timing on full retard (if a manual advance retard is fitted)

2. Press down on the kickstarter. It slowly turns the engine around, (as air rushes in and escapes from the cylinder).

3. Feel the compression stroke by continuing to push the kick starter until strong resistance is felt. This is the end of the fourth stroke in a four-stroke engine - the compression stroke. The top of the compression stroke is called TDC (Top Dead Centre) when the piston is at the top of the bore.

4. Pull in the exhaust lifter lever (if fitted) and continue to push on the kick starter. The engine will now rotate over compression. Repeat this process by releasing the exhaust lifter and pressing on the kick start until you are easily able to find the compression stroke and have mastered the exhaust lifter control to take you over the compression and into the next cycle.

Two: Starting Up

Riding courses teach a start-up sequence, rather like using a computer or those for pilots. For riders with several bikes, each can have a different starting sequence. It's handy to use the first letter of each action, to form a mnemonic, something like:

F   turn on the **F**uel

A   close the **A**ir-lever,

T   press the carburetor **T**ickler 1-2-3 seconds more or less,

P   use the kickstarter to turn the engine until TDC and then continue forward again to **P**rime the engine, until the next TDC. Ease the kick starter just 'over the hump' of compression using the exhaust lifter, until it just starts down the other side.

The knack is to be only just past TDC, never before it, or on top of it.

I   switch on **I**gnition (retard manual advance/retard control if fitted. Start at about half retard, if the engine does not fire, *gradually* advance the ignition and try again until it does. If the engine 'kicks back' retard the ignition a little)

S   **S**tart. Let the kick starter return to the top of its travel by lifting your foot. Then press down until you feel it just engage, without moving the piston. Then take a slow swing (not a short shove) on the starter. A fast start is unnecessary and in fact impossible, as the flywheel inertia has to be overcome. The kick starter naturally accelerates as it swings down, and the heavy flywheels start spinning. And presto the bike fires!

Every classic bike should start first kick, nearly every time. The mnemonic for this start-up sequence, FATPIS, is memorable if undignified. Some riders make up a mnemonic chit and leave it on their tank in between rides, so they don't forget. One I know writes it on his racer's tank with a felt marker pen.

The secret is momentum. Successful kick starting is less about 'starting up' and more about 'momentum'. It's like a skateboard ramp in neighbourhood parks. Skate boarders generate momentum going down one side, to power up the other and into mid-air manoeuvres.

In our case, we have to swing the starter to do two things. Firstly to move the piston and flywheels to the next TDC, where a spark will fire the charge. Secondly to achieve sufficient crankshaft speed for the engine to gain momentum and push over the next compression stroke. If it doesn't get over that next compression stroke the engine will reverse, kicking back through the starter, and causing a nasty ankle injury before the engine stops. There are two common 'mis-kicks' that lead to injured ankles. Starting the swing before or on TDC, and secondly, starting it a long way past TDC. In the first instance it's impossible to gain enough momentum if the engine first has to be pushed through compression. In the second case, the rider runs out of travel in the starter before the threshold momentum for the crankshaft is achieved.

Start-up Summary

By starting the kick with the piston as far back as possible from the next TDC there's the maximum possible swing-time on the starter to generate the needed momentum. The ignition part is as easy as tossing a match into the cylinder. The hard part is getting the engine up to speed using only the kick starter. It's a bit like our grandfathers with bent backs cranking their model T Fords.

Longer-stroke engines give more swing-time, and are easier to start. Such bikes also tend to be older, with lower compression, making it even easier. On the other hand, they may have heavier flywheels....

Braking Formula

The 'Pudd-ing' formula below illustrates the negative impact on braking effect, from enlarging the wheel diameter

$$\text{Braking } B = Pud/D$$

Where:
B= braking effect
P= drum pressure
u= coefficient of brake shoe friction
d= brake drum diameter
D= wheel diameter.

As can be seen for a given pressure on the brake lever the actual braking effect is inversely proportional to the wheel diameter. As the wheel diameter increases the braking effect decreases in proportion, therefore small wheels provide greater braking effect from the same force applied to the brake.

3 *Where And How To Buy Your First Classic Bike*

"I thought I would do something different by getting my motorcycle licence to explore our fantastic country on the open road. ......I've got saddlebags and feel ready to go exploring again". Dick Smith, Australian Explorer, November 2003.

After reviewing the range of retro and classic motorcycles, and with the choice of bike based upon rider's requirements, the framework is laid to connect with a bike that will give immense pleasure and reliable running. Perhaps the best place to start the search is in a classic motorcycle shop, for many still exist. They can be located through the ads in classic bike and club magazines. Any classic motorcycle club secretary will provide referrals, and any classic bike rider will have two or three names top of mind.

Classic Motorcycle Shops

Despite the demise of the British motorcycle industry, there's a chunk of its original distribution channel in place around the world. This is most evident in Commonwealth countries. The businesses trade on, often under the same owners much as they did thirty years ago, except for the absence of new British bikes for sale. The parts side of these businesses is now their core business. Some shops still offer a British workshop service whilst others have taken on Italian and European bikes or combine both British and Japanese marques. The remaining British-only shops are fiercely loyal. They are encouraged by their clientele of committed single marque riders. This British distribution channel is not unique: it's mirrored by an equally loyal distribution channel for classic American motorcycles, especially Harley-Davidson.

In Australia the best examples of classic motorcycle shops are in Sydney, where Jack Graham (the oldest motor cycle shop in Australia) and Jim Eade thrive. Both businesses are maintained by second generation proprietors. Barry Graham of Jack Graham, specialises in Velocette and Vincent, but capably handles anything British, and runs training clinics for classic owners. He also provides a unique 'finding and fettling' service for those riders seeking that very special bike.

Max Eade at Jim Eade has been in business at Strathfield since the 1940's, with British, American and European agencies. Max specialises in Triumph and BSA bikes and parts for most British makes. If you're a returning rider, then visiting any of these shops is like entering a Star Trek transporter. Push open the front door, close your eyes and inhale….and the your nose is once again steeped in a motorcycle aroma which transports you back into your youth. A palpable amalgam of oily timber floor, Brasso, carbonised metal, cardboard, sweat, rags, rust and rubber.

A shop like Jim Eade seems more like a museum; even Max is not really sure which it is. This can be a defining moment in your search. If you're to be a classic rider, then in places like this you feel just right. Here your choice is clear. You reminisce with old hands. You're delighted. You're back.

Illus. 3.1 The oldest bike shop in Australia, Jack Graham in Sydney, after some 80 years trading.

Illus 3.2 Jim Eade in Strathfield, the last full-line classic parts outlet in Sydney.

Naturally, for well presented bikes from these old masters you expect to pay a premium price. Some of these outlets are diversifying into bikes for restoration as well as restored models, to offer a more complete service to riders. This can be a sensible way to buy, as these shops take the place of the original marque distributor. While there's no 'new bike' warranty, it's possible to negotiate a quasi-warranty. Judicious haggling can deliver a package of arrangements to accompany a bike purchase. These might include free or discounted new parts for restoration, technical literature, support and the master's valuable expert advice. However these outlets are only the very beginning of any bike search.

Newspapers

When buying a car, it's usual to turn to the newspapers, but not for classic motorcycles. In the UK, Australia and New Zealand the press is useless in the search. Classic vendors don't use these media. Local papers in country towns are the one exception. In Australia, the tabloid *Trading Post* has been the first stop for Classic buyers for decades. There are similar papers in the UK but generally it is unusual for them to list classic bikes and spares.

The Trading Post

This publication is published in all Australian states. It features ads from classic riders and executors of estates. It's the choice of sellers with no computer. It's also a place to look for motorcycle parts and clothing. Computer minded and serious shoppers scan the net version, (www.tradingpost.com.au) as it's easier than buying the paper. Bargains are often snapped up on the website before the tabloid version hits the streets on Thursdays. I recently logged on at 8am one Thursday, and bought a cache of BSA spares. By the time the vendor concluded the deal, later that morning, he had five other buyers lined up, some offering to overbid me.

Searching the net version by marque or production year, or by regions is fast. Regional searching is important because of the distribution of the bikes in the country. For example, in South Australia Ariel Square Fours are advertised frequently as the police used to use them. In New South Wales BSA B40's are found in the Hunter Valley, still close to their old army bases. Similarly, BSA sidevalve engines are advertised in farming irrigation areas, after decades pumping water in back paddocks. Their frames mostly became scrap but some are still out there: Western Australia exported BSA M20 frames long after the engines went farming.

Classic bikes in country areas are often cheaper than in cities. In New Zealand, classic bikes are cheaper in the South Island. Prices in the rural states of Australia are generally cheaper than the metropolitan areas, and especially Sydney where prices tend to be higher. The same is true elsewhere, for example prices are generally lower in Canada than the USA. These market quirks can be decisive in the search for a classic bike. On the other hand, while Sydney seems expensive the volume of bikes sold gives 'supermarket' shopping and this is valuable for buyers. Good 'city' bikes sell quickly, but the search gives great comparison shopping and firms up the profile of the eventual purchase. A short-list of makes and models can be made much more easily. Even where bikes are missed, it's good to ask the vendor what price he obtained so that the actual prices realized can be compared with advertised prices. Bikes generally sell below listed prices, often a long way below. Advertised prices thus overstate market prices. This can lead the first-time buyer to purchase competitively in one channel, and later find a cheaper bike through another channel.

Magazines

We have to move on to specialised publications to find classic bike vendors. The newsagent, bookshop or supermarket in most countries stocks thirty or more motorcycle magazines and tabloids, but only a handful are useful for locating bikes for sale.

Certain magazines attract classic motorcycle ads. In Australia, it's *Just Bikes* followed by the *Motor Cycle Trader*. In New Zealand, it's the *Motoring Marketplace*. These magazines provide valuable market research. They often have a net version which is useful for international price comparisons, if you can buy overseas and ship the bike home. These magazines also list classic and marque clubs and useful events including autojumbles (swap-meets). Some also cover secondary purchases including helmets and clothing; such items new can cost as much as the bike and as a result many riders consider buying sound used items. This allows more budget for the bike. Pawnbrokers, for example Cash Convertors downunder, is a popular choice for cash-strapped bikers selling their leather jackets. I bought a new Brando jacket there recently for £12 (Aus $30), it was an unfashionable dusty colour and in split-hide (see Chapter 8 for a discussion of leather types) but a little black shoe colour gave me a classic black leather motorcycle jacket, and a bargain.

The English magazines *Classic Motorcycle*, *Classic Bike Guide*, *Classic Bike*, *Old Bike Mart* and *Real Classic* give useful classic bike prices. UK prices are higher than downunder at present, due as much as anything to the exchange rate, but it's not always like that - motorcycle trade flows reverse from time to time. International trade in classic bikes today is largely one way to the UK. The USA, once the greatest importer of classics, is now the major exporter of bikes. This reduces the supply of classic bikes in the USA and downunder, and leads to price inflation in those markets.

The UK magazines also show which bikes are bargains, as they're less favoured by the wider market. Late British singles such as two strokes, and Triumph and BSA unit singles have been out of favour recently, but are now appreciating. Classic Japanese bikes are behaving similarly. These classes of bike give satisfying classic motorcycling at less cost, especially for shorter club runs.

English magazines are expensive outside the UK - pensioners and self-funded retirees may prefer to ask their library to stock them. By their nature the editorial content of these magazines doesn't date although the ads may. They can be bought at markets for a tenth of their new price, and even less by the bundle. Duplicates are always good to swap with friends or on EBay.

Auctions

Classic motorcycles auctions are popular in the UK, USA and locally in New Zealand. In Australia, classic bike auctions went through a boom about fifteen years ago (see Chapter 12 and The Bonnie Index). It was a time of the 'bubble market' and normal trade flows reversed, with UK bikes again coming downunder. That auction peak ebbed along with prices during the 1990's. Classic bikes rarely come up now in general city auctions. They can be found tagged onto classic car auctions by specialised house like Bonhams (until recently) and Cromwells in Sydney.

Specialist classic auctions are still held in South Australia and Queensland by Bennetts, and sometimes at swap-meets. Job lots of parts can also be purchased at auction.

We live in 'low' currency countries downunder, and in markets with relatively low but increasing classic bike prices. Thus, classic bike auctions attract overseas interest and, perhaps as a result auctions in general provide few bargains for local buyers. The odds of obtaining a bargain are against the punter, as opportunities to inspect and road-test are limited. Also bid decision-making takes place under stressful, rushed conditions. A herd mentality can overtake auction participants. It's useful to visit auctions with the expectation of window shopping. Those I've attended in recent years saw record prices and evidence of overseas bidding. In New Zealand in 2003, at the auction of Tom Dalgleish's fine collection two 350cc Velocettes realised nearly £5,000 each. Two concourse-level restored, veteran 1914 Clynos with cane sidecars were entered with a reserve allegedly at £10,000. A rider on auction day appeared to seize the engine on one of these when apparently forgetting to manually pump oil as he rode round the auction site. The opening bid that day for each bike was £7,000, from the Netherlands. Interestingly, the outfits remained unsold for some time. One of them was the same one used on the cover of Maureen Bull's seminal 1981 work *New Zealand's Motor Cycle Heritage*.

Illus 3.3   A fine Panther outfit parked outside that NZ auction, for private sale.

Illus 3.4 One of the Clyno outfits from the NZ auction.

Retirees with large pension funds will find good restored bikes at these venues, if they're prepared to pay international prices. Riders may be better served tracking down classic bargains in the local neighborhood. One exception is the small country town auction where interesting bikes do turn up, at reasonable prices, if riders are lucky enough to be on the spot.

EBay

EBay and similar internet auction floors around the world are reshaping the market for classic motorcycles. Classic bikes are freely auctioned on USA, UK and Australian EBay sites. In New Zealand the online choice is Trademe (www.trademe.co.nz). Online sale prices vary widely and can be reasonable, but commonsense calls for caution. A long clean vendor track record is vital, unless you can physically visit the bike during the auction, something most genuine vendors invite. International EBay purchasing of bikes is a bit problematic. There are some awful stories of import purchases that went wrong. In New Zealand warnings have been made publicly about the condition of EBay-ed bikes imported from Australia. In Australia, similar stories circulate about American imports. Caveat emptor is still the rule. Moreover, the logistics of shipping a US bike to Australia or *vice versa*, need a good deal of planning so it is worth co-opting a clubmate with some imports under his belt. Motorcycle shipping specialists can also be consulted. One way to reduce the risk is to have a friend in the vendor's country go to inspect and report on the bike during the auction, or even to employ an agent to do an inspection.

EBay is straightforward for worldwide buyers and sellers of classic bike parts. This pathway is revolutionising the sale and purchase of parts and accessories. It makes the restorer's life far easier. Australasian riders can sell parts at international prices. They can also buy in directly from the large US and Canadian parts market, with many reputable US NOS (New Old Stock) vendors distributing worldwide. Freight may count against EBay trade in heavy items internationally, but for domestic purposes it's become the first choice for buying and selling parts. It's proven especially valuable for rural restorers and riders, and those in remote locations.

Fossicking

This is a search method for flushing out classic bikes stored under houses, in barns and on properties in any country. In the UK, such bikes are often called 'barn-finds'. The method is based upon a US sociology experiment, where a letter was given to a person, with instructions to hand-deliver it to an unknown addressee on the other side of the country using only friends and family connections. It took an average of just six pairs of hands and a few days for a 'mutual friends network' to spring up and deliver the letters. The findings indicate that someone close to every rider knows people who know people who know where every classic bike in the country is lying, waiting to be discovered!

Simply asking friends, neighbours, casual acquaintances, business associates and relatives for news of any old motorcycles is a flying start. The strike rate can be rewarding, even if some bikes are unsuitable or have moved when they're tracked down. Fossicking is helped by recalling the demographics of the 1960's classic bike owners. Bikes were then a common, cheap form of transport. To locate those bikes now, it's worth looking at sections of the community who had parents or relatives in those socio-economic groups at that time. Where did they go when they retired? In Australia, from Sydney for example, a lot of people spread out to the Central and North Coasts, and into the Blue Mountains. Classic bikes continue to surface from these areas and I predict a lot more are still under houses there. In the 1970's and early 1980's, classic bike prices were cyclically low (see Chapter 12). Retirees in those decades sometimes bought several classic bikes as sentimental investments. Those bikes are now coming onto the market as they pass on. Their children, who inherit such bikes, often sell them out of disinterest or ignorance, leading to excellent purchases for some riders. A recent, true example was a 1952 BSA Gold Star grass-race bike with a Hagon frame: it sold for just £100 in this way in an antique shop in the Blue Mountains. Once out in the market, it was resold for £400 within weeks at auction (where I was over-bid), and offered to me a short time later for £700 by the dealer who'd over-bid me.

It's worth fossicking in contemporary bike shops, as older bikes can be traded or dropped off, or known about by the shop owner. Classic bike shops often have bikes in poor condition and will negotiate over these 'basket cases'. Some riders put up free ads in these and other shop windows and supermarkets, especially in the areas described. Second hand goods and antique shops occasionally receive a bike. It's worth cultivating selected auctioneers and shop proprietors by, for example offering to assist them with identification and valuation advice for anything they happen to buy. This often happens when auctioneers buy household lots or estate clearances, and a dusty old classic turns up. Sometimes it's just about being lucky, as was a Sydney club out on a run some time ago. At their morning rendezvous, a truck pulled up. The driver had noticed the classic bikes assembled and stopped to ask whether members would like the heaped load of BSA bantam bikes and parts - they were going to the tip! AUD200 (about £80) changed hands and a collection of classic bikes was saved. This sounds like an urban myth, but I spoke to a witness. Other classic clubs and riders around Australasia recount similar experiences. This scrappage must still be happening in many countries.

Motorcycle Swap-Meets

Swap-meets are known as autojumbles in the UK. In Australia, the USA and New Zealand, swap- meets are prime sources of classic bikes and parts. Like tradeshows, they're regular annual events and promoted in the motorcycle press. In Australia *Just Bike*s or the *Australian Motorcycle Trader*, publish events calendars. A pre-dawn start is customary. Often the number of bikes for sale will be small, but there are people about who know of bikes coming up for sale. A friend recently tracked a fine purchase from a chance meeting at a swap meet. He ended up buying most of a BSA A65, with a spare motor and a good big tank, for just £200. The process took months of phone calls, until the owner reached the point where he decided to sell. The buyer was in place to buy before it was advertised, and scooped a £2,000

Illus. 3.5 Southern Spares gloved up at the 2006 Rotorua Winter Swap-meet

bargain. Dealers in classics operate in this way, flushing out bikes, rolling frames and parts caches, and buying at wholesale prices. Any rider can do the same - and have the fun of uncovering their own bargain classic bike.

Illus. 3.6 Cycle Torque chuckle over their movable parts feast at NZ swapmeets.

Classic Motorcycle Clubs

Classic clubs provide one of the best paths for buying a good bike at a fair price. Often there'll be a history for club bikes, as they circulate among the group of members for years or even decades. This can be invaluable for new buyers who are setting out to buy thirty to fifty year old machinery, without a warranty or service history and with the manufacturer long gone. Club sellers tend to be knowledgeable and open about strengths and weaknesses in their club bikes. This is helpful as even worn motorcycles, especially British twins, tend to start easily which can give the erroneous impression that the bike is in good condition. This plus a selectively truthful seller, can cause an unhappy ownership. Classic clubs welcome prospective members as they search for a first bike or other more experienced owners looking for a bike of a specific marque. They'll put free ads in their magazines, and refer buyers to members with a bike to sell. Such clubs, especially single marque ones, have an objective of 'advancing their marque', i.e. keeping the brand name alive. This is treated seriously and buyers receive strong club support as they search for a first classic bike among the marque offerings.

There are a hundred classic motorcycle clubs around Australia. In New Zealand, which pro-rata has more classic enthusiasts than any other country; there are a dozen classic clubs, as well as single marque clubs. In the Bay of Plenty region there are four classic clubs and several other bike clubs, all within an hours ride. That tally doesn't include branches of national clubs with branches throughout the country, such as the Ulysses Club for example. Ulysses is unique in that membership is qualified by rider age rather than machine age. The club appeals to the retiring post WWII generation, and as well as the majority with modern machines it also contains some classic enthusiasts mainly riding Harleys and Triumphs. Ulysses, with about 25,000 members is about five times the size of all the 'outlaw' motorcycle clubs in Australia.

Classic clubs fall into two groups. Firstly, the single marque clubs for Norton, Ariel, BSA, Triumph, Velocette etc. Secondly, the classic clubs welcoming all makes of older bikes such as the VMCC (Vintage Motor Cycle Club) in the UK and many other local clubs. In Australia, these are typified by the Vintage & Veteran MC and the Classic & Enthusiasts MC, both in NSW. In New Zealand, the Rotorua Classic Motorcycle Club is the oldest classic club. It was formed in 1976 when Norton and Triumph were still manufacturing. There is a third category of clubs, those catering for competition with classic bikes. If you've a mind for a classic racer or scrambler, then the competition clubs are the place to shop such as the CRMC (Classic Racing Motorcycle Club) in the UK. BEARS Clubs, (British, European and American Racing) organise circuit racing around Australia, often co-running classic racing events with the Post Classic Racing Association in Sydney. Road and race bikes are often for sale in and around the pits. The Classic Racing Register in New Zealand is another excellent venue to shop for competition bikes. Each February there's a national pilgrimage to Pukekohe, rivaling the exodus to the Isle of Man in the UK. 300 classic bikes and outfits raced at Pukekohe circuit in 2006, and 400 in 2007.

What Defines A Classic Motorcycle?

At first sight it's not obvious how a classic motorcycle differs from a pioneer, vintage or veteran bike. It's a grey area. The first UK Vintage Motorcycle club (VMCC) started in 1946, and set an arbitrary age of twenty-five years for eligible bikes, i.e. those made before 1921. Over time, like some of the present historic vehicle registration schemes, this age limit included more bikes. In this sense, all British classic bikes are now also vintage bikes. Another working definition for classics includes bikes made after WWII and before 1976. The most precise definitions are shown in Table 3.1 below.

Table 3.1	Classic Motorcycles By Time Period*	
Group Name	**Period**	**Notes**
Pioneers	Late 19C - Early 20C	Progenitors of modern motorcycles
Veterans	Pre-1915	
Vintage	Pre-1931	
Post-Vintage	Pre-1946	
Classic	Pre-1960	Now includes any bike over 25 years

* Classic Racing has additional post-classic categories

How To Assess A Classic Bike?

The moment comes when the buyer, the bike, and its vendor are standing around a garage somewhere. It's a heady, scary moment for the buyer. Years of experience buying and selling cars seems unhelpful. There are two tips from old motorcycling hands for this moment.

Firstly, a classic motorcycle is a lot of components held together with nuts and bolts. Unlike a car, most of these components are in plain view. They can be checked to see if any are missing or damaged.

Secondly, human brains ignore detail when looking at something for the first time. Old hands overcome this by looking closely at one small component, a nut or bolt will do. This forces the brain into close-up scanning mode and the entire bike can then be scanned picking up lots more detailed strengths and weaknesses.

Items Required

A torch, a rag to wipe hands, a mirror to check beneath the engine. If possible, a photo of the model to compare components and finish, and a digital camera to email experts for precise identification. A magnet is useful to sort out alloy, filler and fibreglass components. A notebook is handy for jotting down details such as frame and engine numbers. A medical stethoscope lets you listen to internal noises in engine, gearbox and chaincase. A fibre-optic wand torch (available from electronics stores) lets you inspect the inside of tanks, engine cylinder, ports, chaincase, gearboxes etc through any convenient opening. These are great for finding such potential problem areas as for example, rusty petrol tanks, and bargaining the price down. A friend recently was buying a good looking Triumph Bonneville for not much over £1,000. On the test-ride it spluttered and stopped, and my mate pushed it back to the seller. Given this embarrassment he naturally dropped his bid by £400, and succeeded in getting the bike for less than £1,000! Examining the tank later confirmed it was just rust in the fuel lines, and a tidy profit ensued.

Assessing A Bike In Fifteen Minutes

Going over a bike from nose to tail, using Table 3.2 gives a complete idea of its condition. Placing the bike on its centre stand helps to test some assemblies. To make this section authentic and practical some photos and the assessment of a bike I considered buying recently are also included after Table 3.2.

It's important to ask to see documentation on the bike. Careful owners keep a folder of receipts, roadtests etc. Better ones and restorers keep a log or diary of work they've done on the bike. Obsessive ones compile a history of the bike, going back several owners. These records indicate a well maintained bike. There should be workshop manuals, the dirtier the better. It's a real worry if the owner can't produce at least one and a parts list.

Table 3.2   Assessing A Classic Bike In Fifteen Minutes

Item	What to look for
Front Wheel	Does it wobble or go egg-shaped when you spin it? A small amount say 2.0-2.5mm ($1/16$ to $1/10$") is acceptable either way.
	Is it rusty? Any external rust is generally worse on the inside.
	Is the tyre rubber hard or cracked along side walls or in the grooves? Any loose, broken or missing spokes? Tapping shows this.
	Check the wheel bearing by rocking the wheel when held at the top and bottom. NB: Re-spoking and wheel truing can be outsourced at moderate cost.
Suspension	Sit on the bike and push the bars forward on the brake.
	Do the forks operate smoothly and silently, up and down?
	Are the stanchions worn, rusted or pitted?
	Is any oil leaking around the rubber seals or gaiters?
	Check for fork and steering head wear by pushing and pulling on the bottom of the forks with the wheel off the ground. Any slack? NB Any of the above indicates a fork rebuild. Bushes, seals etc are available for most makes. Stanchions can be a costly item.
Frame	Check and note any frame numbers. Do they look defaced?
	With the bike on centre stand take a look from behind. Does the bike look vertical, or is it leaning? Your 'eye-ometer' is accurate.
	Do the wheels look aligned? Check by looking along them with your head close to the ground.
	Inspect the front down-tube, especially the gusset at the steering head, on the top *and* underneath, for accident damage.
	Check the frame tube and welds for cracks and repairs.
	Any sign of penetrating corrosion?
	Sit on the bike and jump up & down to see how the rear suspension operates, especially the swinging arm.
	Note any country identification number plate riveted to frame.
	NB: Frames may have a degree of distortion, but still

function quite well at the speeds found on club riding. Some can be relieved of the distortions economically, but generally frame straightening can be costly.

Engine

Check and write down any engine number. Matching engine and frame numbers can enhance value, and also be forged.

Some makes have numbered crankcases. Check the two halves underneath for matching numbers, using a mirror/torch.

Before you start it up, touch the engine casing. If warm, the owner ran it before you arrived. Why, is a fair question!

Try turning it over to gauge engine compression, and feel any slipping in the clutch or jamming of the kickstart.

Put your ear close to the engine. You expect to hear lots of valve gear noise with alloy engines. Close your eyes and listen for knocking sounds, and any intermittent, odd noises. These can be due to worn bearings or clutch. British bikes are noisy and this is where an experienced friend is handy. However, even a first-time listener soon picks up noisy knocks and rattles that seem unnatural. Time to trust the force, Luke!

Look for broken engine fins, butchered hatch-covers etc.

Any fresh or old oil leaks where the bike has stood?

Any smoke in the exhaust when and after it's started?

Look at casings and joints for damage or fresh silicone.

Inspect engine mounts for casting wear and loose bolts.

Look at rockerboxes for damage, leaks and missing studs.

Check the nuts on top of the engine for burring from slipping spanners, indicating someone ham fisted may have worked on this engine. If it looks crook outside, it'll be worse inside!

Check exhaust pipe & muffler (silencer) for rust and gas leaks. Shine a torch up the pipe for baffles and rust. Rub your finger inside. It should have a light covering of grey-black soot. Thick, greasy black soot means a rich mixture or worse - valve trouble or failing piston rings.

Tanks

Look inside the fuel tank with a torch or wand for rust, dents, filler, welds, splits, debris, or distortion from compressed air (used to blow out dented tanks).

Is the oil tank sound and well mounted?

Is the oil return generous or skinny and intermittent? Bubbling is normal, especially if no oil filter or breathers are fitted.

Do the fuel and oil lines look sound?

Is there a proper oil filter, like a car one, often behind engine?

Is the oil clear and fresh, or gluggy, black and old?

Check for an under-tank strap, (a missing strap leads to a split tank, with a lap of petrol for the rider).

Rear End   While on the centre stand test the wheel bearings by rocking the wheel sideways.

Similarly check the swing arm bushes for sideways slack.

Is the rear chain overtight, too slack, dry or rusty?

Inspect the teeth on the chain sprockets. Any hooked, worn or chipped teeth mean a new chain and sprocket.

Look around mudguard bolts for cracks or tears in the guard, a classic secondary vibration sign in UK bikes.

Check rear wheel as for front wheel.

Inspect rear frame tubes for damage, missing bolts etc.

Electrics   With the engine running, check lights, horn & blinkers.

Open the sidecover or seat and check battery for spills and mounting integrity. This is another good place to spot neglect.

Open the headlight, with a coin and check wiring and switch completeness and integrity.

Does the wiring loom look in good condition for age?

Check the bike's electrical components for casing damage.

Has a kill switch been fitted?

Has any security device been fitted?

Cables & Brakes   Check all bar levers for smooth operation.

Do brakes work smoothly or are cables dry and jammy?

Does the cable and actuating lever to front and rear brake form a right angle? If not there may be badly worn brake shoes. Any fraying of cables or worn outers or nipples?

Are brake linkages sound, with clevis and split pins in place?

Are cable outers worn through or pinched against frame?

NB: Expect to replace cables, as they are cheap and vital.

Paint & Chrome   Inspect all chrome on fork seal holders, stanchions, shocks.

Is the paintwork mostly sound on frame and tank etc?

Look under mufflers (silencers) and pipes with a mirror for dents and rust.

Check for any signs of panel beating on the tank and toolbox cover.

Any cracks that might indicate GRP fillers have been used?

Seat   Does it feel comfortable? It has to support your posterior all day on club rides!

Is the vinyl cover sound?

Is the seat mounting in safe condition?

Can your legs reach the ground?

Toolkit   A basic toolkit was supplied with classic bikes. It's rare to find them with bikes now. You can buy original tools, or make up a suitable toolkit, as discussed in Chapter 9.

Nuts & Bolts   Nuts and bolts are like rings in a tree. They record past owners' care in maintenance, or its lack. If nuts are rounded, washers and spring washers missing, or if there's a mixture of bolt types, or bolts are missing then what's it like inside? Some nuts and bolts to check:

Carburetter nuts, (often overtightened).

Rear wheel adjusters, (for wheel alignment).

Bolts in soft alloy e.g. rockerbox studs, (easy to strip threads), drain plugs, (often butchered or substituted).

Kick starter cotter pin and nut, (if loose, it wears the shaft).

Originality   It's rare for a classic bike to maintain its original equipment and components down the decades. Original build states varied anyway, and previous owners tend to replace items. Compare with your photo to see if major items e.g., engine, tank, paint colour and exhaust etc are authentic. If not, price negotiation should reflect any weaknesses.

After the first look, it's useful to ask the owner about spare parts. Sometimes there's a cache of useful, valuable parts.

In pictures 3.7 and 3.8 is a bike I considered buying recently and so did a thorough pre-purchase check. The poor photos were taken in less than ideal conditions. This bike featured many of the adverse characteristics in Table 3.2 above.

Illus. 3.7 (right) and 3.8 (below)
The TR25W the author
considered buying

The bike was described by the owner as a 1970 Triumph, and proved to be a Triumph TR25W. It was/is owned by a retiree, who stored it for years against his retirement. The bike wasn't advertised, but after a fossicking approach, from a chance contact related to the owner, the bike proved to be for sale. The mooted asking price seemed fair, if the bike was in reasonable condition. At first sight it didn't look too bad for a dry-stored bike. The paint was good, it all seemed to be there, and it even turned over. The owner stated it had been running before storage, had compression, and he'd fitted a new battery as part of £100 he'd spent on parts before abandoning the restoration for health reasons. He'd previously restored classic cars, and this seemed a good sign. I'd not seen this model before but so far, it looked good and I was becoming excited - as you do. However, the excitement ebbed a bit as I forced myself to postpone any decision until I followed the checklist above. Here are my notes from the first and second inspections, sent to a friend.

A Triumph Case Study

First Inspection Notes

Now I just came across a Triumph TR25. It looks pretty complete, looks like a (genuine) 22,000 kms (14,000 miles), stored for many years. No history. The guy started a restoration, but quickly found bowls more congenial and pushed the bike away in his garage about 5 years ago.

It turns over with compression. Paint original blue by the looks. Build date is June 1970 and numbers match, so it'd be almost the last of the 1969 models made. The metal battery cover is the same as the 1970 B44. Headlight is a 6 3/4" job like the one on the '71 T25SS but not so many indicator lights. The headlight brackets are perforated and look like aftermarket.

Chromework has light-to-moderate rust, and would need redoing. Light rust to inside of tank, which has Triumph garden-gate type badges. Comes with the parts the guy started buying before giving up i.e. parts manual & Haynes Manual, new kickstart quadrant & pinion (old ones there and minced up), gasket set and a new battery that is now stuffed. Frame looks straight. Engine has a couple of rockerbox studs stripped and replaced with bolts. The front LHS rocker box bolt was fitted by hacksawing off the top engine fin! Head stud nuts a bit butchered, so I guess it's been apart for e.g. a stuffed big end and the usual B25 nonsense.

Worst Points - First Visit

Bike has been in storage a long time, probably 5+ years. It was started and run up the street when bought.

Bike has 20,000 miles on the speedo, probably original, (and quite a high mileage says SP a marque/model expert)

No history on bike.

Bike has had engine work, barrel stud nuts show spanner slip, 3 out of 4 rockerbox studs changed to bolts after thread stripping (very common on this model, the next year they increased stud size to 5/16" to help this)

Bike is painted blue - originally they were always red.

Some light surface rust to tank inside and over tinware, but not bad.

Couldn't get the bike outside in the sun for a really close look.

Best Points - First Visit

Bike looks complete, with all tinware, speedo, tank, seat, stands etc.

Has £100 parts claimed to go with it, inc kickstart quadrant (£20 say), pinion (£5), Parts book, (£3), manual (£10), battery (£5 and useless) and bulbs (say £5 max). This sums to £50 at most, so he paid too much or there are more parts. I'll ask.

Bike turns over and has compression.

Frame headstock looks straight and after first look, no evidence seen of crash damage.

Muffler and exhaust look in usable order after a quick look in shed. Muffler looks stock, low pipe, BSA job.

Tank looks undented but didn't run a magnet over it.

For parting out, (breaking for spares) many parts fit other BSA and Triumph singles and even some twins. Front brake is 7" TLS, a very good brake.

Second Inspection Notes

After waiting a few days, (so as not to appear too keen), I went over and had a close second look, and it wasn't as good the second time. They never are, but maybe it was still worth buying?

Worst Points - Second Visit

Steering head bearings and/or fork sliders had a lot of play, rebuild needed.

Swing arm also appeared to have side play, but hard to say as rear wheel also loose in the forks!

The LHS duplex frame member was flattened under the alternator, probably hit a curb etc. This raises probability of frame distortion, although it looks straight.

Side stand went too far forward on a worn or bent mount, accident damage? Main stand ditto.

Chromework all had mild to moderate corrosion, some would polish out, but on balance bike may be only OK for a club bike.

Lots of nuts and bolts replaced with non-std items.

One front guard stay missing.

Bike repainted blue vs original red, after checking the Roy Bacon guide.

Oil tank had emptied into sump and still leaking underneath in all usual places.

Seat has tear near front. Mileage shown is 22,000 miles. Speedo bezel is wonky so you can' t believe that.

Rear guard is OK except the grab handle holes are b*****d, the RHS one has been torn out! Front guard looks OK. Both are painted as was original, but now in blue. This probably means crash damage in past?

Best Points - Second Visit

Numbers match as COO886XTR25W. This is unusual, as it's a pre-1969 form of number, yet the bike is described as 1970. The number on its own is a 1968 number. C is the TR25W code for 1968 and the bike is the 886X made. (The production run for the TR25W was about 20,000 between 1968-1970). However, the toolbox cover, front brake, oil pressure switch etc mark it out as a 1969 or 1970 bike. I believe it's from one of those years, hopefully 1970 as that had a better 3 stud oil pump. Or has the engine number been forged onto a replacement engine?

Bike is complete save the front guard stay

Engine turns over and has compression

Gears all select OK

Tank has only mild rust inside, and could see no dents.

Spare parts include photocopies of original Triumph parts book, and Triumph Shop manual, gasket set (paid £12), NOS kick start quadrant & pinion, battery (now stuffed) and bulbs doesn't sound like much for £100!

Wheels look straight but mild to moderate rust to chrome and the front brake gauze is quite rusty and needs replacing. Forks did not appear to be leaking, surprisingly.

Exhaust system is not original. It has a low RHS pipe and BSA B25 muffler. The pipe is in very good condition save a graze from the kick start (frame damage?). The muffler has a graze or two but no penetrating rust and is usable.

Engine mounts all good, although front one had wrong bolt, as elsewhere.

Engine has been apart as described, 3/4 rocker studs replaced with bolts and barrel stud nuts a bit butchered. All sidecover bolts have been replaced with socket heads and not stainless steel.

Rear wheel turns OK on stand, clutch works.

Main stand works OK, side stand has been strained and sloppy, as they often are, but it is the original part.

Conclusion

The bike looks tired and I doubt it's worth restoring - too much work to do and too much for parts needed. It doesn't present well to show to buyers in person, but might be sold off on EBay. He's taken some parts off e.g. grab rail, footrests covers and hatches etc, and these are all there. I'd only buy it to part out, and I think now that $XXX is all it's worth, as virtually all the bits are well worn.

Completing The Purchase

Assuming a bike passes 'first muster', any used vehicle needs to have it's legal title checked. No matter how genuine the owner, it's good business to check for clear title, and for any encumbrances and debts. In the UK both the buyer and seller must complete the form V5C, the registration certificate to alert the DVLA to the sale and the address of the New Keeper. If the person selling the vehicle is not the same as the person registered as the 'Keeper' then seek further reassurance from the seller that he is indeed the owner. Governments around Australia enable free REV (Register of Encumbered Vehicles) online checks. Such things are never taken on trust: as my father told me, it's not a question of trust, it's business.

The next step is a second look at the bike, and a test-ride on the front or back seat so the bike can be listened to and felt operating. If that's impossible, the owner should be happy to start and ride the bike, while the buyer observes. However, it's not essential to ride a bike before purchase. Frankly, if a bike's been in storage a while, it may be better not to run it. Risks can't be avoided. A restorer-friend went through the above steps on a US Bonnie import that looked lovely only to find it soon needed expensive engine repairs. The bike had been ridden occasionally, and when the new owner rode it harder and farther, the oil pump failed and the engine seized. I'd also ridden the bike and found it excellent - who can you trust for advice these days!?

Classic Bike Negotiation

It's surprising how few people have negotiation training when life is a continuing negotiation. After checking out courses and texts, I recommend (and occasionally teach) the Harvard method. The reference is *Getting to Yes*, by Fisher and Ury (Business Books, 1986). It's a classic and still in print after twenty years. Their method can be mastered in fifteen minutes. Their essential four points are recalled with a mnemonic, 'PICO'.

P	People & Problems	Be hard on the problem and soft on the people.
I	Interests	Think about mutual interests,not taking up positions.
C	Criteria	Insist on objective criteria, to avoid being pressured.
O	Options	Invent lots of options, look for the best mutual outcome.

For example, if the seller is old and has owned the bike for years, it's good practice to be 'soft on the owner' and assure them their 'interests' will be served, and the bike treasured by the new owner.

If a price has been mentioned, it's wise to ask the seller what 'criteria' he bases that on. Ideally, research into the model shows what's being asked and achieved for the model. This is where clubs are invaluable, they know what's selling around town. Sometimes the seller says something like "This is what it owes me..." which can be a bit confrontational, and is best countered by recent sales data to show the owner perhaps needs to be a little more realistic in his expectations.

It's productive to be 'soft on the vendor', but report the list of 'problems' from the bike inspection. This tends to shake unrealistic vendors. Costing up the needed repairs, helps the rider appear an old hand. Deducting repairs from the asking price is a useful option for establishing and gaining agreement on a fair market value price. Sometimes this is hard, especially where owners purchased bikes during a boom and now they can't bear to take a loss even as the bike rusts away in storage. It's wise to walk away from such deals. There are lots of other classic bikes about.

A useful option is to ask what else comes with the bike: spare parts, clothing, helmets, gloves and even tools or tyres can be gleaned. Often, it's these add-on items that makes the deal attractive.

In the euphoria, it is easy to forget cautious habits with motor vehicles. In New South Wales the UK and New Zealand, buyers must see the vendor executes the change in ownership papers if the bike is registered. Ownership legally passes to the buyer when he pays for it. Buyers are also legally liable for the bike once they make the purchase. For both reasons it's wise to take delivery of the bike on the spot. Where the buyer does not have a motorcycle licence, the seller can often be persuaded into one last delivery ride. Often the vendor remembers some important information about the bike on that final ride and another classic motorcycle passage has begun.

Illus 3.9 A well restored Velocette recently at an auction in NZ

4 *Licensing, Registration And Insurance*

"In those days you could get fined stupid on your Ls and never really 'lose' your licence, because you didn't actually have one. It was a hiccup in the system which spawned a lot of mature L-platers until it was fixed." Boris, 2003

As more classic clubs and riders embark on international rides, it's timely to consider both domestic and visitor registration as well as rider licensing in the major classic British bike countries. Compliance practices are similar worldwide and involve the bike's entry into a central register, with or without a VIN (Vehicle Identification Number) or chassis plate, and sometimes separate licensing for use on the roads involving a number plate sticker or tax disc. This section provides summary information and noteworthy requirements by particular countries.

UK Classic Registration System

The British system for classic bikes is simple. For bikes made before 1973, the tax or Vehicle Excise Duty, is simply waived but a tax disc must still be displayed even though it is free. There are no special riding conditions as found, for example downunder. Annual mechanical checks (the MoT test) are required after three years as in other countries. Bikes not 'on the road' must suspend registration through SORN (Statutory Off Road Notification). This is useful for classic bikes laid up, used either seasonally or infrequently, or undergoing restoration. An abstract of the UK SORN requirements is quoted below by kind permission of the DVLA in the UK.

"SORN (Statutory Off Road Notification). If you are the keeper of a vehicle and you do not license it because you do not use it or keep it on a public road, you must tell us as soon as you take the vehicle off the road. Telling us about this is called declaring SORN (Statutory Off Road Notification). SORN declarations are valid for 12 months and must be renewed, if the vehicle is kept off road for a further period under the system of Continuous Registration (CR), which commenced in January 2004, it is not necessary for your vehicle to be sighted on the public road for an offence to have been committed...."
Source: DVLA UK.

The British authorities run their older regional registration system in parallel with their new national system, enabling riders of classic bikes to retain their regional registration number (the old, original number) and the original plates. Alternatively they can obtain 'age related plates' which are plates of the same form as the original, once a few conditions are met. This system adds an authentic dimension to classic bikes. (Interestingly some US states e.g. New York State, have a similar system where obsolete plates, bought privately at swapmeets etc, may be reinstated by the state regulatory body. US vehicle plates have become collectibles for young men in many countries. It's possible to speculate on their future re-import to the USA, once their classic value is perceived.)

The USA Classic Registration System

The federal USA system requires classic bikes to be registered at the state level, as in Australia. It's beyond the scope of this book to discuss US registration for all fifty US states. US classic bike registration is easier in the USA than in most countries. Vehicle registration is also cheap for US residents, with ordinary motorcycle registration fees as low as £5 (US$10) per annum. Even so, many states have conditional registration schemes, for 'historical vehicles' aged 30 years or more. In some states such as Alabama and Montana where Mr. Barger (of Hells Angels fame) now rides, he can register his classic Harley-Davidsons for under $10 each per annum! That seems to be the cheapest motorcycle registration in the classic world.

Australian Classic Registration System

In Australia, there are eight state bodies regulating classic motorcycling around the continent. These comprise New South Wales, Victoria, Queensland, South Australia, Western Australia, Tasmania and the two territories - the Northern Territory and the Australian Capital Territory. Here motorcycle regulation borrows from the UK system. However, over the past century each state has developed quirks in their policies. Classic bikes are first registered in a State Vehicle Register which issues VINs (Vehicle Identification Numbers) and number plates. This amounts to official recognition that the vehicle exists in the country. Next the machine is licensed, which entitles the owner to take the machine onto the roads. Interestingly, Australian authorities have no counterpart to the UK SORN, or the equivalent New Zealand MR24 procedure.

Each state has conditional registering of classic bikes. In all states bar Victoria, (which has the greatest density of classic bikes), any bike over 30 years old is regarded as a classic. All such bikes are eligible for conditional, or concessional registration, at a substantial saving. For £20-£40, riders receive 12 months registration, licensing and third party insurance. The riding conditions vary by state and include the requirement to join a classic club and ride the bike mainly on club or other associated outings. The system works on an honour code, and riders are expected to be reasonable, and avoid exploitation. Daily commuting is vetoed, but the number of commuters on classic bikes is small anyway. In addition, riders are entitled to ride whenever they feel like testing the engine, carburettor, suspension, tappets, timing, tyres, fuel and oil consumption. Depending on the state, a 10-40kms (6 to 25 miles) radius from home is regarded as reasonable by authorities for testing - and isn't every ride on a classic bike a challenge if not a test? Frankly, a 10-40km radius around a rider's home contains much of his travel. Where longer rides are anticipated, say for measuring the range of a full tank, an email to the club secretary advising of the ride, is all that is required. Other acceptable ride purposes include runs to repair shops, roadtests, processions, displays, ceremonial and educational uses, classic bike events, races etc. It's not difficult to maximise enjoyment and the bank balance with conditional registration. With an ounce of planning nearly every ride can be a complying ride. Some riders bridle at accepting any conditions and pay five or six times as much for ordinary registration. They spend much of their riding on club rides with other conditionally registered bikes. Puzzling, that.

Providing one has title and a club mechanical check (unlike the UK the inspections are organized by the clubs in Australia), registration is plain sailing for all classics. Originally the clubs issued plates, registrations and MoTs and this may explain why bike identification and provenance is less an issue in Australia than in New Zealand or the UK.

For readers who've not yet ridden in Australia, imagine a country with very low traffic densities away from the coast, a dry climate (annual rainfall is only as deep as this page) and excellent roads and infrastructure. Nearly everywhere is within a vintage tankful of the next service station. There is much wonderful scenery, and genuinely friendly inhabitants. To be honest there is also a range of dangerous and venomous animals and insects that share the best motorcycling regions and roads. There is extreme danger in riding at dusk, dawn or at night in some places. Australia has a range of nocturnal animals , and some are so large they're fatal to hit on a bike. Peter Thoeming in his book *Motorcycling in Australia* (Bear Faced Books, 2001 and a must-have for any rider visiting Australia) compares the nocturnal wombat to a sack full of bricks - when hit by a bike! I've hit two kangaroos at night and now never travel on a motorcycle at dawn, dusk or night outside urban areas!

New Zealand Classic Registration System

Uniquely, New Zealand retains flexible motorcycle registration and licensing procedures. Registration is the entry in the Motor Vehicle Register, and causes the issue of a VIN chassis plate along with a number-plate. Licensing is the fee for the use of the number plate on public roads. The two functions are often confused. The authorities are vigilant on classic bike identification and provenance. A barn find, a special or a grey channel import are all difficult, even impossible to register.

A friend recently bought a grey-channel Japanese classic and was refused registration as customs duty and clear title to the bike were 'involved'. In desperation, he purchased a frame from a write-off that had been registered. He stripped his bike, and rebuilt it onto the used frame purely to obtain registration. Other restorers buy an old plate for the bike, declaring it has been sitting in their barn for thirty years to explain it's absence from the register. Wasn't it Clausewitz who said 'for every strategy, there's a counter stratagem'?

The requirement to rivet a VIN plate onto classic motorcycle frames is one reason for the low registration rate in New Zealand. A more conservationist approach to this would be to do as other countries and use the frame number as the Vehicle Identification Number.

A hangover from the time New Zealand had the oldest vehicle fleet in the world, even older than Cuba, is the Warrant of Fitness (WOF) test. This *six monthly* check is the equivalent to the British MoT. Another quirk of the New Zealand system is that it is possible to license a classic motorcycle for a day, a week or a year.

New Zealand's MR24 system enables riders to suspend their bike licence for up to two years. Like the UK's SORN, it is free and useful for laying bikes up over winter or for a rebuild, without running the risk of losing the plate. This is one policy initiative authorities in Australian states should copy. Another Kiwi advantage is the facility for combining the MR24 suspension with the similar MR27 for changing a vehicle's license date so that renewal comes at a more convenient and financially more advantageous time for the owner. The dual MR24 and MR27 process enables classic riders to minimise running costs. This is a factor in the high retention rate for classic motorcycles in New Zealand (see also Chapter 11)

New Zealand is backward in its conditional registration of classic motorcycles, as their scheme cuts in at forty years, versus thirty years in other countries. This encourages workarounds by resourceful riders where post-1966 bikes are registered from an earlier time.

It is interesting to note that by 1902 local councils in New Zealand were passing bylaws for motorcycles. Magistrates enforced these as in the UK. Public opinion went against motorcycles, as riders breached these bylaws. It seems to ignore history to claim that poor public perception of motorcycles began in the 1940s with the Hollister fracas, or in the 1950s with Mods and Rockers in the UK. The public image was formed decades before, at least in New Zealand. My father recounts a 1920s example of this in his memoirs.

How the Whakatane Motorcycle Club Formed in New Zealand

"Along with his fellow riders in Whakatane, Lyle preferred a straight, two inch diameter exhaust pipe, replacing the BSA fishtail silencer. This gave an exhaust note Lyle described as 'kicking up Hell's Delight'. It's interesting to record the modus vivendi over exhaust noise, between the traffic warden, a County official named Marks, and Whakatane riders. Lyle describes Marks as "a miserable bastard if ever there was one", who delighted in catching motorcyclists by hiding under farm hedges and bridges and even in drains near favoured corners. He would leap from hiding and fine the riders for racing, speeding or excessive noise. Marks became such a nuisance to Whakatane riders, they decided to form a club to put their racing beyond Mr. Mark's reach (At that time a Club could legally hold road races on public roads, whereas individuals could not!). This is how the Whakatane Motorcycle Club formed. The Club's rules allowed straight pipes on member's bikes, providing they avoided a heavy throttle-hand in town. The rules also required members to push-start their bikes inside the town limits, apparently to reduce noise, although I can't see how this measure helped much, unless they started in say, second gear. Perhaps it also enabled members to leave the area quickly, and avoid identification! Members apparently complied with this push-start requirement, and Lyle reported a truce which was long respected by Marks and Club members..."

Rider Licensing

Rider training and licensing programmes differ internationally. Every country is intensifying and stretching their training programmes in an effort to reduce the number of accidents, especially those by newly licensed riders. The number of symposia devoted to motorcycle accidents, training and licensing is impressive, with academic reputations being enhanced along the way. Returning classic motorcycle riders who have let their licence lapse, are caught up in complex training and licensing hurdles erected by authorities. From some angles, these programmes look like an effort to discourage potential riders. In this section, we set out to assist such riders negotiate these hurdles and obtain a riding license at the first attempt.

The complexity of country rider licensing systems (USA apart), means a number of grey areas or loopholes exist. One of these is the inclusion of classic bikes for learner riders. This is based upon the lower power and greater weight of classic bikes compared with contemporary machines. We see arbitrary power to weight ratios of for example 150 kilowatts/tonne quoted and rules that dictate permissible bikes by cylinder capacity. It was this simplistic decision-making that saw the British 250cc learner rule in the 1960s, that so aided the Japanese machines in taking over the British market. Now, in an eerie reprise, it's happening in reverse. Due to questionable numbers on power calculations, in many places learners can legally ride classic 650cc twins including for example Bonnevilles, Spitfires and Lightnings.

All the countries of interest use a blend of theory, practical training and assessment in their rider licensing arrangements. Some countries are trying the fashionable Hazard Perception Technology (an interactive video training system pioneered in Japan). It seems sensible, but some video-based trials resulted in motion sickness. Most schemes involve the new rider in a graduated training process, trying to impart the skills and attitudes necessary for survival on modern roads. The costs are born by the rider, and it's interesting to compare the cost of a motorcycle licence in the UK, USA, Australia and New Zealand. Currently it costs £79 more or less, in the UK to obtain a full licence although rather more once the Compulsory Basic Training is included. In Sydney it's £100, while in New Zealand it's £110. The UK has the most complex and expensive training and assessment whilst New Zealand fosters the youngest riders with 15 year olds eligible to ride. In the UK it's 17 years and in Australia, it's 16.75 in Sydney. The USA is the cheapest place to gain a motorcycle licence. For just 15p in Montana, you can have your car licence appended with a motorcycle licence. Even in the Eastern states, the complete licence training package including theory and roadtests can be had for under £9 in New Jersey. Either licensing and registration in the USA are being subsidised by government, or riders in other countries are being ripped off once again.

In the spirit of squaring the slate for riders, here are some tips for exploiting weaknesses in national licensing tests which should help ensure riders pass first time. Born-Again-Bikers often fall into the 25% of candidates who fail. This is because they recall the simple licence testing of their youth but nothing could be further from today's testing, than the perfunctory 1950s test order to "Ride round the block, young fella, and stop here when you get back."

The Duffers Guide To Passing Your Motorcycle Test

This generally breaks into two parts, the theory and the practical or riding tests.

Passing The Theory Or Knowledge Test

The first advice is, Don't Panic! It may be some years since school exams, but preparation is still the best antidote for panic. Compared to school exams the licence tests are deliberately simple and trick questions are uncommon. The questions are designed to help riders pass. In some countries the knowledge test is the first step. In others such as Australia, it's taken after an initial rider training course. This test is nearly the same for car drivers and sometimes it's the same test with a few bike questions added.

The best way to ensure a pass is to read and re-read the handouts given to learners. Look for the topics and points that lead to single number answers, speed limits for example. Look for any quirky areas where the state or country may have some distinctive driving practice or rule, such as how to navigate roundabouts, signaling and traffic lanes etc. There are a limited number of motorcycle-specific issues and questions on lane-sharing, pillions and speed limits come up again and again. It's useful to talk to a relative or friend who's recently taken the car or bike test and pump them for the type of questions and topics covered.

Increasingly this test is a multiple choice questionnaire with 30-40 questions, taken at a computer terminal. The multiple choice format is easiest as it reduces 'exam stress' and there's no distraction. In some jurisdictions there will be sample questions available for study, or even a dummy self-assessment test to take on the net. Sometimes the actual questions are published as they are in New South Wales where eighty questions are listed on the NSW website. The actual test is always a sample of these.

TIPS

In this case it's quicker and easier to memorise the answers to each of the questions, than it is to read and remember the whole handbook. This saves time and effort, and a 100% score is possible without much effort or stress.

If it's a computer terminal test there'll often be a time limit. Estimate how much time for each question, and skip any that can't be answered straightaway. This way, there's time to return to the hard ones. Often, at the end, the outstanding ones are now easy as intervening questions have suggested the answer. To gain this second chance... it's useful to set a watch beside the PC, to watch the time.

Every question should be attempted. With multiple choice there's a good chance of guessing the right answer, especially if one or two of the answers can be excluded as clearly wrong. It's a bit like the technique used on TV quiz shows.

Pass The Road Training And Fly Through The Riding Test

Most but not all places require the rider to show he can ride a bike. Whether a newby or just returning to motorcycling, there are steps that ramp up the chances of flying through the road test. Up to one quarter of candidates fail roadtests, because they're unprepared. It's humiliating to re-book and re-pay for a second attempt in front of the next class. Knowing they know you've failed once makes it harder to pass the second time, and you don't always get course practice before your second effort.

TIPS

Anticipate the tester is not going to go on public roads and test candidates at road-speeds. It won't happen. Riders are hardly out of first gear all day. They'll focus on these slow speed skills - right angle turns, braking, emergency braking within a set distance, U-turns inside a box, slalom runs and, if the trainer is good, they'll provide guidance on posture and weight distribution.

Do the training with a single cylinder offroad or trail bike rather than a road bike. The reason for this is the lighter weight and it's better low speed maneuverability and steering lock. There's a greater chance of passing the training and road test on a 250cc single off-roader, than on a Harley. Also, faired sports-bikes tend to be long and low, with a seating position unsuited (and often unsighted) for the slow, tight turns on the training course. If you can't borrow a suitable bike, rent one for the day. You'll save the rental fee by avoiding another training and testing fee.

Choose a short wheelbase bike. This pays off on the training ground where most of the training is conducted at low speeds. A shorter wheelbase bike lets you fly through the tight, right-angle and U-turns favoured by the test protocols. Avoid using any long wheelbase bike like Harley-Davidsons. Heavy bikes with a long wheelbase are far more inclined to 'fall inwards' into the tight, slow turns on the training courses. Why make it harder than it has to be?

Make sure the clutch and brakes are well adjusted. The only way to stay upright and pass some of the really slow-speed tests is to ride at a trickle with the clutch semi-engaged, while on the brake. Master this beforehand.

If possible, book a female trainer/tester. For some reason, every male trainer I've experienced, from L-plates to Advanced level, has acted like a barrack room sergeant. Female riders make better trainers, and more sympathetic testers! Works for me anyhow.

The more time on the bike...the more likely you are to pass the ride test. If allowed, skip the breaks and put in the time on the course.

TIPS (cont)

If the only bike you own is British and pre-1971 but you are riding a modern machine for the test, then make sure you are comfortable with turn indicators and their cancelling method. I once went through a road test with my right blinker going, as I had no idea how to turn it off. It is also necessary to know about kill switches and left side gear shifts. Testers have little sympathy if you change gear when you're supposed to be performing an emergency stop! Nor will they take kindly to an inability to turn the engine off.

Be prepared to use the front brake far more than on a classic bike. The trainer will insist on it, as it's the fashion these days. Humour them till you get back on a proper bike!

Make up a starting mnemonic for your bike, as the trainer may well insist on it. Unless you're an aircraft pilot, and used to such start-up sequences, then you can be put off your riding by this unfamiliar notion. A typical classic bike start-up mnemonic is 'COFIN' where C=Choke, O= Oil tap, F=fuel, I= Ignition and N=Neutral and see the advice on starting in Chapter 2

Lastly, the BIG secret is that you've actually passed the riding test...before you've taken it! How can this be? The training is broken down into small steps that you master sequentially. As the steps become more challenging you progress to a level of competence one step beyond the actual test! When you take the test, it's supposed to be an anti-climax, yet a percentage still wash out.

Classic Motorcycle Insurance

Motorcycling has always been attractive, partly because of the risk attached to riding unstable machines. This is explored further in Chapter five. The road accident statistics show not much has improved in the risk department since classic bikes came off the production line. In fact, it's a lot more hazardous riding now than it was a generation ago. That's why regulatory authorities insist on insurance for classic bikes, along with other vehicles. Some package third party insurance cover along with their low-cost Historic Vehicle registration. This is the case in Australia and makes conditional registration even more attractive, even so a lot of classic riders never take out additional, fully comprehensive cover. Why is this? It can't be just the cost of insurance. Insurance companies increasingly see classic motorcycle riders as a target demographic for insurance generally. They offer low-cost classic bike comprehensive insurance as a loss-leader product, to get us on their books. £20 a year buys £2,000 of bike cover, including salvage and other benefits downunder. Similar benefits and cheap insurance are offered by specialist insurance companies in the UK. This is great rider value and smart marketing by the insurance industry. It's worth shopping around, as insurance companies may offer even cheaper coverage for classics under restoration.

Certain insurance companies recognise that COBBERs (Cross Over Bikers) are growing in numbers and affluence, and extend cheap classic bike insurance to some new bikes as well. Harley-Davidsons are an example of this. From the company's point of view, this makes good sense. If you can afford a Harley-Davidson, there's a good chance you've other assets and property to produce juicy premium income for the insurance company.

Given the expansion in classic vehicle insurance, it's worth checking for new products every year. It's surprising how many riders know little about the insurance and road service packages available at cheap prices. For example, the National Roads and Motorists Association (NRMA), in New South Wales offer a splendid package through their Veteran, Vintage and Classic Insurance group. £20 (Aus $50) buys one years comprehensive classic bike insurance that includes accident damage, theft, storm, fire, hail and flood damage, windscreen and glass damage, as well as bike accessories and personal baggage. Even better, it includes towing and bike storage costs, even if you're towing a trailer, and even includes legal representation and liability cover up to £8,000,000. Now couple that with a basic club membership and you've covered most of the things that can disable you on a long run, short of mechanical, tyre and electrical problems.

I'm surprised some larger classic clubs haven't moved in to this classic insurance area. It would be simple for a large club to form an insurance pool for members at affordable premiums. The concept is sound, even at the level of an extended family grouping with a dozen cars and a few bikes. When you add up the annual premium outgoings, for a classic club or a large family, it's tempting to think what could be achieved with that cash each year, by keeping it in the club. Some day an enterprising broker will package such a scheme and indeed, in the UK both Carole Nash and Footman James offer clubs special packages for their members.

Breakdown And Salvage

In many countries there are private networks providing motorcycle transport services, including breakdown and extrication. Road America in the USA is a good example, with a national network of providers supplied to other organisations including HOG (the Harley Owners Group), other motorcycle clubs and motor insurance companies. Downunder, the state motorists associations in Australia and the Automobile Association (AA) in New Zealand, provide a competitive package of insurance and roadside services. In the UK, the AA and RAC amongst others offer excellent roadside assistance and recovery services. Specialist classic insurance companies, such as Carole Nash for example, include European wide breakdown insurance as part of their standard comprehensive insurance package.

For classic club riders, the situation is normally covered on club rides, with a salvage vehicle or a buddy system. However, where long solo rides of 500 to 3000 miles (1,000-5,000kms) are made, it's worth considering a roadside assistance package. It's a small price to pay to assuage that terrible sinking feeling as you coast to the roadside in the middle of nowhere as dusk falls.

Motoring associations used to provide roadside assistance for a cheap membership fee that covered classic bikes as well as your car. Nowadays some of these companies marketing departments are charging memberships by the vehicle, and that disadvantages riders since it is rarely cost-effective to enroll several classic bikes individually, as well as the family car: but a few, such as the UKs AA, still offer multiple vehicles per member.

International Aspects Of Licensing, Registration And Insurance

Reciprocal Motoring Association Memberships

It's possible to legally exploit loopholes that have opened up as motoring associations have become increasingly international. For example, you can choose to take a motoring association membership in a country which continues to offer multiple vehicle cover per membership, and employ the reciprocal membership provisions to obtain roadside assistance in other, more expensive countries - namely the one in which you spend most of your time. This can be a real money-saver, as well as providing emergency assistance at no extra cost when you travel in the issuing country, or indeed in any other country within the reciprocal network. It's worth noting the reciprocal network includes all the countries discussed in this book. The only catch, is you need to carry the issuing country membership card, plus a printout of your membership receipt to show in any country where you require road service. This can of course, be done over the net in a few moments: you just print copies for each vehicle you operate and keep a copy in the toolbox. It's worth noting this reciprocal cover covers borrowed or rented vehicles of every kind, including cars.

Motoring associations issue international licenses (International Driving Permits), at a small cost. It's useful having one to ride or drive in different countries and mandatory if they're non-English speaking places. Having two licences is cheap insurance against having one lost or stolen, especially when riding in countries where one could be confiscated in order to extract a bribe or fine. It's nearly as good as a passport for identification. In the event you lose your main licence, say for a serious traffic infringement, you can continue on with your surviving licence, and sort out the mess when you get home.

Shipping Your Bike Overseas And International Documentation

It's surprising how much experience there is among classic road and racing clubs in shipping loads of club bikes in containers for overseas travel. For example, there are regular New Zealand classic club visits to Tasmania, and a growing flow of classics going the other way from mainland Australian clubs. I'm told it's possible to ship a load of classic bikes from New Zealand to Australia for as little as £200 per bike, if the loading, unloading and documentation are handled by club members. To achieve this sort of cost, container loadings need to be maximised by loading the bikes in two layers. There are tales of woe where bikes have come adrift in transit when simply stood and strapped to container sides, damaging the tinware. It's preferable to pack the bikes in recycled bike shipping crates. The Harley-Davidson crates are outstanding for this as they are of welded steel construction, so there are no quarantine issues with timber, insects and fumigation etc. The crates or cage-frames come with tie-downs and a strong heavy board-stock cover that can be re-used by screwing it onto the frame. As with the professional shippers, these frames can be screwed into the container floor, preventing movement during transit. They're forklift-friendly from the sides and ends. A friendly Harley-Davidson dealer may furnish these if approached the right way. For a 'no hands' approach and where clubs are able to pay a good deal more, then packages are to be found in the motorcycling magazines. 'Get Routed' has blazed the trail between Australia-New Zealand, and Australia-England over the past eight years, and averages a container every two months to Christchurch, New Zealand, from Sydney with more leaving from Brisbane and Melbourne. They use proper bike cradles that are screwed into the container floor, preventing movement and transit damage.

Documentation issues vary by country, and can include a Carnet, basically a visa for the bike, freight and customs procedures, as well as temporary registration, licensing and insurance in some destinations, like New Zealand. Carnets are organised through motoring associations, who can also advise on the shipping process. For classic clubs interested in the idea, a good way to start is to invite one of the experienced organisers from another club to speak, or persuade them to send a copy of their overseas trip reports from their newsletter. Such capable folk are usually happy to take time out to brief another club on how to set it up. The key thing is to find a reliable, cost-effective freight forwarder. And when its all done and your bike arrives the other end, there's nothing like the thrill of riding your own familiar classic bike in another country.

What of the future? It's not difficult to envisage the streamlining and packaging of international bike movements by the freight forwarding, shipping and insurance industries. Perhaps specially equipped 'ride in-ride out' shipping containers will be developed, exploiting the available shipping economies of scale internationally. Entrepreneurs may study the information in Chapter 11 on survival statistics and develop cheap international packages for classic riders. Even in a 'small' classic bike country like Australia, there are thousands of classic riders shipping their bikes overseas each year, and the business is growing rapidly. The major international rider packaging groups like Dave Milligan's accurately named 'Get Routed', reports an annual doubling of business over each of the past seven years, while the Harley-Davidson 'Fly-Ride Programme' continues expanding internationally.

5 *Bonding With Your Bike*

"I've always had a big passion for the line; for me the line is like a poem. My focus is always for my lines to be within the same centimeter every time for 20 laps." V. Rossi

The classic motorcycle literature refers to a special link between motorcycle riders and their machines. These references are always brief and tantalising even though experienced riders instinctively know of this link. It's time to describe this connection so that it can be passed on to wives, sons and grandsons. Last weekend I took our eldest son pillion on his first ever motorcycle run. He's 32 years old and for the first ten kilometres was grinning under his helmet, and didn't know why.

Whether British, American, Aussie or Kiwi, riders know that a favourite motorcycle evokes an emotional response. Modern bikes do not seem to evoke quite the same reaction. I enjoy the Sportster, but have a different association with my BSA B44SS. Why is that? We might expect aviation pilots to experience a similar connection with their favourite aeroplanes but experienced pilots advise they have no emotional link with their aircraft, whether military or civil. Their relationship is 'purely operational' they say. Modern aircraft, like modern motorcycles, apparently no longer evoke these feelings. Classic aircraft, say the Spitfire or Tiger Moth may trigger these reactions in their pilots. Here are three quotes. Two are from classic motorcycle riders, and one from a classic pilot, about their machines.

Quote One "I took the machine in hand...I have never forgotten the first sensation, the feeling of travelling over the ground without effort was delightful. The machine did not seem to go fast enough...at length I burst upon the astonished company... I shut off the petrol...and dismounted as gracefully as I could. From that moment I became a staunch believer, and predicted a great future for it..."

Quote Two "It was a beautiful machine and I shall never forget the thrill of that hair-raising... I really came to love that..."

Quote Three- "All my life, I shall remember my first... the clean lines, beautiful engine, a real thoroughbred... I adjusted my helmet...dazed.... I went through... murmuring the ritual phrase... with a sound like thunder, the engine fired, exhausts vomited, the throb of the engine ticking over was like the beating of a winded race-horses flanks....how beautiful the machine seemed to me and how alive! A masterpiece of harmony and power, even as I saw her now motionless.....Softly as one might caress a woman's cheeks, I ran my hand over her.... cold and smooth like a mirror... which would hold my life within the narrow confines and which I would love like a faithful friend..."

One description was evoked by a Douglas motorcycle, one by a Spitfire (Supermarine not BSA) and one is from a Pioneer rider: turn to the end of the chapter, page 69 for the answers if you can't guess.

Fred Hoyle (the Nobel prize winning cosmologist and occasional science fiction writer) points to the starting line in the search for answers with his rule of prediction "...look for the commonplace, as that's what most people overlook". The commonplace starting point seems to be why men ride classic motorcycles in the first place. The seminal research into why men ride motorcycles was recently completed by Jamson from Leeds University (*S Jamson, K Chorlton and M Conner, The Older Motorcyclist, Department for Transport, London 2005*). Parts of their research could have been re-titled, 'The Classic Motorcycle Rider'.

In table 5.1 below are the reasons British riders gave for purchasing their bikes. Although classic riders weren't the focus of this 2005 research they do comprise 20% of UK motorcycles. Given that the ages of classic bikes and riders correlate, classic riders can be placed in the 'Long-Term' and 'Returning' riders in the table below.

Table 5.1	Reasons For Buying Your Latest Bike[*]	
Rank order	**Long-term rider**	**Returning rider**
1	Love of motorcycles	Love of motorcycles
2	Independence and freedom	To engage in leisure activity
3	To engage in leisure activity	Independence and freedom
4	To avoid congestion	To avoid congestion
5	Motorcycle maintenance	Image associated

* extracted from 'The Older Motorcyclist', Jamson et al, 2005. Table 11, p37.

One classic biker tell-tale is the strong reporting of motorcycle maintenance by long-term riders. It's very likely these respondents were riding classic British machines, as Jamson unknowingly elaborates.

"The motorcycle is reportedly an 'image associated' commodity that could reflect a certain 'way of life'. The long-term rider still bases purchasing decisions upon a motorcycle's appropriateness for 'engaging in a leisure activity' but does not rank the importance of image highly. Motorcycle maintenance is instead ranked highly...."

It's interesting to contrast this with other recent British findings into motorcycle 'keepers' i.e. how long a bike stays with one owner. That research found 48% of classic motorcycles are still with their first owner! (*Transport Statistics Bulletin Compendium of Motorcycle Statistics, DfT, 2004*) Clearly there is a group of extremely long-term classic riders out there. Jamson also found their subjects admitting to love affairs with their bikes: some classic riders even give their bikes affectionate names. So much for the image of the British being emotionally undemonstrative! These researchers unfortunately missed the obvious differences between classic and current bikes and their riders; engine capacity and engine power; speeding and motivations etc. Their 'good-news' finding of the long-term 14% decline in UK motorcycle casualties, was also left un-explored. They, like most motorcycling researchers focus on motorcycle mortality statistics, instead of balancing their research with the positives of motorcycling. Researchers too must sing for their supper. Overall, the Jamson research is masterly work, and long overdue. For this bonding enquiry, we can include those aged fifty years plus, who have continued riding throughout their life, as 'Long-Term' classic riders. Jamson's 'Returning' category includes classic Borne Again Bikers (BABs).

Both rider groups give independence, freedom, leisure, love, and avoiding congestion as the reasons they ride. The points of difference are maintenance and image. The researchers found maintenance a positive goal, which points to classic bikes. Contemporary bike riders are insulated from maintenance by distributors and warranties. For classic bikers, apart from some narrow aspects in originality to concours levels and period clothing, image doesn't enter their motorcycling. Classic riders often turn out in unmatched period clothing that is prized for it's patina and battle scars, rather than fashion kudos. Image is a tell-tale sign of contemporary bikers, and especially the Harley-Davidson community. Yet that battered classic riding gear is chosen by many and it also projects an image.

This British research contains more useful information about classic bike trends. For example it shows a seven-fold increase over the 1990s and 2000s, in riders returning to biking. These include BABs returning to classic motorcycling, but the research model was not designed to detect this. Equally suggestive are the age breakdowns of BABs, when viewed together. This shows classic BABs are not just pensioners, as the age groups are 30 to 65 years. The bike sizes reinforce this by showing bikes in the classic engine sizes i.e. 500cc-650cc, are mainly ridden by older riders. This equates with what we see in clubs - classic British motorcycles exert a fascination for younger as well as older men, and some women and therefore incidentally shows classic motorcycling has a great future.

A definitive motorcycling study was done by Elliott et al in the UK in 2003. (*MA Elliott et al. Motorcycle Safety: A Scoping Study. Prepared for the Road Safety Division, DfT. TRL Report 581*) This shows why people ride bikes, and extends earlier US research. Elliott found fifteen reasons for motorcycle riding. These include hedonism, escapism, the dynamic aspects of biking, performance aspects of biking, exhibition riding, rivalry, thrill and adventure seeking, flow effects, identifying with the bike, safety behaviour, control beliefs, social aspects, economic aspects, independence, and convenience. Eight of these reasons relate to classic riders:

Hedonism

All motorcycling gives a good feeling, and classic bikes   give an even better feeling, one Elliot describes as 'autotelic'

> "*A particular kind of experience that is so engrossing and enjoyable that it becomes autotelic, that is, worth doing for its own sake even though it may have no consequence outside itself.*" (*Csikszentmihalyi 1999*).

Escapism.

Classic riders are escapists, though they normally return home to spouses after the ride.

Dynamic Aspects.

Elliott means acceleration, speed, power, mobility, cornering and the physics of the motorcycle, things classic riders also enjoy.

Flow Effects.

Elliott introduces Csikszentmihalyi, who captures classic motorcycling as a 'flow state':

> "*...where attention is narrowed down to a limited field, the self loses meaning, nothing disturbs the flow of action and complete control over the course of events seems to be present in highly practised, intrinsically motivated and competently executed activities...*" (*Csikszentmihalyi, 1988*).

T. E. Lawrence could have written that. Self-aware motorcycle riders speak of feeling 'smooth'. Smoothness and flow are the same motorcycling state. It seems 'Mr Chicks Send Me High' (his pronunciation) can help us with this bonding enquiry.

Identifying With The Bike.

Elliott quotes Hobbs (1986) that 62% of riders believe riding is a way of life, and that older riders are using the motorcycle to regain their youth and their experiences of riding at an earlier age (the 'born-again bikers' effect).

Thrill And Adventure Seeking.

Classic bikes offer thrills and adventure, but this doesn't mean risky riding. Elliott reports 72% of riders disagree with the statement, 'you have to take your chances when riding a bike'. Elliott speculates the thrill comes from the mastery of risks through skill. This points again to Csikszentmihalyi and flow, and leads to control of the bike.

Control.

Elliott nails classic motorcycling, as *"something about the dynamics of controlling a motorcycle appeals to riders. The same aspects motivate riders to take risks"* but he has mixed feelings about control, and speaks of it's dark side

"control is attributed to riders who believe their riding qualifications are perfect. These people believe that they can control themselves, the vehicle, other road users and the situation all of the time...."

Social Aspects.

The mateship in talking, maintaining, restoring and riding classic bikes is magnified by club membership, balancing the aloneness of riding. Many riders belong to several clubs. Elliott, like every other motorcycling researcher, overlooks the classic bike community. Three more reasons must be added to redress this:

Maintenance. This is an integral part of motorcycling with classic bikes. For some it's as important as riding. Shed time gives a sense of anticipation for the next ride perhaps to try out a new setting. And it's a well known fact that after every oil change and greasing, the bike seems to run better.

Restoration. This is the highest calling in classic motorcycling. Restorers become honoured figures and are acknowledged as such at club concours awards. Restoration is a way of communicating the nostalgia riders feel for the classic period.

Conservation. The more a bike is ridden, the more it wears out. Conservation is an issue with classics in their second century. Many riders now see themselves as stewards of these old works of art. Vintage and veteran bikes are still ridden and hard, but not as frequently. Several strategies are developing to marry conservation with riding. Firstly, by adding a second classic bike to take the load off the 'best bike'. Secondly, by trailering the best bike to rallies. Thirdly, by adding a post-classic or Japanese machine to share the load. Fourthly, buying a new 'classic' bike for the longer rides e.g. a Royal Enfield, Triumph or Sportster. This also opens up long-distance and circumnavigation riding. By such measures riders keep riding classics whilst conserving them for sons and grandsons to ride, and avoid what nearly happened in the true story of...

The Aerial Ariel

There's a reason no one ever rides my bike, and it has to do with a summer evening in 1964. My brother was stationed at RNZAF base Whenuapai, outside Auckland, New Zealand. After an exuberant evening in the officers' mess, we adjourned to town for more action. My brother, a keen rider, and without a bike, asked to ride my Ariel Huntmaster into town. We went ahead in the squadron car, and waited at the city limits…and waited… but no bike or brother. We backtracked to find my crestfallen brother and a bent Ariel. He'd taken a sweeper a bit hard, run off the road, up an embankment and through a Coke billboard. I think Bryan Brown could've been inspired by this, for his famous Ferrari scene in 'On the Beach'. I rode home hanging onto the broken throttle cable, with the damper down hard to control the wobbling suspension. It cost my brother half what the bike was worth to repair, and it was never the same. My helmet was cracked, but was far too valuable to throw away and I used it for years.

The eleven reasons for riding apply to classic bikers, while Elliott's other reasons (performance, exhibition, rivalry, safety, economic, independence and convenience) apply more to new bikes. Having established why people ride classic bikes, we can dig into how they might be 'bonding with their bike'. Mihaly Csikszentmihalyi points to the start line with his concept of 'Flow'. Flow also comes up when motorcycle racers talk racing. Csikszentmihalyi conducted 250,000 interviews around the world, including 'bosozoku' outlaw bike clubs in Japan. In 1975 he described the characteristics of autotelic activities (fun activities like riding). His work indicated riders experience a dynamic state he called 'flow', and described as: *"the holistic sensation that people feel when they act with total involvement"* (*Csikszentmihalyi, Beyond Boredom and Anxiety p36, 1975*). By 1988 he had mapped Flow as:

Intense involvement

Clarity of goals and feedback

Deep concentration

Lack of self-consciousness

Loss of a sense of time

Intrinsically rewarding experience

Transcendence of self

A balance between skill and challenge

He saw this balance between skill and challenge as:

"a sense that one's skills are adequate to cope with the challenges at hand…Concentration is so intense that there is no attention left over to think about anything irrelevant or to worry about problems. Self-consciousness disappears, and the sense of time becomes distorted. An

activity that produces such experiences is so gratifying that people are willing to do it for its own sake, with little concern for what they will get out of it, even when it is difficult or dangerous." Csikszentmihalyi (1991, p71)

Farmer, who heard Csikszentmihalyi speak in Sydney, described Flow as:

Completely involved, focussed, concentrating

Sense of ecstasy, of being outside everyday reality

Great inner clarity, knowing what needs to be done and how well it is going

Knowing the activity is doable, that the skills are adequate, neither anxious or bored

Sense of serenity - no worries about self

Timeliness - focused on present, don't notice time passing

Intrinsic motivation - whatever produces 'flow' becomes its own reward

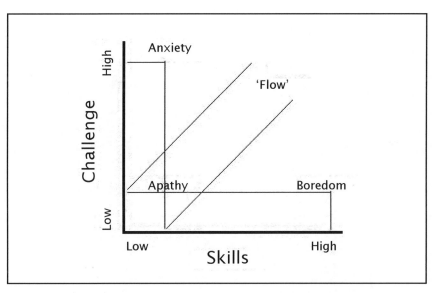

Illus 5.1 The Flow Concept I (from Farmer 1999)

Farmer (*Notes on the 18/3/1999 lecture by Csikszentmihalyi*) depicted Flow in Illus. 5.1 above.

Flow is a channel that develops from challenges mastered by new skills, for example advanced rider courses. Boredom is avoided by moving into the 'Flow Channel' where the experiences are so enjoyable they make us want more. One essential is the balance between a riding challenge and riding skill. More about Flow is shown in Farmer's second illustration Illus. 5.2.

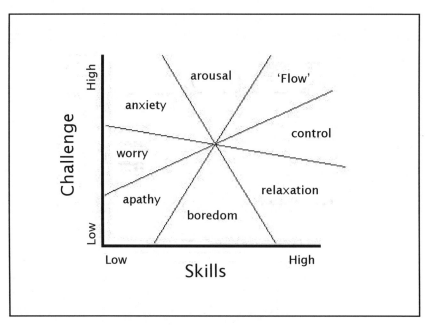

Illus 5.2 Flow in Context (from Farmer, 1999)

From Illus. 5.2 above, 'Riding-Flow' is about riding within one's limits. It lies beyond anxiety and boredom, between arousal and relaxation. It's about effortless control of the bike. In Farmer's 5.3 chart, Flow relates to everyday activities, including riding.

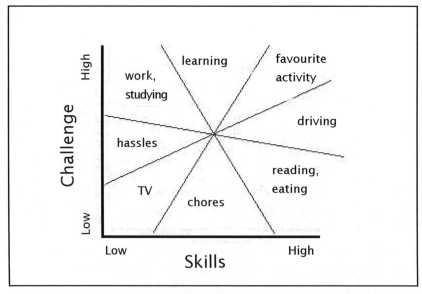

Illus 5.3 Flow in Daily Activities (from Farmer, 1999)

The charts in illustrations 5.1-5.3 show Flow is found in favourite activities. It's better than driving, reading, eating or learning. It's practical. It's about a ride through beautiful countryside with see-though sweepers, like the roads behind Cumbria, or Putty, or the Delaware Water Gap or the Rotorua lakes. Ideally riders would drop into Flow as they kicked the bike over, but life isn't like that. Riders are lucky to feel Flow on a few rides, and so they stand out. Motorcycle racers are aware of Flow and MotoGP champions have ways of moving into Flow. Racers define success not in terms of speed, but consistency. Rossi works out the best cornering lines, and aims within a centimeter on every corner on every lap. His racing line is the shortest, fastest way round the circuit. His skill keeps his tyre within that centimeter for the entire race. That means lap times vary by 0.02%. How does Rossi achieve Flow for his sublime riding? In his autobiography he discloses how he prepares for a race. Firstly, he surrounds himself with people he trusts. Then he isolates himself with a nocturnal lifestyle. He personalises the bike paint finish from what is otherwise a factory bike. He spends time alone communing with his bike. His insurance sticker stamps each bike with a personal touch. His tight sequence of waking and dressing leads him into his Flow channel for the race. His pre-race bonding with his bike, where he meditates in his helmet, crouching beside his bike and finally, his de-wedging adjustment on the warm-up lap is the last step in a sequence for him to enter Flow, when the lights change.

Flow has similarities to Stress. Both were 'invented' by Hungarian scientists looking for the secret to a better life. Both worked in America. Mihaly Csikszentmihalyi invented 'Flow' and Hans Selye invented 'Stress'. Both became world authorities. Flow and Stress seem to be related, and connected with riders bonding with their classic bike. Selye stumbled upon 'stress' in 1936, describing it as...

> *"the response of the body caused by unpleasant or pleasant conditions...distress (Latin 'dis' bad), and eustress (Greek 'eu' good). During both eustress and distress the body undergoes the same responses...eustress causes much less damage than distress... it is 'how you take it' that determines whether you adapt successfully to change."*

Stress itself isn't bad, but too much of the good 'eustress' ends up damaging the body in the same way as too much bad or 'distress'. Selye put his discovery into a chart shown in Illus. 5.4.

Selye explained how the body passes through three stages, coping with stress.

Alarm, as the body prepares for 'fight or flight'.

Resistance, as the body copes with the stressor.

Exhaustion, if it continues too long and sickness or death follows.

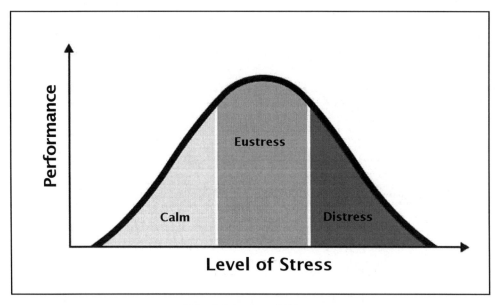

Illus 5.4 Stress and Distress

In illustration 5.4 above, as the stressor builds up (say on a long ride on dirt roads), our bodies pass from calm into eustress, where we enjoy the ride as we rise up the stress curve. As the ride continues, we get dehydrated and tired, go over the top of the curve, and fall down into distress. To illustrate this, Robertson and Porter (1987) found 60% of motorcycle riders reported muscular stress, 33% thermal stress, 27% noise stress, and 22% vibration stress. Classic riders on long club rides would be more like 80% muscular stress, 70% thermal stress, 60% noise stress, and 100% vibration stress! Elliott notes stress increases accident risk as it dulls responses, increases reaction times and fatigue, and impairs motor responses and perception. These are very hazardous issues for riders.

Both great Hungarians seem to have discovered a universal phenomenon, one that Rossi and classic riders both put to very good use. To illustrate this, by comparing Selye's Stress curve in the chart shown in Illus. 5.4 with Csikszentmihalyi chart in Illus. 5.1, the Selye curve rises north-east into his good-stress state and lies inside Csikszentmihalyi's 'activity channel' also rising north-east to his desired Flow state.

Selye's vertical chart axis measuring Performance matches Csikszentmihalyi's vertical axis of Challenge. They appear to be measuring the same human state - performance rising to meet a challenge. If the vertical axes measure the same thing, then the horizontal axes might also be related. A Skill for Csikszentmihalyi equates to a Stress reaction for Selye. That means Selye with his biochemistry tools was measuring Csikszentmihalyi's Flow. In effect Selye measured the biochemistry of Flow and human happiness.

Joining Flow with Stress opens up a body of practical knowledge for motorcycle riders to access Flow. Stress has long figured in medical research and ways of controlling stress exist. Being aware Flow and Stress are connected, allows stress-coping measures to be applied to create a Riding-Flow state, perhaps on demand. Most approaches to controlling stress involve some form of relaxation exercises or meditation - neither being practical on a bike. Breathing and muscle relaxation techniques are other proven ways of moderating stress. These can be performed with eyes wide open and senses alert. They offer practical ways of moderating stress to encourage Riding-Flow on the ride. Walker (2005) working with the Royal Canadian Mounted Police, described a simple breathing technique developed for use by SWAT teams to restore calm during action - the 'Five-Four-Five' Breathing technique. This is a three-step 'Breathe In - Hold Breath - Breathe Out' approach. Everyone who's ever had a chest X-Ray has done precisely this.

5 - Breathe in through the nose, 1-2-3-4-5, saying 'Breathing In, Relax'

4 - Hold your breath, 1-2-3-4, saying 'Calm, Centered, Ready'

5 - Breathe out through the mouth 5-4-3-2-1, saying 'Exhale Tension'

For something closer to Transcendental Meditation, a mantra can be substituted for the words. Marque names might make an effective mantra - Sunbeam, Panther and Gnome Rhone owners may have a head start with this approach.

These techniques can be developed for motorcyclists, with Stress and Flow knowhow enabling riders to achieve Riding-Flow on every ride. They can be used before a ride, to put us into the start of the Flow channel. Late in the ride, when Flow fades due to fatigue, we could use these techniques to pull back from the downside of Selye's distress curve, and reinsert us into the Flow channel. For classic racers, these techniques might be pushed further and a Race Flow Training Programme developed. I wouldn't be surprised to find MotoGP teams pushing into this area.

With an awareness of Flow and Stress, and also the reasons men ride classic bikes, it's possible to see how riders might bond with their classic machines. The bikes are interwoven with memories of extraordinary life events. Bonding seems to involve seven key riding aspects forming a special connection between bike and rider, one that sometimes sees the rider personify the bike by giving it a name, so enabling a relationship to commence. These seven aspects are:

Hedonism.

The favourite classic bike becomes interwoven with the unique experiences of years of memorable rides. Every blemish and battle-scar conjures up a splendid past ride in a way no photo can.

Escapism.

The favourite bike is a constant invitation to take us away from humdrum daily existence, for as Tolkien said it best 'the road goes ever on'.

Dynamic Aspects Of Biking.

A rider and his favourite bike ride a line along a favourite stretch of road. Mike Hailwood even, wouldn't be able to copy that line. The rider's skill adjusts to the challenge, so the line is different for each ride.

Flow.

Like a golf handicap, Flow sees riders competing only against themselves. On a good day they push the envelope and surprise themselves with skill and drive, even into their 60s and 70s. On a flow-less day, riders take almost the same satisfaction, circulating with less effort and strain.

Identifying With The Bike.

Younger classic riders are placed into a time machine where they relive their father's and grandfather's motorcycling through their hands on their father's bars. For older riders, it's a Rocky Horror Frankenfurter time-slip, where they offload the years and reconnect with themselves as young men. Old riders operate the twistgrip exactly as they did when young. And wasn't it Ulysses who said 'And tho' we are not now that strength which in the older days, moved earth and heaven...[but] that which we are, we are'.

Control.

There's something about the dynamics of controlling a motorcycle that appeals to men. This is a male brain thing. Men have powers to focus on riding in a way that amazes many women. It's pure and transcendental to focus your mind on just the ride. The other dimension of control lies in the intimate knowledge riders build of their machines. They're a bit like Walter Kaaden, who could listen to an MZ passing the pit off-song, diagnose the problem and issue tuning instructions on the spot. As Csikszentmihalyi says, the mastery of such knowledge is self-reinforcing and leaves the desire to spend more time in that satisfying place. Who can blame riders for that?

Social Aspects.

The classic club multiplies the bonding impact. After spending one or two years restoring a classic bike, it's a unique feeling to have concours judges reward the bike on the day. But it's not essential - the rider would have done it anyway.

So that's it. Bonding with that bike is real. It's bound up in the reasons we ride classic bikes. Riding is bonding. Bonding is riding. As Pierre Closterman said *"A masterpiece of harmony and power... which would hold my life within the narrow confines...and which I would love like a faithful friend"*. That's the classic motorcycle and it's rider, at the end of the day on a road somewhere...

Illus 5.5 The James 7R at Paeroa

Answers to quotes on page 57 and 58

    Quote One is from H.O. Duncan, H&W 1894.

    Quote Two is from Rev. B. Shergold, Douglas 1987.

    Quote Three is from Pierre Clostermann, Spitfire pilot 1951.

6 *Global Resources For Classic Motorcycles*

"Few people bother to put a vacuum gauge to their crankcase. When you do, you find your typical British bike is running a small vacuum in there, providing your breather is working." RB.

Of the major classic bike manufacturers, only Royal Enfield (from India), Triumph (phoenix-like), Harley-Davidson, BMW and Ducati survived the Japanese takeover of the 1960s-1970s. The first question for the today's classic owner is therefore, who to see for parts and technical advice? The answer opens up a world of resources unimagined by riders of these bikes in their heyday. Much of the technical, service and engineering data, even the production and shipping records of the classic British companies survives. The material has passed into the public domain, and has a legal standing similar to public domain software. Thanks to the conservation efforts of many individuals, an industry has sprung up collating and publishing this vital technical information for riders through print media, CDs/DVDs and websites. Classic Japanese bike restorers are also well served by their marques' continuity and continuing supply of parts.

Email, the internet, websites, web forums, magazines, the postal service and EBay have proved ideal tools for this industry to flower in each country where classic motorcycles survive. This industry enables classic riders to access a range of parts, service and technical advice beyond the abilities of the original classic dealer network. In a real sense, riders of these machines are better served today than our fathers and grandfathers.

EBay

Parts supply channels were discussed in chapter two, in the context of searching for a bike. The same channels are even more important for buying parts, whether new or used. EBay is progressively penetrating the parts supply channels, and many predict it will become dominant in this role. I'm not as sure. The immediate impact of EBay is to dramatically boost the volume of classic parts in circulation. It has introduced through it's virtual trading floors a new global market for cost-effective parts supply on fairly secure terms. This marketplace has been growing exponentially for the past five years, and is likely to for years yet. By its auction nature, it alerts sellers and buyers to the effective market price of parts, and this disturbs the established price levels of retailers. It also changes the pattern of demand retailers experience. For example where once a rider needing to undertake major maintenance would price the parts at retail and often postpone the work due to costs, he can now shrink and spread the cost by buying items off EBay around the world, reserving his retailer for cherry picking certain items, perhaps bulky, heavy, rare or expensive ones, which are impractical to buy on EBay. This enables more work to be undertaken by more riders, more quickly, and this must increase total parts sales through all supply channels. In turn, these trends allow more bikes to be restored - bikes which may in pre-EBay times have not been cost-effective to restore. The net effect is to boost the available classic bike supply numbers to meet the increasing demand. These activities help support the statistics presented in Chapters eleven and twelve which show continuing growth in the market for classic bikes. These changes also alter the geography of classic bikes. As a keen EBay buyer and seller, I'm struck by the frequency of parts buyers located in the remote regions of Australia and other countries. Such riders are avidly restoring classic bikes and funneling parts from many countries into their remote locations. Net relationships develop that transcend the initial buyer and seller roles and they are fashioning a 'new world' classic bike society.

Other Electronic Channels

Internet search engines such as Google, allow users to group related data, and move across the intersections between topics, as well as vertically within topics. The internet has proved addictive as well as useful for classic riders seeking advice or parts. Classic bike net forums leverage the classic bike technical and troubleshooting help available to riders. All that's needed is a start point which Google provides. The days of traditional classic motorcycle maintenance knowledge being restricted to printed books is over. There is a definite place for both electronic and print media in classic motorcycling as it is hard to refer to a PC beside the bike in the garage with greasy hands. A photocopy or printed manual still works better as an assembly guide.

Autojumbles, Swap-Meets, Field Days And Auctions

Despite the growth in electronic trading, the urge to get up before dawn and go fossicking in boxes with a torch is still formidable. I've visited swapmeets and bought parts in several countries. There's no difference in the dynamics, even if the events go by different names (autojumbles in the UK etc). Traditional bazaar rules still apply, and here are tips gleaned from the USA/UK/NZ/Australian swap-meet scenes.

Illus. 6.1 A well-prepared swap-meet shopper in New Zealand

Guide To Swap-Meet Etiquette

Despite the tales of Goldstars bought in the dark for very little, it's pointless to enter a swap-meet until there's natural light to read by. (Australians seem prone to ferreting around in the dark, UK autojumbles rarely start much before 10.00am). It's easy enough to mistake parts and their condition in the daylight let alone the dark. Once I held an interesting conversation with an unknown stall vendor in the bitter, pre-dawn sleet of the Rotorua swap-meet, one of the best in New Zealand. As first light developed into dawn, we were surprised to recognise each other. We were in fact, old friends.

- It's worth taking a cheap plastic vernier, and a note of key dimensions of any parts being sought. Dimensions always appear more appropriate at the meet than when the part is on the garage bench. If mislaid the plastic vernier is cheap and easy to replace.

- A backpack holds bargains whilst keeping both arms free. Plastic shopping bags and classic parts don't mix. The pathway back to the carpark is lined with small parts dropping out of shopping bags.

- Men seem to have a natural inclination to focus on a single item and analyse it. This is a weakness at swapmeets, they become so focused looking for one part they ignore or put back many parts they afterwards regret not bringing home. The rider in Illus. 6.1 seems to be taking notes on the content of the entire table, so as not to overlook anything.

- It's worth looking for parts to buy and resell on EBay, as well as parts to keep, and parts for friends. That also helps explain to spouses, why the car is so full.

- A shopping wish-list is handy. Not having one leads to anguished indecision, and parts that are gone when the buyer returns to a stand.

- Seek out one-time sellers, rather than regular traders whose parts may have been well picked-over at prior meets. Often the best shopping is towards the periphery of the swapmeet, where such sellers are frequently found. They often arrive late and are in places long ago passed by the early birds. Look also for those who've completed restorations and are selling off surplus parts. Also ancient gentlemen who are exiting the sport, and who may be selling rare tools and parts for very little. Those selling on behalf of others can provide great bargains.

- It's permissible to ask to borrow a part from one stand, to see if it fits an assembly on another stand. If the tape and vernier are forgotten, this can help a decision.

- Where a very low price is quoted for a part try to assemble a job-lot of parts from that stand to obtain a further price cut from the low base prices. Vendors are often uncomfortable in a sales role and do silly things. Bulk discounts are always there at swapmeets, often for as few as three to five parts. Also, for five to ten parts or more, it becomes difficult for the seller to price things individually. They are more likely to give away a group of bargains if you make an offer for the lot and pass them the cash.

- Take enough cash and then some, and have someone there to borrow from if that really great bargain surfaces. This happened recently to a friend who found an early Goldie in boxes in the back of a van, late in the swapmeet. He'd spent most of his cash but was able to buy it for £36(!!), only because another friend staked him.

TIP: If you push money at someone, they automatically take hold of it, and this leads them to say 'yes', when they should be saying 'no' to a silly offer. This hardly ever fails!

Pattern Parts, NOS Parts And Used Parts

Classic magazines carry articles declaiming against pattern parts as poorly made, ill-fitting and often inferior to factory-made NOS (New Old Stock) parts. This is a criticism that can also be made of some factory parts. There are branded pattern manufacturers who, in some cases, can trace their company back to their origins as OEM suppliers (Original Equipment Manufacturers) to classic marques.

These companies own their own brands and constitute an elite group in the pattern parts league. It's hard to generalise: companies and quality change with proprietorship and with generations of staff. Yet in many cases some proud link back to the old days can still be some assurance of quality, as it is in the old British distribution chain around the world. The ethics persist. For British bikes, it's easier to assess such parts makers from inside the UK. Downunder, riders tend to rely on recommendations from the British classic magazines, and mates who have visited the companies. Increasingly these companies are sorting out distributors downunder. In Table 6.6 below, the parts choices for riders are ranked broadly by quality and price.

Table 6.1 Parts Types, Sources, Prices, Qualities-Rank Order

Parts Type/Source	Quality/Goodness of Fit	Price Level
New Old Stock	OEM specification, more or less	Very high
OEM seconds	Compromised, by definition	High
Factory Refurbished	Can be virtually OEM spec.	High
Branded Pattern	Often as good or better than OEM	High -Medium
Generic Pattern	Quality variable, sometimes good	High-Medium
Cooperative made	Often meets/exceeds OEM spec.	Varies
Used Parts	Variable, depending on wear	Low

Most price levels in Table 6.1 above, are rated as 'High'. This reflects the slowly declining supply in NOS parts, although this isn't always obvious. It's masked in the short term by US parts caches from companies such as Cycle Hub topping up the market, although such supply must eventually run out. It also reflects the small scale of pattern parts manufacture. Classic bikes are worth more as parts, and this provides an incentive for parting out or breaking bikes: a practice usually condemned except by the buyers. Yet it's always been this way. Back in the classic heyday downunder, dealers bought new ex-factory bikes and stripped them for parts to supply their shops. There were savings to be made buying parts as whole bikes. This explains, for example why new, number stamped crankcases are advertised. There is nothing suspicious about this and in fact it can legitimise some parts, by relating them to a shop. They are effectively NOS parts, as they've never been on the road, even though they've been stripped off a bike.

My experience with branded and unbranded pattern parts has been excellent, and I wonder if there's more smoke than fire in the argument over pattern quality. Harley-Davidson source components from Asia, in particular from Japan, Taiwan and Korea. They don't distinguish the country of origin in their pricing of components. Indeed, so many Harley-Davidson motorcycle assemblies and their accessories are now made outside the USA, (wheels from Australia, carburettors and suspension from Japan, aftermarket components from Korea and Taiwan) that it's better considered a 'world bike' than a US bike. As elsewhere noted, all the world's major motorcycle and component manufacturers are now based in Asia, (and that doesn't include Japan). The better plants are developing expertise in parts manufacture. It would be surprising if this failed to translate into classic bike parts manufacture of steadily increasing quality. After recently purchasing some excellent pattern products from the Sparx range made in China, I feel we can look forward with optimism.

Supply is one thing, but the challenge remains over recognising good parts from bad, good NOS from worthless NOS, good pattern parts from bad pattern, and good versus bad used parts in general. Parts selection comes down to having a part in the hand and facing the choice of either putting it back or buying it. Some decision factors apart from its source, are as follows.

Part Identification

How likely is it that it is the right part for the bike - 50% or 80%? Rarely will it be 100%, unless it bears a part number and there's a parts book handy. Even then, it may be correct for the bike but for a model a year before or after the year required.

Appearance

Does it look right? Is it consistent for age? A NOS part will have been held as inventory for 30 years or more. Over this time, it'll have developed battle scars, dirt and corrosion that can make it look worse than a used part - but NOS parts generally clean up OK.

Parts To Avoid

Is it in the category of NOS parts that have 'time-based' wear. Examples of older capacitors, rubber and paper items come to mind where the compoenent will deteriorate with age whether or not it has been used.

Hazardous Parts

Is it obsolete for good reason? Brake linings are an example of such obsolescence. Asbestos brake linings should be left untouched.

Quality Of Manufacture

Many parts were originally sourced from UK cottage industries. Quality in such environments varied. Its worth recalling that British and US manufacturers practised 'parts selection' during bike assembly i.e. parts were not manufactured to a tight specification, but to a description, and with fairly wide tolerances. The British and American assemblers often tried parts from a box until they found one that fitted in with the existing assemblies. It was an art, and uneconomic compared with manufacturing to tighter tolerances.

Defects And Wear

Is it straight and true underneath it's grubby appearance? Will it clean up once it gets home, or is there damage under that dirt? As discussed in purchasing, it's vital to focus on the details of a part. This calls for practice, and it's best learned from friends who've developed the knack. Some people immediately spot a defect in a part, defects others find impossible to see until they're pointed out. Some things *are* almost impossible to see. For example how can we see if the hardened outer layer of a gear part is worn through, when the layer is measured in microns? I don't believe the average rider can and, depending on just how worn the part is, will it matter greatly on a club bike anyway, where engine noises are legion and another note from the worn gear may pass unnoticed?

Passing Inspection

A preferable approach is to confine inspecting a part to some indicators of quality. Threads are a good example of an indicator of wear and abuse. On externally threaded shafts and sliders etc it's easy to see how sections of the thread may be worn down, where the hills and valleys are eroded away. This is important when buying used factory tools such as clutch and other pullers. Such items are expensive, and may well have seen one or two service lives. If the tool can't be engaged with the component because of a worn thread, it's wasted money: a new, but inferior pattern tool would do a better job. Internal threads are hard to assess without a fibre-optic light inserted in the recess. However, if the price is right on say a fork slider, it may be worth buying to attempt to clean-up damaged threads or use a helicoil-type insert on damaged mudguard bolt holes which bear little loading for example.

Parts That Defy The Experts

Anonymous gears and pistons are examples of parts that even experts seem to pass over at swapmeets. Unless you've the old part with you, or a chart of piston makes and numbers, it's a shot in the dark.

Otherwise, it seems largely a matter of experience. Having once seen good and bad examples of a part, a yardstick is established for future shopping. That's the fun of it all.

Custom Making Parts

For riders of earlier classics and vintage bikes this is a familiar path, by necessity. The technology in a classic bike is after all, largely basic metal working for tinware, exhausts, and other components. Commissioning one-off manufacture of some items by an engineering shop can be a cost-effective approach. It gets better if a batch of the items can be ordered through a club to spread the overheads for example on barrel spacers or gearbox shims or even more complex parts. The reconditioning and remanufacturing of components is now well established in the car industry and is also useful for classic bikes, for example worn carburettors are cheaply re-sleeved at a quarter the new price.

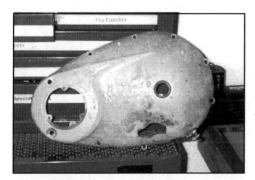

Illus. 6.4 (top left) Defects, like the typical left footrest through the chaincase, are welded up more or less well. It's worth closely examining the inside surface for repairs.

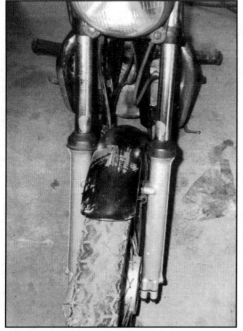

Illus. 6.5 (bottom left) shows tell-tale abrasions of these fork stanchions, pointing the stanchions being bent, possibly from impact.

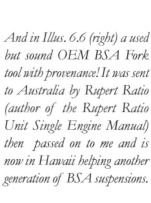

And in Illus. 6.6 (right) a used but sound OEM BSA Fork tool with provenance! It was sent to Australia by Rupert Ratio (author of the Rupert Ratio Unit Single Engine Manual) then passed on to me and is now in Hawaii helping another generation of BSA suspensions.

Tricks Of The Retail Parts Trade For Canny Buyers

- If you are a visitor or tourist in a country, concentrate parts buying into the 30 day period before flying out of the country. That way you get a 10% GST or VAT tax rebate when you leave. Always consider buying parts abroad as the tax saving on parts can subsidise the travel.

- Ask the retailer to stockpile parts over the weeks and months before the departure date; then pick them up a few days before leaving.

- Establish yourself as a professional classic motorcycle restorer. There's often a fine line between a hobby and a business. If you have several bikes and basket cases to restore, that can qualify you as a trade account for parts suppliers and for a 20% wholesale trade discount. It's useful at tax time also, as vintage motorcycle restoring is an honorable, if little-known pursuit to accountants and tax authorities.

- There's often idle talk at the club about particular retailers being high priced, and best avoided. Because of this, a lot of riders avoid some shops. The result is that these shops accumulate lots of very rare parts that have sold out elsewhere.

- It's cheaper to centralise buying at one shop perhaps even despite high prices. You save time, petrol and postage chasing around the world and on EBay, when for a little more, you can shop locally. The parts can also be inspected before purchase, and their identification and condition confirmed. Returning or exchanging parts that happen not to fit is straightforward. Add the tax saving above and those high-priced NOS parts can start to look competitive with other sources, including Ebay.

- Look for contemporary Japanese bike shops that had a prior business selling British bikes many years ago. You sometimes find a stock of British parts out back and they are happy to get rid of them, as no one knows what they are, or what they're worth. For starters, it's worth obtaining the original British manufacturers' distributors lists for your home country, and for others visited, and check if there's a motorcycle business still trading at the old address. I've been in luck in several countries using this approach.

- In such shops, it's good to question the owner about the price of one British part. If he goes to his computer screen, you know his old British parts have made it across into his new accounting system, and the chance of bargains decreases. However, if he stays with you and hesitates, you know he has no records and probably no clue what to charge. He may cover this by asking you to make an offer. If so, offer what's on any old faded price tag on the parts, as it's probably the 1960s price. If you feign disinterest or doubt over the part's suitability, often the reward is a bargain.

- You tend to get the best prices when you buy several items, or a box of old stuff at the same time. Either making an up-front silly offer, or asking for a bulk or trade discount of 20%, can be productive. It becomes a win-win for both parties, and cements an ongoing relationship. Most likely you'll become a regular and that encourages him to look after you on prices, especially if he regards you as a fellow dealer and a potential trade account.

- Take a pragmatic, cost-averaging approach to parts. When say, hunting for a sub-assembly like pistons, rings, gudgeon pins, circlips and small end bearings, accept that the needed parts may have to be bought at more than one location. For example my brother recently assembled a NOS piston assembly for a classic twin, avoiding retail piston costs of £60 ($150), in favour of £12 on EBay. He then cheerfully over-paid a retailer for the gudgeon pins and small end bearings that were nearly unobtainable anywhere but at that one retailer. Overall, he got his needed complete assembly, and at a bargain price.

- Know the market. To become a classic bargain shopper a keen knowledge of parts prices is a must, also the different levels of parts prices such as what the same part costs at retail versus a swap-meet, or via a club member.

- When coming across rare parts at a retailer, especially bona fide NOS parts, always try asking the price for one, and then the price for two, or even five. It's often better to buy several of the item, if you know it's scarce and in demand. That way, you can obtain both at a discount, keep one and sell-on the other at a slightly higher price for your trouble to a clubmate, or possibly a lot more money on EBay. This is another way to achieve competitive prices from retailers with high-priced reputations. With trade standing, of course it gets even better.

- Make offers. No matter how good the retailer's accounting system may be, and how long he's had the part in inventory, when you make an offer, he makes the profit that he may have waited years or decades to see.

- Often it's better to buy a grubby NOS or factory reconditioned part that needs cleaning up, versus a shiny new NOS part still in its box. Better prices are negotiated this way.

- I deliberately buy in contrary ways. By this I mean, shopping for makes and models that are not the mainstream business for that particular shop. An example would be shopping for BSA single parts, in an outlet that specialises in Triumphs and Nortons. The latter are mostly twins, and often staff don't bother to keep their singles inventory information up to date and a bargain is therefore more likely. Chapter eleven is a useful starting point in this regard. Knowing the top ten classic brands by country can help when checking out a maker's old distribution channels when visiting a country on business or holiday. Researching their old distributors and their locations, can give valuable information on where the surviving parts are likely to be today. Bargains can be found in the most unlikely of shops which bears out the old axiom, that there's a bargain in every shop.

Australian Motorcycling Resources

Despite the strength of classic motorcycling downunder, it lacks the developed communications and networking infrastructure of the UK. This is partly because there's been no dedicated Australian classic magazine for a long time. My last copy of the Australasian magazine *Classic Motorcycling* is from 1991. The UK classic bike media such *Classic Bike, Classic Bike Guide, Old Bike Mart, Real Classic* and *The Classic Motorcycle* help fill this hiatus. However, they do not extend their full service to Australasian readers, nor for example can the Australian VMX magazine going in the other direction. There is a new Australasian classic magazine, the promising *Old Bike Australasia*, launched in June 2006 by a well-known author Jim Scaysbrook. Hopefully, this magazine will have the right recipe to appeal to the large Australasian readership. At the time of writing, *Old Bike* announced it is increasing publication frequency to a quarterly for 2007, a very good sign for all.

As we'll see in chapter eleven, Australia and especially New Zealand are repositories of classic motorcycles. Given the differential pricing in the Southern hemisphere markets for both parts and classic bikes, readers in other countries may well wish to tap into the cost-competitive downunder suppliers. Increasingly they are set up to trade globally, via the net. Airmail delivery to the UK, Europe and North America is only a week, and airmail prices from Australia recently dropped.

The easiest and most congenial way to source parts and service advice is still to walk into a retail outlet. Surprisingly, there are still retail outlets about that have traded continuously since before the British industry demise. Often these are still under the same ownership, and even the same proprietor. Frequently, these shops have the patina of an antique, the atmosphere of a museum, and a fragrance that transports you back to your youth, For example there are three such retailers within an hours ride of my home - Eades, Northcotts and Grahams. How many are left within an hour of your home? Will they continue trading indefinitely? You may be surprised once you start digging for them. To assist in the search for parts, here is a rundown on one typical classic parts shop - Eades, in Sydney Australia.

Illus. 6.7 The range of discounted parts at Eades.

Max Eade recently closed his workshop but kept the spares business. (The workshop moved to Sovereign Classic Motorcycles where continuity of service is provided by Norm who ran the workshop for many years at Eades.) Max maintains an astonishingly wide parts assortment, especially for Triumph and BSA, the mainstays of the Australian classic market. Many of these are NOS parts. NOS parts often are expensive, but to be genuine, they need to be. The retailer has paid to keep them in his inventory for decades until we walk in and want them for a pound or a dollar or two. Max also stocks aftermarket and pattern parts and will often point out the strengths and weaknesses of each type for you, when he's not on the phone. Eades supplies many other bike shops around Australia with classic parts and advice, thus assisting interstate riders. His phone runs hot. Used parts are also sometimes available. In addition, a continuous new and used spare parts market runs in the front of the store, with Max delving deep into his archives and producing new dainties to tempt all British riders, and at big discounts too.

For overseas tourists and business travelers to Sydney it's worth bringing your wish-list of spare parts, as many of us do. Set aside a day or two to visit Eades, then go on to call on Barry Graham (for Vincent and Velocette help) and also Bruce Northcott. Northcotts in Western Sydney have been trading under the same ownership for fifty years. Bruce Northcott used to race BSAs and his shop is decorated with photos of his wins. After the closure of the British plants, he took

Illus. 6.8 Northcotts in Western Sydney

up a Suzuki dealership and is now a major supplier of NOS Suzuki parts, as well as technical information. Deep in the recesses of his shop are residual British parts, mainly BSA and Triumph. If you've struck out elsewhere, it's worth asking Bruce before you give up. He also maintains a stock of pattern parts to suit British riders.

While in Sydney, also give Patrick Ryan a call up country. Ryans are another old-time Sydney classic outlet to remain trading. In 2001 they moved from their Parramatta site to the country in NSW and now run a mail-order business specialising in British parts. Between the four outlets you're bound to fill your list. You can then take advantage of the Travellers Refund Scheme. This is modeled on the UK VAT Refund scheme and gives a full GST (Goods and Services Tax) refund for all goods bought in Australia within the previous 30 days. The only requirements are that you present the goods at the airport, with one statement for each shop covering all their goods; and that you take the goods out in your personal baggage. You could find a trip to Sydney nicely subsidised by tax savings on the parts if you're based in the UK or USA.

Table 6.2 is a list of classic retail outlets where, as of 2006 you can find parts for classic motorcycles in Australia.

Table 6.2   Australia Classic Retail & Spare Parts Outlets

Business	Contact	Product Range
NSW		
Jim Eade*	02-97987822	Triumph/BSA/Norton
Jack Graham*	02-95674703	Velocette/Vincent
Metropolitan M'cycle Spares	02-97487400	Classic Japan Parts
Motociclo	02-95577234	Italian & Enfield & Parts
Bruce Northcott*	02-96221091	Suzuki, some British
Redfern Motor Parts	02-42846733	Classic Harley-Davidson
Ryans*	02-65588195	Triumph/BSA/Norton
	www.ryansmotorcycles.com.au	
Noel Shipp	02-42291030	Classic British Parts
Victoria		
Central Motorcycles	03-95400866	British & Japan Classics
	www.centralmotorcycles.com.au	
Classic Motorcycle warehouse	03-97735500	British Bikes
	www.classicstyle.com.au	
EuroBrit Motorbikes	03-94326886	Vincent/Ducati/Triumph
	www.eurobrit.com.au	
Modak*	03-96021229	Triumph/BSA/Norton
Motorcyclists Emporium	03-54751584	Triumph/BSA/Norton
	www.mcycle.com.au	
Royal Enfield	03-54221277	Enfield Parts & Bikes
	www.royalenfieldaustralia.com	
Union Jack*	03-94996428	Triumph/BSA/Norton
	www.unionjack.com.au	
Vintage Swapshop	03-57221457	Triumph/BSA etc
Queensland		
B.J's Bikes & Bits	07-33917322	Triumph/BSA/Norton
	www.britishmotorcycle.com.au	
Pioneer Cycles	07-54915344	Most makes
	www.pioneercycles.com.au	
S. Australia		
Bill's Bits & Bikes	08-85685756	Most makes
Britbikes	08-84433771	Triumph/BSA/Norton
Vee Two	08-92487500	Classic Ducati
	www.veetwo.net	
W. Australia		
Vintage & Modern	08-94598981	All Classic Makes
Tasmania		
Ambrit	0417-786600	Triumph/Harley/BSA

These shops are among those trading since the classic British heyday.

In addition to the parts resources above, there's an extensive network of specialist classic niche suppliers around Australia. These are listed in Table 6.3 below.

Please note these listings are by no means exhaustive. Smaller suppliers especially change over time. The lists include those Australasian businesses that make themselves visible by promoting their services in the print media, through clubs and at swapmeets etc.

Table 6.3   Australia Specialised Classic Resources

Business	Contact	Product Range
Autobookworld	02-92996669	Classic books
BEARS Spares	08-92960225	BEARS parts
Peter Boros	02-99206658	Instrument repairs
Bookworks	02-97406766	Classic books
Brankos Auto Shop	02-43561800	Classic Harley repairs
Carlel Pty Ltd.	02-98999439	Classic breathing specialists
Carstrip	03-93578936	Bike bead blasting
Chrome4Cruisin	02-97691991	Chromeplating
Classic Fasteners	08-83469838	Classic fasteners
Cobs Classic Spares	02-65539442	British parts
Ezy-Movers	1300-722477	Bike transporting
Ghostriders	0428-922700	Bike transporting
Alan Graham	02-46327202	Amal carburettor service
Bill Green	0419-280650	BSA M20 parts
Headworks	03-95685226	Cylinderhead work
Norm Jeaneret	0417-077697	1946-62 Matchless & AJS
Draggin Jeans	03-96961622	Classic Kevlar clothing
Impact Glass Beading	02-96713696	Bead blasting
Lightfoot Engineering	03-98983677	Wheel building
Link Powdercoating	02-96226205	Bike powder coaters
Marquebooks	02-95283737	Marque books
MAW	02-96342014	MCS and accessories+
MCA	02-96331296	Harley & Zodiac accessories
MIS	02-96218190	Gauge rebuilds
MMT	02-96370277	Classic mechanics
Moose Racing Products	03-57951828	Shocks and wheels
Motociclo	02-95577234	Classic accessories
Moto Graphix	02-97483164	Classic decals
Motorbooks	02-91444799	Classic books
Motorcycle Specialties	07-33756600	MCS pattern parts

Table 6.3 (cont.) Australia Specialised Classic Resources

Business	Contact	Product Range
Motorcycling Australia	03-96840500	Rider & Industry Assn.
Mountain Motor Books	07-33976845	Classic books
Nat. Motor Racing Museum	02-63321872	Racing museum
Don Newell	07-33531874	VMX, Metisse, Wasp
NRMA Veteran Insurance	1800646605	Classic insurance
Old Bike	02-94189225	New Classic ANZAC mag
Lionel Otto Instruments	07-32773888	Gauge repair
Pacific H-D Trading Co.	02-43221666	Classic Harley-Davidson
Jim Parker	03-98095599	Indian support
John Parker	03-98793817	Amal parts
Pitstop Bookshop	1800-622422	Classic books
Puds (Four) Parts	03-51966190	Classic Honda
Peter Scott Motorcycles	02-96241262	Magneto service
Road & Race M/CEng.	02-43884211	Classic Italian Parts
Shannons	134646	Classic insurance
SOS Suspension	02-47325533	Suspensions
Sovereign Classic M'cycles	0400-468043	Mobile service & repairs
Superior Spokes	02-96425838	Wheel building
Technical Book Shop	03-96633951	Classic books
Terry Prince Classic Motorbikes	02-45682208	Vincent & TPV
	www.classicmotorbikes.com.au	
Veliss	043-331578	Bespoke stainless
Vintage Dirt	02-63660138	Fibreglass & seats
Wheels of Time	03-97923944	Classic manuals

New Zealand Resources

While New Zealand has more classic motorcycles on a pro-rata basis than any other country surveyed, the small size of the country and its excellent freight service mean there are relatively few significant retailers. British Spares is by far the most significant of these and their business would probably rival that of the larger US and UK suppliers. They have a slick export mail-order business that can be breathtakingly fast - even overnight to Australia at times. You save GST if you are ordering from overseas, and they offer 10% discount for internet orders. Their high service level, coupled with their competitive pricing and wide 16,000 product line range, contribute to their large overseas business. They have plenty of competition from other home companies though, and this all contributes to the vigorous New Zealand classic bike scene. The main competitors are shown in Table 6.4.

Table 6.4 New Zealand Classic Retail & Spare Parts Outlets

Business	Contact	Product Range
Anderson Motorcycles	07-3470804	Classic Japan spares
Ash King Motorcycles	06-7536789	British & Japan parts
Best of British	03-3487332	Classic British parts
British Spares	04-9398819	16,000+ British parts
	www.britishspares.com	
Classic Cycles	04-5279608	Classic British parts
Custom Chambers	09-2741155	Classic exhausts
Cycle Colour MC Painters	07-8266871	Classic paintwork
Cycle Torque	07-8465099	Classic spares & repairs
	www.cycletorque.co.nz	
EconoHonda	07-8848810	Classic Honda parts
	www.econohonda.com	
F1 Motorcycle Works	07-8476990	Custom classic parts
	www.rapidartnz.com	
Franklin Cam Services	09-2384067	Classic camshafts
Hamco Industries	06-3248345	Classic wheels
Hanes Engineering	07-8299741	Indian spares
Joe Hannah Motorcycles	04-2330989	Classic British parts
Kitney Engineering	06-7647565	Classic repairs
Motoring Marketplace	06-3688945	Classic books & mags
	www.motoringmarketplace.co.nz	
Park Ave Cycle	025-2805919	Used British parts

Table 6.4 (cont.) New Zealand Classic Retail & Spare Parts Outlets

Business	Contact	Product Range
Royal Enfield NZ	09-4158453	Enfields & parts
Southern Spares	07-3463120	Classic Triumphs, SRM parts
Technical Services	07-5422616	Classic electrical
Twin Cam Motorcycles	04-9025006	Classic British repairs
Trevor Hall Motorcycles	07-8703423	Classic British parts
Vintage Motorcycle	09-4222638	Classic British parts
Alan Wakefield	06-8354052	Classic tinware makers
Wheel and Spoke	09-5760312	Classic rims & spokes
	www.wheelandspoke.co.nz	

Illus 6.9 An early Hobart of about WW1 vintage sold recently in NZ

United Kingdom Resources

The UK supply position is of course amply documented for UK riders. Here the focus is on those major UK suppliers who are known and patronised by riders downunder and elsewhere and tends to include mainly those without an agent downunder, but with whom Australasian riders can deal direct. UK and Northern hemisphere readers may be surprised to find a supplier or two whose abilities are appreciated downunder, but with whom they may be as yet unaware. Table 6.5 lists these suppliers.

Table 6.5 UK Selected Classic Retail & Spare Parts Outlets

Business	Contact	Product Range
ABSAF*	+31 596620254	GS/G85CS repro engines
AJS Motorcycles	(0)1264 710074	VMX
AJS & Matchless OC	(0)1536511532 www.jampot.com	AJS/Matchless parts
AMC Classic Spares	(0)1462811770	AJS/Matchless parts
Barleycorn	(0)1379586728 www.barleycorn.co.uk	Stainless BSA classic parts
Boyer Bransden	(0)1622730939	Classic ignitions
Bri-Tie	(0)1558668579	Classic BSA parts
BritBits	(0)1202483675 www.britbits.co.uk	Tri., BSA, Norton parts
BSA Owners Club	www.bsaoc.demon.co.uk	Parent BSAOC
Burton Bike Bits	(0)1530564362	Classic British parts
C&D Autos	(0)1217062902	Classic BSA parts
Draganfly Motorcycles	(0)1986894798 www.draganfly.co.uk	Ariel and BSA parts
Richard Hacker	(0)2086594045	Tri., BSA, Norton parts
Hagon Products	(0)2085026222 www.hagon-shocks.co.uk	Classic suspension
Hamrax	(0)2089695380	Classic parts and repairs
Tony Hayward	(0)1244830776	Belt drives esp. Triumph
George Hopwood	(0)2083009573	Tri. performance parts
Norman Hyde	(0)1926497375 www.normanhyde.co.uk	Tri. & Norton C'mando
Inter-Moto	+44 (0)1252613680	Cheney kits
K&S Frames	+44 (0)1306889538	Replica BSA frames
Laverda Intl Owners Club	(0)1844238269 www.iloc.org.uk	Laverda Owners Club

Table 6.5 (cont.) UK Selected Classic Retail & Spare Parts Outlets

Business	Contact	Product Range
Bruce Main-Smith & Co.	(0)1162777669 www.brucemainsmith.com	Classic manuals
Merlin Books	(0)1403257626 www.merlinbooks.com	Classic bike books
Mill House Books	(0)1205354848 www. millhousebooks.com	Rare classic books
Sammy Miller M'cycles	(0)1425616446	Bultaco & trials
Motomecca	(0)1202823453	Guzzi & Laverda parts
Muttz Nutz Products	(0)1344874763 www.themuttznutz.com	Conical brake extenders
Norton Owners Club	(0)2380693262 www.nortonownersclub.org	Parts and tech help
Norvil Motorcycle Co.	(0)15 43278008 www.norvilmotorcycle.co.uk	Norton parts
The Norvin Centre	(0)1708470526 www.the norvincentre.com	Vincent, Norton, Triumph
Panther Publishing	(0)1494534778 www.panther-publishing.com	Classic publishers
Pazon Ignitions	(0)1795 470126 www.pazon.com	Classic ignitions
Rickman Motorcycle	(0)1453758026	Rickman frames & parts
David Silver Spares	(0)1728833020 www.davidsilverspares.co.uk	Classic Japan parts
SRM	(0)1970627771 www.srm-engineering.com	Exquisite engineered parts
TMS	(0)1159503447	Tri., BSA, Norton parts
Unity Equipe	(0)1706632237 www.unityequipe.com	Manx Norton racers
Vin-Parts	(0)1597851542 www.vintech.co.uk	Vincent parts
Norman White	(0)1264773326	Norton racing parts
L.P. Williams	(0)1926408822 www.triumphspares.co.uk	Unit Triumph parts
John Wyatt's	(0)1423358004	Classic Japan parts
Zodiac*	+31 297288621	Classic Harley-Davidson

* Turn right at the UK for downunder visitors!

North American Resources

The situation with parts suppliers in North America is similarly well documented for local US riders. Given the longtime popularity of off-road riding and racing in the USA and Canada, there's a greater emphasis on these sectors of the sport in the US and Canadian parts distribution channel. Again this list is confined to the major suppliers of significance to international readers shown in table 6.6 below. Some EBay sources e.g. 'queeng' are thus not included.

Table 6.6   N. America Selected Classic Retail & Spare Parts Outlets

Business	Contact	Product Range
Accessory Mart	+1 5138711678 www.domiracer.com	British & European parts
Barnett Tool & Eng	+1 8056429435 www.barnettclutches.com	Classic clutches & cables
Barrington Motor Works	+1 6036642673	Classic BMW parts
Baxter Cycle	+1 7127812351	Classic British parts plus
Bench Mark Works	+1 6624656444 email:vechbmw@aol.com	Classic BMW parts
Blue Moon Cycle	+1 7704476945 www.bluemooncycle.com	Classic BMW parts
Bob's BMW	+1-800-BMW-BOBS	Classic BMW parts
Bob's British Bikes	+1-5099912815	Tri., BSA, Norton parts
British Bike Connection	+1 5852884546 www.britishbikeconnection.com	Tri., BSA, Norton parts
British Cycle Supply Co.	+1 9025427478 www.britcycle.com	Classic British parts
British Only M'ycles	+1 7344229253	Tri., BSA, Norton parts
British-USA	+1 713-9447951 www.british-usa.com	Tri., BSA, Norton parts
Buchanans Spoke & Rim	+1 6269694655 www.buchananspokes.com	Wheel building
Circle F Exhaust	+1 7134671488 www.circlefexhaust.com	Classic exhaust systems
Cycle Hub	No longer active	Just for old times sake!

Table 6.6 (cont.) N. American Selected Classic Retail & Spare Parts Outlets

Business	Contact	Product Range M.A.P.
Cycle	+1 7273811151	Fine British parts & belts
MG Innovative Prods.	+1 8144591173 www.MGInProducts.com	Classic British & Japan
Old Britts	+1 3608252192 www.oldbritts.com	British parts
Rocky Point Cycle	+1 9373769792 www.rockypointcycle.com	BMW/Norton/ Triumph/BSA
Speed and Sport Inc	+1 5707846831 www.yamatopdog.com	Classic Yamaha parts
Sterling Cycle Works	+1 651 290 0889	Vincent & TPV
Vintage Husky	+1 7607448052 www.vintagehusky.com	Husqvarna parts
Vintage Jap. M'cycle Club	n/a www.vjmc.org	Classic Japan support
World Vintage M'cycle Sales	+19052764050 www.classicbikes4sale.com	British & European

7 Riding, Survival And Shibboleths

"Boanerges, T.E. Lawrence's name for his favourite Brough-Superior is derived from the Greek and Hebrew, and means Sons of Thunder" RB

Who Rides Classic Bikes?

Talking with the leaders of bodies representing motorcycling to governments and traffic authorities, shows just how frustrated they have become. Regulatory bodies rarely contain motorcycle riders, so few legislators and regulators have first hand experience of conditions from the motorcyclists perspective and even less experience, at first hand of the invisibility cloaking riders on the roads. They thus see no need for change. Buried inside this official disinterest, are 300,000 classic and vintage riders, who have never been recognised as an identifiable, large and homogeneous body of intelligent voting riders. Of many national motorcycling accident papers published over recent decades, I've not read one where the researcher admits to any riding experience, evinces any real awareness in classic motorcycling, or has much empathy with riding. Part of this is circumstantial. Much motorcycling safety research is performed by university researchers and consultants. Motorcycling generally and classic motorcycling in particular, is a 90% plus male pursuit. No academic research model or plan recognises and includes classic motorcyclists as a distinct grouping in motorcycling. Nor does any recognise that we are the stakeholders and stewards of each country's motorcycling heritage. We seem to be as invisible to the researchers as we are to car drivers on the roads. It's not as though classic riders hide from academics making their reputation via the limitless government road safety funding programmes. I urge road safety researchers everywhere to recognise this opportunity and open up a fresh dimension: we're ready and waiting for you.

Sometimes we are half-recognised in academic reports as the 'older riders' or riders of 'traditional or naked' bikes, neither of which are terribly meaningful. A researcher now and then will evince some passing regret that her research model failed because of such a dimly perceived group. This is more surprising given the numerical significance of classic riders. In Australia and in the UK, a cursory study of classic bike and rider numbers indicates they comprise up to 20% of total motorcycle and rider numbers. If outlaw bikers are the '1%'ers' and the fringe

Christian and Ulysses clubs with colours are the '10%'ers'; then classic motorcyclists can be fairly described as the '20%'ers', yet get less media and government attention than either of the other types of clubs.

In an endeavour to fill this research vacuum and lay down a trail for academics and consultants to follow, I sifted through a lot of the Anglo-Australasian research that our licence and registration fees have paid for in past decades, and have distilled a profile of the 'Classic Motorcycle Rider'. As I'm writing downunder, this has an Australasian flavour but most of us are riding British bikes, and from what I can see in the UK research, I'd be surprised if the demographics are very different in the northern hemisphere. So who exactly rides classic bikes?

Table 7.1 The Downunder Classic Motorcycle Rider Profile

Who are they?

Gender	91-93% Male.
Average Age	45 years
Age Range	21-70 years
Riding Experience	20 years plus

What do they Ride?

Bikes manufactured	1900 to 1978 approx.
Australia (top brands)	Triumph, Harley-Davidson and BSA
New Zealand	Triumph, BSA and Norton
UK	Triumph, BSA and Norton

Where do they Ride?

Annual Mileage (approx)	2,500kms (1,500 miles) per year or 100kms (60 miles) per week or less.
Suburban Riding	1,800kms (1,000 miles) per year.
Back road scratching	400kms (250 miles) per year.
City Freeways/Expressways	100kms (60 miles) per year
Rural Freeways/Expressways	100kms (60 miles) per year

When do they Ride?

Weekend mileage	60% approx.
Recreational rides	80% approx. or 2000kms (1,200 miles)
Non-riders	*50% of licensees say they don't ride.*

How Safely do they Ride?

Classic accidents	0.6 accidents per 100,000 kms
All Riders	1.0 per 100,000kms
Chance of an accident	2-4% per annum for Classic Riders.

Do Classic Riders Take Riding Training?

Every second classic rider returning to bikes after some absence has recent training on L-plates. Only one in five classic riders have taken refresher or advanced rider training. The above profile is borne out by what we see around us in classic clubs, both downunder in Australia and New Zealand, and in the UK, as outlined by Jamson's excellent 2005 UK research. Classic riders tend to be a little older on average than bike riders in general, but by no means are they all greybeards. Classic bikes continue to appeal to riders across all age groups and demographics, as they have always done. Annual mileages are less than average. This is consistent with the increasing value of most classic bikes, their age and growing conservation awareness. It's now commonplace to have some bikes trailered to rallies and annual days rather than being ridden as previously. More riders have multiple bikes, for example one for regular club rides, one for concourses and another, perhaps a modern bike for other riding. Classic riders focus on recreational road riding, in and around our towns and cities, with a fair amount of back-road scratching. This is borne out by a scan of club ride calendars which show an emphasis on weekend rides, but still includes a considerable amount of mid-week riding. Commuting and work riding of course is insignificant now. Accidents are also below average and this is a subject which needs to be explored further.

Few riders bother to do refresher or advanced training with their bikes. This is partly due to practical issues with advanced training courses such as frequent stops and re-starts, with lots of first gear manoeuvres, hard brake and clutch work: not the sort of things classic bikes really cope with easily. Here there may be an opportunity for enlightened trainers and educators to package a classic riding training product and market it to classic clubs.

Motorcycle Training and Accident Risk

Safety and training is the most contentious, politicised, and misrepresented area in motorcycling. Motorcyclists are often described by those who write road safety reports, and in turn by Joe Public, as a selfish group that tests society's tolerance by behaving poorly on the roads. They are labeled as taking crazy risks, leading to their being injured and killed - and annoying good folk in the process.

Now a classic bike book author is responsible only to his editor and is judged by his readers. We are likely to be independent and technically experienced in the subject, or at least appear so. The cadre of academic consultants, who write the streams of commissioned bike safety reports for regulatory authorities, can be neither as independent nor are they likely to be as practically experienced. Incidentally, why do the road and traffic regulatory authorities across the UK and Australasia farm out their motorcycling safety research studies to consultants and universities? Is it an admission they don't understand motorcycling and/or have no suitably trained staff to prepare these reports in-house? Isn't that their core business? Isn't that what we pay them for, i.e. as public servants to be in charge of, and be most knowledgeable about the subjects of roads and vehicles and safety?

Illus 7.1 This vintage Harley outfit was lucky to escape when its tow vehicle driver nodded off and rolled in central Australia last year.

Therein lies the problem for motorcycling. Too many research reports written for policy-makers, are written naively and by apparent non-riders. As mentioned above, there's difficulty finding a recent, decent motorcycle safety report in which the authors evinced they rode motorcycles, or had done so as they prepared for their research project. Too often the research models are poorly designed, with poor questionnaire design technology, and as a result fail to provide policy-makers with the wise counsel they sought. Some recent high-profile motorcycle reports are so poorly prepared they would face rejection if submitted to a proper scientific journal.

How are classic riders to find a way through this? There have been a few beacons in motorcycle risk and crash research over the past twenty years, and they stand out against later research offerings. Their virtue is often in their brevity, best summed up by Rothe and Cooper who back in 1988 concluded that

"...the lack of riding skill is not the major problem. Attitudes, personality and awareness of others are..." (See Rothe and Cooper Motorcycles: image and reality 1987 Ins. Corp of Brit. Columbia)

The amount and type of exposure (time on the road) were found to be the most important determinants of accident frequency, and they went on to state that no evidence could be found to support a conclusion that formal motorcycle training was effective in reducing subsequent motorcycle accident risk. Most of the later research derives from this study, which is why it's the most quoted research in motorcycling safety. Unfortunately this conclusion seems to be mostly ignored by the regulatory bodies. The awareness that motorcycling is a solitary pursuit, where skill develops largely in a 'learning by doing' way, is too often overlooked.

Rothe and Cooper recommended *"Motorcycle rider training courses should be more attentive to education than training... (and)...should use instructors who are better prepared to implement the education-oriented programs..."*

Fifteen years on, Elliott et al in 2003 (*Motorcycle Safety: a scoping study, Road Safety Division, Department for Transport, TRL581*) could still not find evidence to demonstrate whether 'skill training' was effective in improving riders' knowledge or skill. Elliott is another of the distressingly small number of credible motorcycle accident research studies that offer worthwhile reading. Huang and Preston in 2004 drew heavily on Elliott in their fine review of UK motorcycle accidents and programmes. (*B. Huang and J. Preston, Literature Review on Motorcycle Collisions, 2004*) This report was commissioned by UK Police bodies. If readers only want to read one recent paper on the subject, Huang and Preston is the right paper to select. This is recommended because the report is from a credible research group, The Transport Studies Unit at Oxford University. It was *not* commissioned by the usual regulatory bodies but by two quasi-private bodies, the Association of Chief Police Officers (ACPO), and the Police Foundation who requested a review of the literature on motorcycle accidents, user demographics and trends in the motorcycle market. They also reviewed the types of motorcycle accidents, their causes and primary and secondary prevention.

Unfortunately, as in 1988 no one in government was listening in 2003, and so to this day, motorcycle education takes a pillion seat to skill training. The Australian rider licence programme is almost completely a skill training exercise, as it is in other countries. The pay for motorcycle trainers is £7.60 an hour in Sydney this year. Wasn't it Sir Peter Abeles who coined the phrase, "you pay peanuts... you employ monkeys"? This pay rate is about one quarter of comparable casual teaching rates. I suspect a lot of motorcycle trainers would rather donate their time than work for such a low pay rate. The main focus remains the discredited MOST or Motorcycle Operator Skill Test. The only vaguely educational part of this is a knowledge test, worth about 40 minutes out of three days of skill training.

If there were an alien motorcyclist visiting Earth, it would conclude from Australian training that earthly bikers rode habitually in first gear, at walking pace, and were constantly steering around obstacles....but very skillfully indeed.

This is a puzzle because although some early 1960-1970s studies optimistically reported that skill training reduced crashes, later researchers could never rediscover the connection. As far back as 1981, the failure of the MOST test to prevent accident involvement was attributed to the absence of testing for danger perception and risk-taking. After another decade of MOST skill training, Crick reported:

"The MOST test is still geared towards the acquisition of basic vehicle control, a fact which inevitably influences the content of elementary training courses aimed... at equipping novices to pass the test" (Crick & McKenna, 1991, p.104).

After a further 15 years, it is still just like this in 2006 for all new riders, and across many refresher courses. The most plausible explanation for this lack of emphasis on education is that governments fail to understand why people ride bikes, see no votes in this fringe activity, and therefore give it no priority. However, that does not excuse those academics and consultants who have made a living for decades writing lucrative reports for governments on motorcycle road safety. Too often their reports comprise recycled overseas material with little original or relevant local input, or substantive, actionable recommendations.

Too often there is a failure to ask the right questions from these quarters, either because the customer is always right, or there's been simply a knowledge gap. One of the biggest gaps in comprehension is in defining the risks involved in motorcycling, especially where the researchers are not active, experienced motorcyclists. Bellaby and Lawrenson pointed to this in 2001, noting that a lot of motorcyclists disagreed with the experts' assessment of risk. Many riders stated quite accurately that, *'we are not so much risk-takers as the risky situation is often imposed upon the rider, i.e. from oil or gravel on the road, and drivers who fail to look etc'*.

The US MSF (The Motorcycle Safety Federation) has been a long time advocate of education-based programmes and ongoing education. Their Rider Education and Training System (RETS) is the most outstanding international role model but has, since 1973 unaccountably been ignored downunder. Why this hasn't been taken up in Australia is a puzzle when the country derives so much from the USA in other social areas.

The situation is different but mainly in degree, with the so-called advanced rider training area. Most courses focus on the same riding skill set, but often at speeds that enable second or occasionally third gear, and using road or race circuits. These are extremely valuable for classic riders, though the caveats on using your classic bike still apply - there's an awful lot of stopping and starting and brake and clutch work that simply isn't friendly to many classics. You may want to borrow or rent a modern bike for the day, and burn out their clutch!

There are a few signs that this is at last changing. The recent controversial Victorian Motorcycle Safety Levy, a surcharge applied only to motorcycle registrations in the State of Victoria since 2002 (but which excludes Classic bikes on club plates), has at least seen funds earmarked for education rather than skill training. Even more encouragingly, funds are being allocated to highlight proven 'Black Spots' for bike accidents and to ameliorate some of the more dangerous road sections in the state. At last we seem to be recycling research from the UK that might actually help to reduce rider accidents and mortality downunder. It's only taken 20 years to recognise the obvious. Goodbye training, hello education.

Classic Riders And Accident Risk

Classic motorcyclists are caught up in the criticism of motorcyclists generally as an unidentified, unresearched but important sub-group of riders and stakeholders. Even when they are almost recognised, they are often mixed in with a group whose accident record is far worse. Here's a typical, recent example from Australia. Haworth and Mulvihill 2006 noted in their influential 2006 Australian report to government *Crashes of Older Riders*, that returned riders:

"rode less... but in circumstances associated with increased crash involvement; they were more likely to ride in rural areas, were more severely injured in crashes...were also less likely to have undertaken training... However, it is somewhat surprising returned riders... have a lower crash risk… Perhaps the returned riders were avoiding riding in more hazardous conditions...or are riding more conservatively?"

What Haworth and Mulvihill were almost certainly sampling and unknowingly describing is the group of returnees with big-engined new bikes mixed in with the classic club riders. Both rider bodies have similar demographics and are from comparably sized populations, but ride fundamentally different kinds and vintages of vehicles - even if they are of similar makes (BMW, Triumph, and Harley-Davidson etc).

These rider populations have a dissimilar accident record. Returning riders of large, modern bikes ride the same country roads as classic riders, but they fall off more frequently. This is based upon experience in riding with both groups. There are always more hospital notices and walking wounded at, for example Ulysses meetings, than at classic club meetings. Returning riders may consider joining a classic club first and then migrating on to say Ulysses or HOG once they've updated their riding approach.

Classic riders must avoid being tarred, with the 'accident-prone' brush. This is a potentially dangerous and expensive trap for classic riders, as they may be slugged with licensing, registration and insurance restrictions and levies, when they aren't appropriate or deserved. We should be extremely concerned to see Haworth et al recommending to governments that

"Reducing the amount of the activity being undertaken (often termed exposure reduction) ... to reduce exposure in high-risk situations may be the best approach to reduce crash involvement, at least for... returned riders...."

Essentially, they suggest the best way to reduce motorcycle accidents, is by reducing the amount of the activity i.e. to take riders off the roads! These authors then reach back into the 1960s for that comfortable, false mantra...

"The main rider-based measures to prevent motorcycle crashes are:

* Rider licensing requirements

* Rider training

* Enforcement of rider adherence to road rules...."

What about education? What about listening to riders? What about asking better questions? Trying to be creative? Thinking laterally? Or even thinking originally? These are all normal consultancy skills expected by clients, who in this case are us. Which group appears to require more skill training, the riders or the researchers? It's frustrating enough reading and writing about these things. How much worse is it for those riders working in riders rights umbrella bodies who are hindered, rather than helped by much of this inept research?

I suggest classic riders, indeed all riders examine the track record of consultants involved in future motorcycle safety studies, before agreeing to be interviewed or participating in group discussions. Your contribution may unwittingly lead to tighter restrictions and costs imposed on fellow riders and on our favourite pastime.

The facts on classic riding road safety at the club level are for the record, clear. Classic riders from all demographics ride in one or more clearly defined classes of motorcycles, grouped under the classic rubric. The vehicles are all more or less old, but are often quite high performance bikes in well maintained condition, and capable of being ridden safely in today's traffic. The classic riders ride them competently. They ride them on suburban and rural two-lane roads, which are admittedly dangerous but they know that, and take it into account in their riding style. They ride them generally within the speed limits. They value their bikes too much to crash them, because in most cases, they restored them and they're more or less irreplaceable. They sometimes ride them on 500-5000 mile (1-8,000km) runs. One of their few admitted road risks is that they ride them less than in former days, largely for heritage and conservation reasons. That is no cause for alarm by the wider community. There are over 40,000 of these riders in Australia, and 300,000 globally. They are dedicated individuals who conserve a significant part of each nation's transport history, and often demonstrate that heritage to an appreciative public. Sometimes, even careful riders get into situations that are labeled accidents, but really are impossible to classify, like the true story of:

The Hautapu Railway Trap

In 1964, having left home in remote Gisborne, New Zealand for the big city in Auckland, I rode the 330 miles back home for my 18th birthday. It was a cold Winter and that rainy Friday night, I had no screen on the Ariel and the wind chill was vicious. My fingers and nose were numb after 100kms. At Hamilton, I refueled, smoked and burgered, and set off again. Unfortunately, as is easy to do leaving a service station, I became disoriented and turned North-East, rather than South. It was foggy and took a while before I noticed the road didn't feel right. I was lost, without a map or compass. Across the paddocks a house was still lit, and the kindly farmer soon gave me directions back to the main road. I was anxious now and declined the offer of tea. I later found out my way took me through a map dot called Hautapu, and as I closed on a road junction, the head-light happened on a sign. It pointed left to Cambridge and the road for Auckland. Relief. I turned left at the sign and the road dissolved in a Brigadoon-like fog and became a railway line. I rose up over one track before I knew what was happening, and soon established that a tight steering damper is not ideal on wet railway tracks. We slithered to a halt between the rails. The bike cut out in gear. I paused to collect my wits and loosen the damper. It was too far, dark and slippery to push back to the road in reverse, but turning the bike round in the pitch dark and fog on the permanent way seemed a bit dicey. It would not be easy forcing a wheel up and over the slippery wet rail at an angle, and then to stop dead to avoid carrying on down any invisible embankment which happened to be lurking in the dark. Then I'd have to chance it again, going the other way... to end up back between the tracks, facing the road. What a quandary. It was pitch dark, the land was low-lying and I felt sure I was on an embankment of some sort. At that apocryphal moment, I noticed a single headlight traversing the land ahead. Panic was immediate and fortunately followed by inspiration. I leapt off, and hauled the bike up on the centre stand over a sleeper. By tilting it up on the left stand tang, with the rear wheel elevated, I was able to rotate the bike, as if it were a train on a turntable. Fortunately the Ariel started first kick, and we bounced back to the road, fearing a whistle behind me at any moment. The rest of that trip was an anticlimax. I bought a windscreen soon afterward, and some inner gloves.

Coincidentally, and forty-four years later my wife and I were following a friend's shortcut to Cambridge, and unknowingly came up on that same Hautapu junction late one foggy Winter's night - and yes, I followed that damned sign again, and turned the rental car up the railway line. They really have got to do something about that sign.

Are Classic Riders Put At Risk By Today's Rider Training?

Late starters and BABs should expect parts of the training they receive to be fashionable and politically correct. Some of the skill training and competencies are inappropriate for classic riders, and could increase their riding risks if uncritically followed. They should expect to discard these parts of their training from their riding behaviour once they leave the training ground, in the interests of rider safety. Here are just four examples to watch for in training courses.

Throttle Friction Control

This refers to the throttle twist grip friction adjusting screw on the right side of classic handlebars. Current Australian rider training is against any use of such a throttle friction aid (see *Stay Upright* and *HART*). The argument seems to be a confused variation of the 'dead man's handle' argument for train drivers, that is should the train driver have a heart attack and take his hand off the throttle, the train stops. Grafting this argument onto classic pre-1971 bikes creates a real hazard for classic riders in urban areas. If the throttle closes when you need to give a hand signal in traffic, for example when turning right at a road junction, the bike suddenly decelerates before you can get close to the junction or traffic light. This early and unexpected deceleration manoeuvre, coupled with the distraction of an unfamiliar hand-signal, can cause cars behind you to pile into your rear.

Here's another common classic scenario. Out on country roads for a longish club ride, it's not uncommon for older riders of classic British bikes, especially singles with lots of secondary handlebar vibration, to experience cramps in the hands or fingers. If a sudden cramp hits you while rounding a corner, and you're forced to straighten your fingers or lose your grip, then the throttle snaps shut... and you career off the road.

To illustrate that this and other aspects of current training are nothing more than fashions, let me quote Warwick Schuberg, an ex-police riding instructor and founder of the *Stay Upright* rider training course. His was the first such course and was mandated by the NSW government as the first compulsory license training scheme in Australia. In his 1982 book *Stay Upright*, Warwick recommends *"a throttle friction screw be fitted if possible and that riders should make use of hand signals as a valuable safety measure....I would prefer the engine braking to take place under the control of the rider..."* Most classic riders would agree with Warwick. Why then do his trainers now veto the use of throttle friction? You might also ask Harley-Davidson, who still routinely fit them to all their 2007 range of bikes.

Many riders might expect, after seeing enlightened classic bike registration and licensing policies, that this official empathy flows through to rider training. Afraid not. At least in NSW, this is blocked by a Roads and Traffic Authority (RTA) interpretation of their own admirable policy. The perverse RTA view, is that classic bikes cannot be used for rider training and MOST testing, even if they are road-registered on club plates. The Ombudsman and I failed to obtain a commonsense outcome. Some classic bikes do squeeze into the programme. I know one Bantam and rider who passed the course recently.

Braking Techniques

Classic riders made more use of the rear brake than is generally the case for modern bikes. Indeed I hardly ever used the front brake on my Ariel, considering it unsafe on the metal (dirt) roads of the 1960s. Today, the main brake training emphasis is on front braking. This is based on load shifting to the front, and thus more effective front wheel braking. I suggest that this is as inappropriate as the advice on throttle friction for classic bikes. The major reasons for this are discussed in Chapter two, and relate to the marginal performance of classic front brakes, especially from the earlier classic period. The combination of small brake pad area and a large front wheel diameter greatly reduces effective braking. Classics often have narrow front rims, older compound tires, and only basic front suspension. Training classic riders to focus first and hardest on front wheel braking, to the detriment of the rear brake, places them in harms way. One braking point in our favour with drum brakes compared to some discs can be superior performance at lower speeds with lower lever pressures, and in the wet.

Today, with better tyre/road cohesion and hydraulic disk brakes, a greater emphasis on front wheel braking is sensible for many modern bikes, but even here, the current training prescriptions can be perilous for some classes of modern bikes. For example cruisers and especially Harley-Davidsons have two thirds of their weight over the rear wheel. The front of the bike is always light, and the load shifting argument has far less going for it in these bikes. Accentuating this, the rear tyre is often nearly twice the width of the front, with correspondingly more braking weight and rubber on the road. For these reasons, I suggest contemporary training nostrums on braking be treated sceptically by classic, chopper and cruiser riders. When riding a Harley-Davidson for the safest riding, I choose classic rear-wheel braking with little use of the front brake.

Cornering Lines

The 'racing line' was *de rigeur* for young riders cornering in the 1950s and 1960s. Peeling into a corner early, shaving the corner apex, and drifting wide across the exit, with the throttle on and staying in the road lane with difficulty was fast and fun. While it is still a fast way through a bend, the classic rider's priority these days is not speed and our suspensions may not be as they once were, for bike or rider. Today's training varies by country but typically includes cornering advice. For left handers the advice is to start wide, exit close. This means you ride wide, close to the white line (if it's safe to do so) as you enter the corner and stay wide until you can see the corner unwinding. This way increases your chance of seeing round the bend before selecting an exit line, which should be reasonably close to the left kerb. On right hand bends a similar technique is used. Start wide and near to the left hand kerb as possible until you can see around the bend. Then take the corner exiting nearer to the centre line than the kerb.

These days, while out of favour with trainers, echoes of the racing line are seen in the syllabus for right hand turns. Here an earlier corner entry can be acceptable since visibility through the corner is opened up down the right hand lane, and this lane also increases the corner's radius compared with left handers.

However, for left hand turns, entering the corner late and wide, and exiting in the middle of the lane is now recommended. This makes sense in hilly and rural roads where the geology, coupled with disinterested local councils, can also leave a lethal gravel film on corner apices. However in urban and suburban areas where much classic riding takes place, the advice to enter wide and late, should not be uncritically accepted either. For example:

- In towns, riders starting late from the white line and sweeping across left handers, may provoke road rage in drivers from such 'show-off' behaviour.

- Similarly, moving across to the white line before a left hander opens up the inside of the lane, inviting drivers into the space vacated. Cars also split lanes!

- Current training effectively reduces the radius of left handers versus the racing line. Classic riders must bank further to take left handers using today's training. If we do hit gravel on skinny tires, today's training can make it easier to fall, so take it easy.

- Late corner entry to avoid apex oil-film is not as relevant now as in classic times. Cars are more oil-tight, transverse engines distribute oil across the lane and vehicle widths vary.

On balance, cornering lines vary depending on road and traffic conditions. In heavy town traffic, dominating the middle of the lane makes more sense in order to stay conspicuous and discourage lane splitting. In the country with blind corners, entering wide and late opens up visibility and preserves options. And where wide open sweeping corners are found with perfect vision, Keith Code's 'Two-Step' approach to the old racing line, may safely be revisited. See his website on www.superbikeschool.com.

Signalling

The modern training syllabus no longer includes hand signals. This is a serious omission for all riders and especially commuters who, like classic riders, ride in traffic. Hand signals address the problem of the Klingon 'cloaking device' that surrounds all bike riders in traffic, and which is discussed in the next section.

Top Tips For Classic Riding Survival

Older and returning riders are criticised for being accident-prone. This is said to be due to older riders returning after long absences, not updating their training, and then riding powerful bikes infrequently and on more hazardous roads. In NSW there are five times as many licences as registered bikes possibly indicating that many former riders are planning to return. (This begs the question...why do men pay for decades to retain a licence when they have neither bike, nor immediate plans for one?) This may indicate that many men have a retirement or goodbye-plan involving a dream motorcycle, and for many that is a classic British bike. If so the future demand for classic motorcycling seems in safe hands.

Top Survival Tips

- **Do refresher training**, or re-do licence training before starting on any serious riding. When the L-plate trainers argue it's more dangerous out there than it was in your former motorcycling days, they should be believed. The injury rate for bikers in the UK runs at thirty times the rate for car drivers, i.e.at 147 KSI (Killed or Seriously Injured) per million kilometres ridden. A long clean car driving record does not carry over to BABs when they take up riding again. Instead, new riders resume their level of riding expertise from where they left it, twenty or thirty years past, except that it's now decayed from disuse, and what's left is insufficient to keep them safe on today's roads.

- **Hazards are different.** Recognise that on any stretch of road, motorcyclists face the same hazards as car drivers plus another set of hazards unique to riding a motorcycle. These relate to the condition of the road surface and include leaves, gravel and melted tar patching in Summer, slippery man hole covers in the rain and so on. This is also the reason why motorcycle riding is so much fun. Riding a bike over a much-travelled road is like riding that road for the first time, every time. All motorcycle riding is a joyous odyssey, because every time on every road is a fresh adventure. That helps us maintain concentration for long periods; something hard to do in a car.

- **Become a show-off.** Making yourself deliberately conspicuous can be a life-saver in urban, suburban and motorway traffic, as Hancock found in 1990. They noted two key factors that explain why car drivers fail to see motorcyclists.

    > Firstly *sensory conspicuity* or the physical aspects of an approaching vehicle that distinguish it from the background. Motorcycles have poor 'sensory conspicuity', due to their small size and silhouette. People identify objects by their size, shape, colour and motion. From a distance motorcyclists are similar to pedestrians or bicycles except for their speed. Drivers distinguish small bike silhouettes

by picking out their movement (speed) and estimating their distance. A bike merged in a traffic stream, does not muster a speed differential against adjacent cars, so drivers cannot easily pick them out, especially at a distance. That's why they *really don't see us*. It's like a bird noticing a worm once it wriggles. Classic bikes are often smaller than modern, fully faired bikes, and painted in darker colours, so they can be harder again to pick out. This is why it's better to ride with another rider, or in a convoy so that the effective size and silhouette is increased and more likely to be noticed by car drivers.

Secondly, *cognitive conspicuity* or the degree to which the car driver's experience or intentions lead them to notice an approaching bike. Motorcyclists now have very poor 'cognitive conspicuity' as there are relatively speaking far less on the roads than in earlier days. In the UK motorcycles comprise just 3% of vehicles, down a whopping 84% from the peak 19% share of all vehicles in 1960. Only at weekends are motorcycles seen in the same sort of numbers as in earlier days. We are more likely to be seen by drivers at weekends *because they expect us to be there*. For this reason, the accident rate involving cars and bikes should prove to be lower on weekends, when standardized for the number of bikes and cars out there. This is another safety question researchers could usefully explore.

- **Hand signals.** Always use hand signals when turning or changing lanes in town. Hand signals draw attention to invisible bikes buried in a traffic stream. They address both 'conspicuity' issues above. First, a sharp, affected gesture with the whole arm to the right or left turns the 'sensory conspicuity' problem into a lifesaver, by changing the bike and riders' size and shape. The bold arm-shift and speed is so different to that of the traffic flow, it draws the drivers' eye to the rider. We can change our shape to be seen, just like a frill neck lizard puffing up, or a cockatoo erecting it's comb! Second, it deals with the 'cognitive conspicuity' issue as drivers aren't used to hand signals, except for road-rage signals and police signals to stop. We can exploit the power in police gestures to draw attention to ourselves in traffic. It may feel silly at first, but it becomes second nature after seeing car drivers fall back on seeing the signals. That proves they see us. An unfashionable white or multi-coloured glove intensifies the power of hand signals.

- **Noise and the benefit of a loud exhaust**. Car cabins are insulated, and a vehicle has to be very noisy to be heard over the iPod. It's another way to overcome Hancock's sensory conspicuity trap. The exhaust noise laws have been relaxed in NSW, and have never been applied to classic bikes.

There is no real way of defining standards for classic exhaust volume. In New Zealand the attempt to have police rate bike exhaust noise has proved impractical. For classic bikes, the lesson is clear.

- **Bright clothing.** A riding wardrobe should be selected for more than comfort. Studies such as the 2004 New Zealand Wells study show a 37% risk reduction from wearing fluorescent clothing; a 27% accident risk reduction from having headlights on, and a 24% fall in risk from wearing a white helmet compared with a black helmet. I own both a black helmet and a white one. When I wear the white one, cars fall back and I associate this with 'cognitive conspicuity'. If I add a fluorescent vest the effect on cars is more pronounced. Drivers associate the yellow vest and white helmet with postmen or motorcycle police. They fall back while they work out the answer. I dress like a police rider, and am searching for a pair of CHIPs blue cotton NSW police jodhpurs. They provide no leg protection to police legs, and are a rotten example of safety clothing to riders, but they outfox car drivers.

- **Crashbars**. In Harley-Davidson speak 'engine bars'. Originally classic bikes commonly fitted crashbars, but they fell into disuse. There is evidence they reduce lower limb injuries from legs forced into the bike during accidents (Ouellet 1990). Nairn 1993 advised leg injuries are lessened by crashbars in half the crashes where leg damage occurred. Crashbars can also enhance bike appearance and protect the tank if the bike falls over. They're handy for mounting mirrors, cable/helmet locks and pumps. They increase sensory conspicuity. Pillion crashbars are also handy. Front and rear bars are becoming popular downunder in stainless steel.

- **KUFO and FIFO.** These are acronyms standing for 'Fit In or F*** Off' and 'Keep Up or F*** Off'. They're self explanatory and easily addressed by moving to a better club. KUFO is lethal: it causes riders to exceed their comfort zone keeping up with a speed set by an inept ride leader. Any decent club knows members have varying speeds, and caters for them by providing for faster riders to rejoin the group at way-stops.

Do Crash Helmets Cause, As Well As Prevent Injuries?

The evidence on balance suggests they do. Despite compliance with standards testing, helmet designs vary making some more suitable for classic riding. As Huang engagingly says, *"lthough protective helmets have been used to advantage for more than three millennia, the first systematic investigations of helmet function and effectiveness appeared only recently, in England in the 1940's"*

As in the 'training vs accident' debate, Cairns and others reported positively on helmet protection. Yet by the 1980s researchers found evidence of injuries caused by helmets. Today, there's sufficient evidence for every rider to reach his own conclusions about helmets. Unfortunately this requires wading through anatomical, epidemiological, engineering and statistical evidence which few will enjoy doing. It's possible to distill the evidence into some classic rules of thumb:

- In most places helmets are mandatory so we should wear one.
- The main helmet aim is to reduce the brain impact speed, when it hits the inside of the skull, and so avert a brain injury. Above quite low impact speeds 10-15mph (20-25kph), no helmet really achieves this.
- Above 10-15mph the risk of neck injuries caused by the helmet increases.
- Softer helmets and linings may better protect the brain at slower classic speeds by better cushioning the decelerating brain.
- Harder helmets and linings may better protect the brain at higher speeds.
- Lighter helmets help to reduce neck injuries, caused by heavy helmets.
- Full face road helmets with hard face bars can give a fatal brain injury via the chin strap and lower jaw, transmitting force to the base of the skull and fracturing it.
- Full face helmets can reduce facial damage, in some accidents.
- Open face helmets give more face injuries, but less of the fatal brain injury of full face road helmets. Open Face helmets with a separate tilting face-bar may offer a safety compromise. Off-road open face helmets with softer face-bars offer another classic compromise.
- One effect of mandating helmet wear is reduced bike registrations.
- A 'Drop Test' may assist in helmet choice. Helmets that bounce less may absorb impact with less rebound impacts on the brain. The dealer should have used helmets for this test rather than trying their new stock. In Illus. 7.2 below, Sam at MAW in Sydney, demonstrates how a laminated helmet rebounds less than a moulded plastic type. This can indicate different helmet deformation characteristics and may guide the choice for classic riders. While helmet manufacturers and testing agencies use sophisticated testing equipment, they all involve impacts with the helmet.
- Prices do not reflect the above factors, and some cheaper helmets may be preferred by classic riders.

To avoid doubt, I do not recommend any particular type or brand of helmet, but hope to provide better information to aid in selection. Helmet weight is a key factor to protect the neck and those under 1.5kgs may be better. Manufacturers seem remiss in not labeling helmets with the above information. This needs to be corrected.

TIPS

It's not just a question of head protection. The lighter the helmet, the less risk of neck injury. The way the face-bar collapses could help minimize damage to the brain.

Helmet criteria for classic riding might include low speed crash performance, easy deformation, soft padding and light weight.

Thermoplastic helmets are cheaper, as they're injection moulded and less labour-intensive to make. While these may generally be harder, some of these may deform more easily at lower impact speeds. Choosing one of these with a softer polystyrene liner may lead to a choice that meets the above criteria. Whether these are the right criteria, is up to each rider to judge. It's determined by the nature of the crash, and this is unknowable. However, going by the reported statistics and observations of accidents and patients, it's possible to describe a typical accident demand on the helmet as it protects the brain during a sequence of impacts and sudden movements. In a common single vehicle incident, where a bike runs wide on a corner, the front

wheel goes and the bike drops, while the rider follows training and steps off, or high-sides. The helmet first protects the head from a glancing blow as the rider drops on the road. Next it scrapes along the road, grinding away the outer layers sacrificially as it protects skin and face. If the rider slides head first into a tree, rail or a structure, this may be the third helmet impact, and the most severe. The rider has decelerated and often hits at an angle, so avoiding an immediate stop. The outer helmet now deforms, and the lining compresses, cushioning the brain as it slams into the skull.

The rider may continue sliding with another impact or two before stopping. The helmet protects against further skin-loss

Illus 7.2 MAW's Sam in Sydney shows how a laminated helmet bounces less.

and heat from road friction. The neck has been alternately flexed, extended, compressed and violently twisted along the way. The heavier the helmet, the more the combined weight of head plus helmet which can act like the head of a sledgehammer, swinging around on the flimsy neck. In this kind of accident, the open face helmet with a softer, tilting face-bar may be a better choice.

The helmet base at the rear, extending down the neck also has an impact on safety. It's possible in hyper-extension for this to impact the spine and contribute to injury. This might happen if the helmet is loose, and is hit in front and pivots up. If it worries you, then select a helmet which is scalloped out at the rear, so the helmet base finishes in line with the base of the skull. On the other hand, this exposes your cervical spine to impact from items waiting in the landscape. You take your pick.

In Table 7.1 below, the helmet types are ranked as a reference, based upon the above analysis. Naturally, each rider must make their own choice in this life and death area. It's too important to leave to others.

Table 7.1   Available Helmet Choices for Classic Riders

Rank	Helmet Type	Strengths	Weaknesses
1	Open-face, tilt face-bar	Some face protection	High speed impacts
2	Off Road, face-bar	Some face protection	High speed impacts
3	Open face	Less base-skull injury Less neck injury	More face injuries
4	Full face	Face protection	Skull-base injury Neck injury

There are other important helmet factors. Firstly in Australia and other hot regions of the world, the best flow-through ventilation is a must, both for comfort and to help avoid hyperthermia. Helmets with a fog visor i.e. a visor liner, are preferable to avoid misting during kick starting and, in the UK and NZ they're very useful in the wet and on cold days. A nose guard also reduces misting up on cold days and protects the exposed nose on hot sunny days. A peak provides more nose protection and glare reduction late in the day and in the morning, when heading into the sun. With full-face helmets, it's important in cold weather to maintain airflow through the air-space behind the visor. This avoids carbon dioxide being re-inhaled, which can quickly reduce oxygen supply to the brain, whereupon the rider passes out! Wearing bulky neck-warmers or scarves can contribute to this hazard.

A more insidious and undocumented hazard, is interruption to the brain's blood supply from tight helmet chin-straps causing the rider to become giddy or to faint. This can arise from any helmet with a chin-strap, but is more likely with some designs and rider anatomy. The problem occurs where a chin-strap is over-tight and the straps and padding press on the sides of the neck. It's a design weakness in modern helmets that chin-straps pass behind and under the jaw. This means they cross the internal and external carotid arteries just above where these branch, i.e. below the angle of the mandible (the right angle made by the lower jaw), on the side of the neck. The carotid arteries supply the brain and it takes only a small reduction in flow for a short time for the brain to starve from lack of oxygen, and the rider to become faint or pass out.

Its worth checking helmet adjustment to see that padding and straps do not bear too firmly over these pumping arteries - they must never be compressed. Helmets with narrow, hard straps and hard, unpadded side-flaps can be the worst offenders. It's an item to check when a new helmet is being purchased. Also, where riders start to feel faint or giddy on the road, it's always worth loosening the strap. I became aware of this hazard when doing some road-testing recently, using a popular white open face helmet. I was looking down at the engine breather as I rode along, became faint and nearly passed out. After I pulled over and loosened the strap, the symptoms vanished. The combination of helmet design, a firmly tightened strap, and looking down (which tightened the strap over the carotid arteries), restricted the blood supply to my brain.

There's one more clinching argument on classic helmet choice. It's the time when helmet choice affects survival after the accident is over. This is when a rider is lying at the roadside with a neck injury after an accident. The rider is having difficulty breathing and a mate is trying to save his life by mouth-to-mouth. He's well trained and doing the right thing by leaving the helmet on, but he's facing a life-and-death quandary. It's hard for the first aider to get the mouth inside the face opening of a full-face helmet in order to give mouth to mouth ventilation to the downed rider. Trying to kiss the wife while wearing a helmet demonstrates the problem. If that appears hard, try also putting a hand inside the helmet to pinch off the rider's nose whilst giving mouth-to-mouth! The choice facing the first rider at an accident scene can be this: to remove the helmet and risk making the rider a quadriplegic or withhold ventilation and hope the rider starts breathing again. The conventional view is that it is better to take the helmet off, even if he puts the patient into a wheel chair, than leave it on while the downed rider turns blue and dies. I suggest taking a long hard think about it, before removing a helmet.

One of the most pervasive urban myths about helmets is that they have a finite life. Rider training groups instill this into new riders, as if the helmet somehow has a use-by date. In fact there is no law in Australia governing helmet age. Nor have I found any convincing evidence to suggest there is a time-based wear factor in helmet technologies. For example, if a helmet is sitting on a shelf it may last indefinitely. The only practical result I can see from this myth is to increase helmet sales. If there is any truth to claims helmets wear out, it's to do with actual helmet hours in the saddle and the knocks and bumps along the way, and not how many birthdays the helmet has seen.

The other helmet myth is that helmets with more stickers, showing they comply with more international standards, are better. That isn't necessarily so. AS1698 for Australian riders, is as good as any helmet standard. Opting for a helmet with multiple stickers can leave riders worse off, financially and safety-wise. From the manufacturer's viewpoint, different certifying groups have different testing criteria. The only way to design a helmet to pass AS1698 plus Dot and Snell is to make a stronger, tougher helmet to meet the hardest of each set of tests. The resulting helmet is likely to have the hardest shell and lining. Some tests e.g. Snell, are said to relate more to car racing where demands are different. One might conclude that any one of the Australian, US and European stickers are better for classic riders [AS1698, BSI, DOT or ECE].

For helmet and visor cleaning, people in the trade say the best thing is the product many Harley-Davidson dealers use to detail their bikes - Mr Sheen household polish.

It's easy to see why GP racers use full-face helmets. They rarely collide at high speeds with objects and given the run-off space on circuits, the full-face helmet is a better bet for the remaining risks of high-speed riding. Their frequent crashes are single vehicle incidents where the rider slides off the circuit due to a tyre losing adhesion. The full face helmet here is less likely to suffer a severe frontal impact causing a fatal hangman brain injury. It also provides abrasion protection for the face, as the rider slides across the run-off gravel. In the racing context it also provides good noise protection. Classic riders face different risks on the road, so racing aspects are of limited usefulness.

Classic Near Misses

Amongst the plethora of motorcycle accident statistics, the incidents classic riders experience pass unnoticed by researchers. Given classic accident rates are low, it's more useful to log common 'near miss' situations.

- **Falling In.** This near-miss occurs in off-road situations such as on service station forecourts, parking stations, concourse events - and in front of club mates. It happens when manoeuvring in low gear, tracing a circular path into a parking slot, or petrol pump. Suddenly, the rider is on the ground. If riders were pilots, it'd be called a stall. In low speed turns, use of the front brake stalls the front while the rear wants to move forward. The bike literally drives over onto the ground amazingly quickly. The longer the wheelbase and the heavier the bike, the more likely they are to fall in. Cruisers are notorious for it, especially with forward controls. Recovery is then harder, as the feet are further from the ground, and legs at the wrong angle to offer salvation.

- **Daydreaming.** It's easy on a club ride in the country, to listen to the engine note, or review an adjustment made that morning. The rider looks up to find the road ahead empty, as mates have turned off.

- **Convoy Riding.** This traps BABs on club runs in a congo line of bikes all watching the ones ahead and behind. The rider falls behind, and strains to close up on reaching a straight. He does so as they disappear round a bend, leaving the BAB steaming into a corner too fast, furiously declutching, braking and changing gear to scrape round.

- **Follow The Leader.** On a club run, it's common to follow one bike for a while, matching his speed and riding in his tracks. Come to a bend where the radius tightens, and the guy in front sails through smoothly. The second rider is halfway through the bend and sees his cornering line is wrong, runs wide, wobbles back to the road, and rides on with a racing pulse.

- **Dressing In Or Out?** It's de rigeur in some clubs to have pants inside or outside the boots. A common low-speed near miss, especially with forward mounts on choppers and cruisers, is to catch the pants cuff on the brake or gear lever or footrest, when stopping in traffic. The rider can't ground the foot, and the bike slowly topples sideways into a car.

- **The Layback Trap.** A 5'6"rider on a club run, stops at a service station to refuel. As riders jockey into position to rejoin the road, a car passes and the rider in front of him stops, leaving our rider straddling the layback or gutter. He puts his foot down into thin air and topples over.

- **An Unkind Slide.** A rider finally gets his bike started at the annual field day, and the Amal throttle slide decides to stick wide open, careering the rider through the assembled bikes.

- **Drat That KIFF!** A BAB regains his license and is taught the KIFF mnemonic (Kill switch off, Ignition off, Fuel off, First gear engaged). Notice this includes leaving the bike in first gear. The next time he starts his classic bike on the centre stand, when he pushes it off the stand the bike takes off with the rider sprawling back over the pillion seat and bystanders roaring with laughter.

Classic Riding Ergonomics

Like any physical activity, riding classic bikes exercises muscles and parts of the body that may not have received any training for a while. Given the popularity of classic bikes among older riders, this can lead to a range of annoying aches and pains, as well as more severe states of unwellness. Below are common problems classic riders face, and suggested remedies.

- **Cramps.** These are common on longer rides. They occur in any muscle group, and are due to the frozen riding position on the bike. When cramp strikes in a leg, it's relieved by a small shift in posture, for example pointing the foot up or down on the footrest. Some riders stretch out a foot and rest it on the crash bar if one is fitted. This sounds dangerous but half a million Harley riders ride this way. That doesn't make it safe. Wasn't it Einstein who said "if 20,000 people say a stupid thing, it is still a stupid thing"? Some riders use the pillion footrests. This is safe on empty straight roads. If cramps are severe, then adding highway pegs to the crashbars often helps. The rider then has a choice of four anti-cramp positions, and cycling through them prevents cramps starting. Finger and hand cramps are relieved by stretching the hand. For the throttle hand, a plastic cruise controls which clips over the twist-grip, as shown in Illus. 7.3 is a handy device to help prevent cramp.

- **Dehydration.** In hot countries like Australia, this is a real issue for all riders. Wearing leather gear and with wind-chill, the body's fluid requirements can top four litres on an all-day ride. It's hard to drink this much fluid at fuel stops on a run, and many riders become dehydrated. As discussed in chapter eight, wearing a hydration back pack can help maintain a fluid balance.

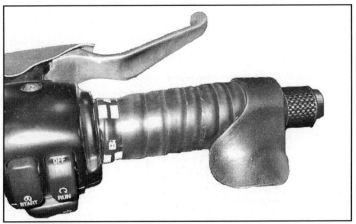

Illus 7.3 The wrist-controlled, throttle control takes the load off fingers.

- **Back Aches.** Most of the population has a bad back, and classic riding can exacerbate it. Kick starting, vibration, and posture are precipitating factors. The starting tips and anti-vibration measures in chapter nine can help. Back braces and kidney belts are covered in the next chapter.

- **Hyperthermia.** This used to be called 'heat-stroke' and these days is often referred to as 'brain fade'. Riders in the Australian summer are especially at risk. If the temperature under the tongue gets past 37.5C, symptoms begin. These include, feeling hot and cold, shivers, extra sweating, headache, furry tongue, confused thinking and orange urine. It's avoided by wearing summer riding clothes and taking in clear fluids, not coffee or alcohol. Downing a water bottle at each fuel stop works. First Aiders point out it's vital we sweat to cool our bodies. In fact not sweating is more serious than sweating a lot. Their advice to Firefighters downunder is simple "if your wee isn't clear, drink two glasses of water"

- **Hypothermia.** There's no commonplace name for this condition, where core temperature falls below 36.1C. Older riders are particularly susceptible. All riders in winter face the combined effects of low temperatures and wind-chill. Shivering, losing concentration, and stiff fingers are tell-tales it's time to pull over and warm up with hot drinks

- **Frequent Urination.** Dehydration is a common precursor to hyperthermia in the down under summer. The best indicator is orange urine. Drinking lots of fluids can be irksome on rides, as it entails more toilet stops. One solution is the 'Bangkok Dunny', used by those marooned on Bangkok's elevated freeways. A zip-lock bag taped to the leg, with Penrose tube joining your old fella, avoids bailing out in front of gridlocked Thai motorists. For riders, the chemist supplies a 'Urodome'.

- **Fatigue.** Motorcycling is physically demanding, and classic bikes are more stressful than modern bikes. This is due to the weight, size and wheelbase, suspension (or its lack), vibration, noise and nakedness. Club rides rarely go more than two hours before a break.

- **Riding Position.** Like a car, the positions of bike seating and controls are largely pre-set. Levers, footrests and bars can be adjusted to provide a comfortable riding position. This has the rider leaning forward, to spread weight away from the spine, and reduce wind load. Handlebars are narrow to cut vibration. While the handlebars are normally anchored to the head-stock, bar height and position can be varied by rotating the bars until the optimum handgrip position is found. Hand levers are angled to follow the curve of the arms down through the straight wrists. Once these are set, feet positions can be locked in. For and aft, foot lever positions need not be the same. The gear lever and footrest height should be set so the big toe can nudge the gear lever up and down. The brake lever height depends on rider preference. Some like to lift the foot before applying pressure, others pivot the foot on the rest to control the pressure. Foot settings vary with footwear, and should be reviewed with new boots: even one spline shift in a gear lever adjustment can affect comfort.

Change Blindness And The Visual Scratchpad

Drivers really don't see bikers as discussed above. More accurately, they see them and forget them, putting riders at risk even if they remain in plain sight. This is worrying for riders trained to stay in the driver's rear view mirror and expecting to be seen and safe there. This may achieve little and make us complacent. Fascinating research by Simons (*Simons and Chabris: Gorillas In Our Midst*) showing how drivers fail to see a bike, even if it's right in front of them and even when they are concentrating on their driving. This classic experiment involves an audience watching a video of a basketball game and being asked to count the passes. A person in a gorilla suit slowly walks in front of the camera, pauses and beats her chest, then slowly walks away. Half or more of the audience do not see the gorilla! In another test, a stranger stops someone in the street to ask directions. During the conversation, two people carrying a wooden door pass between the direction giver and the stranger. Behind the door is a third person, who changes place with the original stranger and carries on the conversation. Even with the third man being of different height, build, clothing and voice, 50-90% of people failed to notice the change and carried on the original conversation. It's called 'change blindness'.

Experiments have shown that as soon as they look away, drivers only remember two, three or four vehicles around them even though there may have been several others around at the time. It's as if their visual scratchpad or short-term memory can only hold two to four items. There are obvious implications for road accidents and bikes. Other research evidence shows that people's perception is incomplete, and the brain fills in the gaps to form a complete picture of what we see. This is one reason why eye-witnesses disagree in court. Given this knowledge what chance has a bike of being detected by drivers in heavy traffic?

Understanding the problem is half the solution. There's not much riders can do about change blindness, except expect it from drivers. But we can help keep ourselves on the visual scratchpad by ensuring we are one of the 3-4 vehicles drivers observe. This is the same challenge as sensory conspicuity. Riders must stand out from the background and force themselves into drivers' perception.

Trout Fishing And Classic Road Craft

Surviving on a classic bike employs similar skills to those used in stream fishing. Reading a river when fly-fishing for trout, is similar to reading a road for traffic hazards. The stream fisher looks first for the current because that determines where the trout and their food will be. On a road he looks in the traffic stream, as that's where the hazards will come from. Junctions in the stream are places to pay special attention for trout. Intersections on the road demand the same attention, for darting cars. Sight lines and manoeuvring round obstacles to casting are vital on the river, just as they are on a bike. It's important to cast smoothly on a stream, as it is to feel smooth on the bike. Anglers never hurry on a stream. Quick reaction times are important when a trout strikes, or a car suddenly changes lanes. Fishers have a spot already planned to bring the trout to shore, just as riders plan cornering lines, and have an escape route in mind. Anglers are never rough with the trout letting the rod do the work, just as riders keep a light grip on the bars, and let the bike find its way on metal roads. Each pool along the river is different, as every corner of every road is different. Fishermen read the surface of the water for submerged rocks, eddies, snags and holes... just as they read the road surface for gravel, ripples, oil and holes. Back-country trout fishing on a motorcycle is a doubly satisfying hobby.

First Aid

Motorcycling has its share of injuries, and while these are less common in the classic area than on today's bikes, it's a requirement (or perhaps should be) that someone on club runs has First Aid know-how. There comes a day when every rider is first on the scene, alone with a downed, unconscious rider. Don't panic! There's a window of several minutes in which to act. The first move is to the mobile phone to call for an ambulance. Next, and in the absence of First Aid training, remember 'ABC', as a start-up mnemonic for attending the injured where:

A	Airway.	Check his throat is open and clear of tongues, dentures, mouth guards and dirt.
B	Breathing.	Check he's breathing. If not then resuscitation is needed pronto.
C	Circulation.	Stop bleeding by pressing a scarf or other material over the wound.

In researching First Aid for this book, I was surprised at the changes it's undergone in recent years. The training now includes subjects taken from medical degree courses, with diagnostic and therapeutic approaches you'd expect from your family doctor such as defibrillation, tension pneumothorax, diabetes, stroke, gastroenteritis in babies etc. The First Aid leaflet of yesterday is now a 132+ page medical textbook. How can the typical rider learn and remember to apply such a body of medical procedures? First Aid seems subject to Parkinson's Law, it's expanded to fill the available capacity. Along the way, the essentials have attracted a medical overlay. This information overload could lead to roadside uncertainty. For motorcyclists, the first reservation concerns roadside resuscitation. The advice being published in good faith, looks inappropriate. If followed literally, it could cause injury to the person receiving assistance. Why is this? Perhaps it's because First Aid writers are trying to cover so many injuries and diseases, in a simple way. They distill a range of ill health, diagnoses and treatments into a few lines each. This makes a good reference book, but one of dubious value at the roadside. Motorcycle riders need to focus on the essentials of First Aid, and weigh up what they're taught. Here are four examples:-

- **Danger.** Current teaching says first see it's safe to approach the downed rider, and if he's in a dangerous position, move him. Firstly, riders end up exposed in the road or gutter, but we must help, even if that places us at risk. Secondly, advice to move a downed rider can be bad advice unless you're a paramedic or doctor. In addition to the earlier helmet discussion, there's also the possibility of a spinal injury. If there is one, moving could worsen it. Personally, I'd never move a downed rider. Instead, make the area around him safe. This can be done by parking a bike against oncoming traffic, dragging wreckage onto the road and scattering clothing along the road. Better to be naked and save a life.

- **Consciousness.** Present advice is to shake and shout at the downed rider to see if he's awake. In a common scenario, he's lying injured, shocked, concussed and semi-conscious on the road. His neck may be dislocated and the spinal cord may be stretched across a sharp bone surface. It may not be wise to shake or startle him into sudden movement by shouting in his ear. A less risky way of seeing if the guys awake, is by asking him. It's preferable to assume he's unconscious and start your ABC. If he's awake, he's going to tell you.

- **Rolling Over.** We're advised to roll the rider onto his side, but only if he's unconscious. Riders should be wary of following this piece of advice. It's impossible for one person to roll an unconscious person, in riding gear, onto their side while stabilising their neck and without a neck brace. It's possible to create a paraplegic or quadriplegic doing this. It may be preferable to leave them where they lie and adapt the first aid efforts. If they're unconscious, it's a dilemma and riders make a judgment call. In this case a kidney belt or back brace might be adapted as a neck brace. The type made with elastic nylon and velcro might be better than nothing at all.

- **Helmet removal.** It's hard to get a helmet off another's head without moving the neck, which may be injured in a high speed crash. In rendering first aid at a crash, helpers have no idea at what speed the bike was travelling, or how the rider impacted any surfaces. I suggest don't remove the helmet. They don't do it on MotoGP. It may be better to work around it. Remove or tilt the visor to get access to the mouth or nose; cut the face-bar off with side-cutters, but otherwise wait for help. MotoGP riders have possibly solved this problem with a new helmet design that allows removal of the shell, without disturbing the lining or head inside. Hopefully such innovative designs will carry over into road use, though this seems impractical as it requires training to remove the helmet safely, and bystanders won't have that know-how.

These examples may lead riders to critically assess First Aid training. As an alternate source of advice, groups like the 'Basic Life Support Working Group of the European Resuscitation Council' (http://www.bmj.com/cgi/content/full/316/7148/1870) can be accessed on the net. They have the concept of 'basic life support' to cover the ABC above without using any equipment other than a protective shield. It comprises the elements: initial assessment, airway maintenance, expired air ventilation (rescue breathing), and chest compression. Their useful tips include the following.

- There is a 3-4 minute window before the brain is damaged from lack of oxygen.

- The ratio of chest compressions to lung inflations should be approx 30:2.

- The rate of chest compression during resuscitation should be approximately 100 per minute, (about one tenth the bike's idle speed.)

- When blowing into the rider's mouth or nose, the lungs need about the same volume of air as a 500cc classic engine. Blow in at the rate to fill a 250cc cylinder per second.

In these litigious days, it's worth knowing something of first aid in order to also protect the helper. A good legal defence would be that the helper had training and reasonably followed it. For this reason alone, it's worth riders familiarising with their country's First Aid code. It's unwise to exchange body fluids with strangers. If called upon to resuscitate, a face-shield is handy. This is a plastic sheet with a filtered hole. It prevents an unconscious person vomiting into the helper's mouth.

As well as spinal injuries, other fractured bones are likely in bike prangs. Unless there's a trained person about, or the rider is in an untenable position, it's best not to move him. It's worth keeping him warm in case of shock, although the riding clothing should be adequate. Once the ABCs are covered probably enough has been done to hold out till an ambulance arrives.

First Aid Kit

Space on a classic bike is limited but it's worth making space for a first aid kit. A small kit could include:

Face-Shield	or clean T-shirt
Band Aids	large and small
Sunscreen	insect repelling type does both jobs
Aspirin	for pain and blood-thinning in case of heart attack, (unless they are on a blood-thinning agent or have other bleeding problems). The NSW Ambulance suggests half an aspirin as a dose guide.
Antiseptic cream	for minor wounds etc
Wound closures	butterfly type
Swiss army knife	for blade, scissors, wound probe and tweezers
Tissues	
Antibiotic powder	for open wounds,
Bandage roll	if there's room (otherwise a T-shirt). Vital First Aid also suggests two 7.5cm crepe bandages and two 110cm triangular bandages. These four bandages deal with all situations including fractures.
Thermometer	a tape-type thermometer takes up no room.
Hangover tablet	prudent if silly things happen on rally night.
Electrolyte sachets	diarrhoea treatment is worth packing for extended outback or tropical travel.

Safe and happy riding to all.

8 *From Waders To Kevlar*

"Add to coat and waders a large pair of horsehide gloves, a soft woollen scarf, a stiff-peaked cloth cap and a pair of mask or 'rubber-cup' goggles.....include a pair of silk undergloves...and a pair of waterproof shorts...to keep the crutch dry..."
Motor Cycling Manual 1952

Motorcycle Clothing Of Yesteryear

Motorcycling clothing traces its roots back into 19th Century angling, bicycle, marine and agrarian apparel.

Waders

Our great grandfathers adapted rubber 'waders' to keep their lower halves snug. These waders were more like the rubber thigh boots, used in flyfishing years ago, than the chest waders now used by anglers. These motorcycle 'waders' were worn over the rider's street clothing, shoes and all. Being a flyfisher, I've tried riding a motorcycle wearing my father's old black rubber chest waders, and also his old rubber thigh boots. Both items reduced the sense of touch so much, I couldn't imagine how they operated a gearchange or foot-brake! To be fair, hand gearchanges and brakes were perhaps more common than foot-operated ones in Pioneer and Vintage days.

Riding Coats

For their torsos, the hardy pioneers chose long riding coats made with fabrics of waxed cotton, gabardine or wool, often multilayered and tailored into long 'stormcoats' in dun colouring. For most riders a full set of leather was prohibitively costly, as it is for today's classic riders. (It is still true today that a cow's hide is worth far more at retail than its meat). Even a leather jacket was too expensive for many, and raincoats, army greatcoats, and farm coats were co-opted. In the 1920's with unpaved roads, lower traffic density, lower speeds and lower powered bikes, falling off, or being 'unseated' as it was termed, was painful and more common, but not perhaps as lethal as today.

Entering the 1930's, motorcycling clothing for road use was still much the same as in those pioneer days. I recall my father's brown leather jacket from this period - a short, full-grain, lined jacket (for a discussion of the types of leather see page 135) with just two breast pockets, a button front, lapelled collar and no rear lumbar padding or rear flap to cover your kidneys and the join with your pants. It couldn't have stopped the rain or wind. Interestingly, at least in New Zealand, the generation riding in the 1930's seemed to prefer brown leather coats: possibly they didn't show the dust on the metal roads of the time? New Zealand manufacturers attempted to relaunch the 'dusty-look' in brown motorcycle jackets several years ago, but it wasn't successful. For racing use though, black leather has always seemed to be *de rigeur*. Maybe black didn't show the ever-present oil leaks, working on the same principle as the British Army 'Redcoat' which masked bleeding.

The Brando Jacket

Marlon Brando and Stanley Kramer prescribed us a multi-zipped, black leather jacket in their seminal 1953 motorcycling movie, The Wild One. Motorcyclists around the world discarded their greatcoats and WWII British and American brown flying jackets. They followed Brando into Henry Ford's car colour choice, you can have any colour you like so long as its black. Those of us who couldn't afford a leather jacket, bought new technology, black vinyl jackets, and were disappointed at how easily they ripped, even before you hit the road. However, at least we could join with the better-off riders in this global black jacket fashion trend. Those who couldn't afford even vinyl carried on with the oiled or waxed cotton coats (aka Drizabones), comforted that at least they resembled pukka English riders in their Barbour and Belstaff suits. They even looked like black leather at a distance.

Services Clothing

The Pacific theatre of World War Two supplied motorcyclists with cheap armed forces clothing to go with those ex-army motorcycles. I remember Barwicks Auction Mart in Gisborne, New Zealand in the late 1950s, with piles of army and air force greatcoats alongside NOS crated Indians, the latter selling for fifty pounds. American Tank-Suits and Flying Suits were favoured by some. The British commando leather vest was prized. Later versions continue to be favoured by Harley-Davidson riders.

Leggings And Chaps

Oilskin 'leggings', in stockman-style, were common on roads and had changed little from 19th century farming leggings. These leggings made great sense up to the 1950s, on rigid frame bikes with single bicycle seats. With an army greatcoat draped over your lap and legs to cope with wind-chill, and long equine leather gauntlets you were reasonably comfortable, at least in dry weather. They made less sense as motorcycle seating evolved into the familiar 'dual seat' where the crotchless design of leggings was not very helpful, illustrating that motorcycle clothing design evolves with motorcycle technology, as much as with fashion trends and fabric technologies. Leggings enjoyed a later resurgence as a gay fashion item, and are still favoured by Harley-Davidson riders as a variant on US cowboy chaps.

Waterproof Over-Pants

Oilskin leggings faded from the general scene with the advent of Japara in the 1960s. Japara was really just another treated, or waxed cotton but marketed as a brand name product downunder in fashionable black, it took over the market. Black waterproof Japara overpants were easier to don, having no press-studs or belt loops to locate. They did introduce a sometimes embarrassing delay in ablutions, as you fumbled for that damned elastic waistband with stiff, chilled fingers on cold winter night rides and they never really solved the 'soggy bottom' problem. As dual seats replaced the single bicycle seat, rain collected on the pillion section and water flowed forward under the rider's bottom. The oiled cotton then became porous, rather like a canvas tent-roof if touched inside during rain. Downunder we always rode in wet weather with a damp crutch, never knowing about Motor Cycling's marvellous invention of waterproof underpants in the UK!

Classic Riding Clothing For Today

Today, we're all relieved the 'soggy bottom' problem is only of historical interest. Classic motorcyclists shopping for a wardrobe now face many choices in materials and designs. The range of motorcycling activities these days, and associated clothing designs, means it's important to forecast your requirements before you start shopping. This can be easily resolved by posing yourself a few simple questions such as:

- Will you ride in summer only, and/or in winter in your home country?

- Will you ride daily, weekly or monthly?

- Will you ride at night, or mostly in the day?

- Will your rides be mostly solo or club rides of 100-500kms, or touring for example riding to rallies over 500-1000kms? Or holidaying with the bike?

- How likely are you to want to ride offroad, or competitively on circuits?

For the record, most classic riders I know ride more in summer, perhaps once every week or two, hardly ever at night, and in Australia (but not NZ or UK), never in the rain unless caught by a shower, in which case you all pull over for coffee!

In New Zealand, the UK and parts of America, it's common to ride mainly in summer. Bikes are often mothballed over winter. In Australia, without the rainfall or low temperature extremes of the UK, it's comfortable to ride year-round with lighter clothing in most States. This means only having to double up on some clothing, such as gloves in both summer and winter weights, to allow for wind-chill. In table 8.1 below, are suggested clothing design choices related to ambient conditions, and common classic riding requirements for comfort.

Table 8.1   Classic Clothing Choices

Item	0-10C	11-20C	21-30C	31-40C
Jacket	Leather or fabric lined or heated	Leather or fabric	Split leather summer jkts.	Summer jkts. vented
Pants	Leather or fabric insulated	Leather Kevlar denim	Kevlar denim	Kevlar denim
Gloves	Gauntlets, inner gloves. Heated	Leather, med. weight	Leather, unlined & perforated	Leather, light racing
Head	Balaclava	Neck tube	Light scarf	Neck cooler
Smalls	Thermal, Polypropylene	Boxers or Longjohns	Boxers	Boxers

As summarised in Table 8.1 above, there is a wide range of jackets and materials along the Nylon-Cordura-Kevlar spectrum. Features to check include style, colours, design, composite structures, permeability, lining, waterproofing, vents, armour, padding, pockets, reflective inserts, back-protection, map pockets, belts and epaulettes, covered zips, etc. For warm climates, it's worth looking at some of the ventilation features in jackets. By opening sets of zips, flow-through ventilation occurs, easing the risk of hyperthermia and dehydration. I've experienced both these ailments, even on shorter club runs in summer, and the combined effect erodes your perception and reaction times. Australia is a dry continent with similar rainfall to Western US states, and hence has similar road and offroad riding conditions.

Clothing Technologies

Broadly speaking with clothing materials you choose from an ascending price range, starting with say denim and lightweight nylons, moving up into heavier fabrics such as Cordura, then on up to Kevlar-lined denim and synthetic fabrics like Dinex, Tactel, Sebring, Tex and Dremax; and topping out with many leather grades. Some of the fabrics and leathers will have their basic characteristics modified by a range of treatments, coatings or laminations to alter their moisture permeability, heat conduction, reflectance or waterproofing performance, the so called 'active fabrics'. These include Gore-Tex, Dry Line and H2OUT. A good example of this is the Swiss Schoeller Dynatec composite. This is a two ply material, with a Du Pont Cordura nylon outer layer, backed by a polyamide fabric. It's designed to shed water, oil and road dirt, have good abrasion and tear resistance, and provide a good service life while being comfortable to wear. Polyamides and nylons are well proven in the packaging industry as flexible packaging films, so it's natural to extend their use to wrap up bodies as well as common packaged food products.

Another approach is typified by Gore-Tex, concentrating on their polymer chemistry to deliver outstanding waterproofing performance in coated composite fabrics that breathe (via 9 billion pores per square inch), and are also very comfortable to wear. And yes, it was invented by a man named, Bob Gore back in the 1960s for NASA. Naturally there's a price premium for such composite materials. Depending on the kind of riding you have in mind it may be worth stretching the budget for enhanced air circulation and permeability in hot countries like Australia or Asia, where ambient temperatures are often 30-40+ degrees Celsius. Similarly if riding in countries with a high annual rainfall, like the UK and NZ, then improved waterproofing may very well be cost-justified. Where riding is undertaken in the 0-10 degrees zone, or where high wind-chill can be expected, then removable, insulating and reflective linings are worth examining. Many of these value-added clothes use proprietary technologies whose relative performance is difficult to compare, short of performing controlled laboratory trials, or having friends in the textile and flexible packaging industries. The easiest path is to discuss clothing with other riders, see what their experiences have been, and then to read clothing labels thoroughly. Otherwise you can place some trust in global technologies and brands like Gore-Tex, Dainese, Du Pont, 3M etc. For more basic data on oil and grease soiling resistance you might follow up textile and packaging industry associations in your country. Some friendly wholesalers may provide access to their supplier's technical catalogues for original technical specification data.

At the end of the day, there is much overlap in clothing fabric ranges, with different fabric types, composites, thicknesses and coatings, all delivering everyday riding insulation and waterproof performance. Beyond this remains the crucial question of abrasion and tear resistance against road surfaces. Apart from Draggin Jeans remarkable 'road skiing' experiments to promote their fine Kevlar-denim clothes, we have the proven performance of leather that dominates racing clothing. Watching for example Valentino Rossi bundled from the 2006 Spanish GP by Elias on the first corner of the first lap, and seeing his leathers virtually unmarked afterward, reminds us that traditional, full grain bovine leather is still the leading technology in motorcycling clothing.

Shopping Channels

Having sorted out clothing ideas, it's time to look at shopping channels. The larger motorcycling supermarkets are the best place to examine different ranges and try them on for goodness of fit and comfort. It's worth stepping up a size in pants and jackets, as you may have extra layers underneath, and need room to move around on the bike. The common items are regularly on special, so it's wise

Illus 8.1 1200 riders at Uluru (Ayers Rock) in Central Australia, wearing every conceivable type of riding apparel.

to scour the latest magazines to check for sale bargains. Countercyclical buying is the order of the day, so buy winter clothes in summer and vice versa. Shopping at retailer sales can also let buyers jump up a level in quality for the same price. Often, there's one shop in many cities that specialises in discounting biker apparel. In such shops, there's good 'value shopping' in remaindered lines and last years fashions. Choosing recycled clothing also lets us jump up a couple of product ranges, and after all, motorcycling clothing is designed to be tough and so can last for two owners or more! A lot of clean, sound used clothing can be bought on EBay, Trade Me in New Zealand, the Trading Post and Cash Convertors (pawn shops) stores around Australasia. For example, I recently bought a NOS 'Jet Leathers' split-hide Brando jacket for £12 at a pawn shop. It was a dusty colour, but black shoe dye turned it back to regulation black. Bargains exist for bikers with time to hunt them.

What To Wear

Let's discuss in more practical detail, the pros and cons of the most needed items, starting with the iconic leathers.

Leathers

If budgets are set aside, if you want to project an image, if you also ride very long distances on a current sports bike, if you're morbidly worried about falling off or are seriously interested in classic road or circuit racing, then consider a riding suit of one or two-piece motorcycle leathers. Otherwise they're probably not cost-justified for most classic riders. In fact I can't remember the last classic club run where I saw full leathers worn on a classic bike. Even if not serious, it's still fun to try on a set and imagine oneself on a circuit somewhere! Areas of compromise lie in the twin suits where the jacket unzips, or in buying a used set of leathers from EBay, where they're sometimes cheap, providing key tailoring measurements are obtained.

Motorcycling leathers should have a fabric lining, joint padding and preferably some armour. Also look for a label disclosing the type of leather used. It ought to be full-grain leather, and be at least 1mm thick. Leather toughens as an animal ages, (due to the collagen proteins cross-linking in its hide if you want the full technical explanation). This is why it's worth looking for suits made with older bull hide, cow hide or buffalo hide. Avoid steer or calf hide for this reason. Hide from smaller animals is often too thin and requires too many seams, to be of much use. Goat and sheep hide has poor abrasion resistance. Kangaroo hide is tough and stretches but is likely to have more seams. Leathers, apart from kangaroo, have limited elasticity, so you will need to find a suit that fits your body shape and size. If you are not one of the fortunate few for whom the 'off the shelf' sizes were designed, then you can always have a suit tailor-made, or altered by a tailor. A plain black road leather suit from North or West Asia can be purchased from £240 up. Going up market are multi-coloured racing-style leathers, with lining, armour, hump, knee scrapers, modified waterproofing, elastic panels, ventilation etc. Prices range up to three times the price of an entry-level suit. The first time you try on leathers, you feel like the hunchback of Notre Dame, until you remember that they are cut to fit in a riding position, and can therefore bind in places when standing. As a natural product, no two suits are identical, so it's worth rummaging through racks, comparing hides, assembly, zips, number of sections, stitching, species and thickness, as well as any special treatments the hide may have received. Leather's strengths lie in comfort, low drag coefficient, insulation, wind-resistance, and short-term rain resistance.

Jackets

As mentioned above, is there any choice for classic riders other than the Brando zip front, studded, double-breasted black leather jacket? There is, but for many it's a timeless and practical design, up there with the Irvin flying jacket. The Brando is practical in full grain leather and works well for winter use in most countries, with the collar up. In summer in Australia or the lower US states, its collars down, zips down, and belt loosened to let air circulate. If this is still too hot, then you can choose a thin split-grain Brando jacket, or one with flow-through ventilation. Regular leather clothing is showerproof but not waterproof, so if out on a club run it's unnecessary to take extra wet weather gear. It takes an hour or so untill the rain soaks through leather garments. In the UK and New Zealand however, it can rain heavy and long on any day and waterproof Cordura outer clothing, is more common on club runs.

Summer Jackets

With the drier times from global warming, more riders are adopting 'summer jackets'. These are strong but light nylon jackets, showerproof, well-vented and with open mesh sections to allow free air circulation, without billowing. They're also armoured for crash protection. However, if it rains or turns cold, the chance of hypothermia increases. Under the jackets, most riders wear a T shirt or skivvy in summer. In winter, riders are cruising mountaineering and fishing shops to add a polypropylene vest under the shirt. Polypropylene fabric has a 'wicking' effect that moves moisture away from the skin to reduce condensation. It keeps the skin dry, and the rider toasty. Given sudden weather changes that can be important, as in the true story of:

A Winters Tale

Bill has ridden all his life and still sits on a bike the way John Wayne sat a horse. He once told me the yarn about the time he rode to Sydney from the Snowy Mountains one very cold 1950's winter night. Only lightly dressed, he left later than planned from Cooma, and got caught out by a weather change. The wind-chill was so bad that when he got as far as Collector, he was forced to stop to thaw out. He pulled in to the carpark of the Collector Pub, but found he couldn't move his feet from the footrests. They were frozen immovably, and he couldn't lift them off the footpegs to ground the bike. His only option was to ride in circles around the carpark, yelling lustily till he either ran out of gas, warmed up or patrons came out to see what the ruckus was. Eventually after a lot of ribald remarks, a couple of patrons took pity on him, ran alongside and supported him so he could stop without toppling over!

Recycled Jackets

Despite the array of jacket choices, classic riders often favour old and valued items over fashion. Why is that, I wonder? On a recent ride with the BSA Club, a new member happened to ask about clothing. When we all 'fessed up', we were surprised to find each of us wearing recycled jackets, for which none of us had paid more than £12! This often comes about because a durable leather jacket may be thrown in with your bike purchase, and even sometimes a helmet and gloves. Such a windfall can save up to half the cost of a first bike! Many returning riders are also happy to wear an old leather jacket, as it doesn't advertise they're a newbie.

Leather Vest

There's one other popular leather top, and that's the ubiquitous vest, often laced and dressed with Harley regalia. I have friends who prefer these on short club runs, and have noted them on riders 1,000kms from home. I suppose they provide some protection to your torso, but nothing for your arms and shoulders. They're often teamed with leggings in other non-riding quarters.

Gloves

Despite the textile industry's advances in fabrics, most riders still choose leather gloves, (fabric mitts excepted). The 1mm ($^1/_{32}$") unlined leather gloves are fine in summer, offering protection along with great sensation, but they leave wind-chilled fingers in winter. Hypothermia in fingers is easily missed on a ride, as attention is focused on the road, and a gradual loss in digital sensation passes unnoticed. As we age, peripheral blood flow to the fingers may reduce, so it's wise for older riders to budget for summer and winter gloves. Proprietary insulation in winter gloves such as Thinsulate works well, but there's a trade-off between insulation and a loss in sensation and grip. Women seem to be more cold-sensitive in their extremities, and should consider insulated or heated gloves, the latter hooking into the electrical system, assuming the bike has a decent alternator. Look for gloves with yellow Kevlar stitching and reinforced palms, finger-joint and knuckle protection. In a spill, riders automatically reach out the arms and the hands suffer on the road surface. Cheaper gloves are imported from Pakistan and Korea with mostly good leather quality, providing its 'full-grain' leather.

It's worth shopping in the Motocross section for bright coloured gloves. These are often discounted. More importantly, on a pre-1971 bike, there'll be no indicators and bright gloves give more visible hand signals to drivers behind. Bicycle shops stock reflective stickers to fix to the backs of gloves, a godsend at night when hand signals are invisible. Glove length and width should allow for the jacket cuff so that it can fit over the top of the gloves at the wrist to stop drafts and rain. Winter gloves are often discounted in warmer climes like Australia. Older and retired riders can benefit from this by picking them up at a discount. Converting winter gloves to summer weight by removing the lining layer can also save money.

Trousers

To experience the classical waders mentioned at the beginning of this chapter drop by a good fishing store where you can choose from light and heavy-grade neoprene thigh boots and chest waders. Some will fit inside the boots while most have boots built in, as in the early days of motorcycling. If you have any medical condition affecting blood flow to the legs, these waders might be worth considering. Lighter plastic thigh boots can be bought more cheaply, with boots attached. You'd certainly be a talking point at your classic club, and who knows, you may restart the wading trend!

Leather trousers are still a popular classic choice, even if they don't come cheaply. It's worth considering a two piece leather suit, if you're thinking of leather pants, as you can mix and match later, or even go racing. Some leather grades have improved waterproofing as in jackets. It's also worth looking for used leather pants, so long as you've no hangup about hand-me-downs. It also saves wearing them in. If you have a micrometer, it's worth taking it shopping, as trouser leather should be of full grain hide, and about 1.5mm ($^1/_{16}$") thickness. Thicker leather gives more protection, but it becomes a trade-off against comfort, as it's stiffer. Better manufacturers offer more comfortable designs with thicker pieces in front and softer sections at the back of your leg where it conforms better to your flexed legs on the bike. Trousers should be lined, as there's nothing worse at the end of an exhausting ride then stumbling round trying to remove sweaty trousers that are clinging to your legs. Longjohns worn inside can avoid this problem.

Setting aside leather and rubber, there are many ranges of fabric trousers and overalls using nylon, Cordura and composite materials, as discussed above. The cheapest nylon clothing is bright, lightweight and rainproof, but of less help if you come off. They're handy to scrunch into your bag as over-trousers on a rainy day. Heavier weight nylon pants, especially if padded and armoured, provide more resistance to impact and weather. Upping the budget, a better performance mix is found in the heavier and multi-layer materials e.g. Cordura. These types offer good waterproofing and better wind-cutting comfort. They may have armoured sections, made of foam and hard plastic, to cushion your pelvis and thighs in the event of a spill, and possibly Kevlar kneepads. Good motorcycling pants have a removable padded liner which is useful for colder countries, but this lining can induce hyperthermia in hot summers.

Bib and braces overalls are a popular riding choice, as for some body shapes they're more comfortable, and drier in the rain. They also offer overlap with the jacket and avoiding exposing your lower back. This can be useful as I found on a long run last year where I wore a moneybelt. My shirt tails were billowing in the wind and following riders had a great view of my secret moneybelt.

Looking around a typical club ride in Australia recently, I counted two riders in Cordura overalls, one in leather pants, and the remaining riders in denim jeans.

Most riders wore black leather jackets that day, so really little had changed since the 1960's on that run. In New Zealand, more classic riders wear heavier clothing, given the climate, and heavier nylon overalls are favoured. One striking innovation in motorcycling wear are the Kevlar-lined 'Draggin Jeans', allegedly named after the tough skin of dragons. These were invented downunder by Grant Mackintosh, who manufactures a range of Kevlar-reinforced clothing. With these Kevlar-jeans, you can combine 60's 'street cred' while keeping skin where it belongs. They probably outperform full-grain leather when sliding across a road surface, and in heat transference. In this regard, we should sympathise with Police motorcyclists in Sydney. The remaining sixty odd riders are issued with CHIPs-type elastic jodhpurs. They may look good on Police legs, but are useless as leg protectors. Their Police-issue leather jackets are lightweight and lack armour. They provide a poor role model for safe motorcycling clothing, and deserve better.

One clothing aspect rarely covered in motorcycling books, is what do you wear under your motorcycling gear? Assuming we dress partly to survive an accident, then we dress to cope with abrasion and impacts with objects. Abrasion is covered with Cordura and Kevlar, but what about impacts, not just with car bodies but also with sharp objects like handlebars, footrests, wing and bar mirrors, branches and fences etc?

A lining beneath the outer clothing makes the same good sense it did to medieval knights who wore padding under their chain mail armour. According to recent trials, the two layers of mail and padding were more effective in stopping sharp impacts than mail alone. Similarly, padding serves motorcyclists in the same way. In addition to sharp impacts, motorcycle incidents involve rolling across a road surface, causing friction and intense heat next to your skin. An insulating lining seems sensible, but not of materials with a low melting point such as some synthetic fabrics.

Helmets

In chapter seven, we covered helmet designs and detailed safety analyses. Here, we'll look at the remaining aspects of helmets, as part of clothing. The choice of helmet in the 1960's was either the 'pudding basin', the 'Jet' (open face) helmet, or riding bare-headed before helmet laws came in. I confess reserving my costly pudding-basin helmet for long runs and never wore it in town. Now we're told most accidents occur within 3 miles (5kms) from home: how did we survive? Yet I cannot recall any serious injuries and no deaths among my circle of young and aggressive riders. A lower traffic density alone does not explain this group survival.

Classic riders still frequently choose the open face helmet, given their lightness, better visibility, familiarity and cost. They let you feel the breeze, enable a sun visor to be fitted and they are cooler than wearing a full-face job. You also get to wear MkVIII flying goggles, still available from the original Halcyon and pattern manufacturers. Pudding basin helmets are still made but do not always meet country safety standards. Complying basin helmets are mostly sold by Harley-Davidson dealers.

Most riders adopt full-face helmets. They protect the face but are heavier, and you feel it in your neck muscles. Your nose gets burnt in summer, unless you have a nose-guard, or wear sunscreen cream, as there's rarely provision for a peak - unless you opt for a motocross version. Full face helmets have top and bottom face vents and the visor can be cocked to cool off but beware, at dusk moths can find their way into your mouth. It's worth noting modern visors produce a loud bang when hit by insects at speed. You'd swear a conrod has broken if a cicada hits your visor at 60 or 70 mph (100kph or more).

My BSA B44 started making an odd noise one Spring, as I rode through the Blue Mountains villages west of Sydney. A high-pitched, scraping, ringing sound developed in the engine. I thought of engine fin resonance, a broken valve spring, or worse, my clutch working its way off its shaft. After a time I noticed the noise seemed to ebb in the villages and return in the bushy sections of the road. It dawned on me...cicadas! A similar sound effect used to occur in England, where picket fences were common along narrow roads. Engines developed a chuff-chuff-chuff noise as a single's exhaust echoed back from the pickets. My own picket fence produces this effect on my BSA single still.

Visibility as well as hearing, seems more restricted on full face compared to open face helmets. Perhaps it's just a perception, as your face is surrounded. If you're concerned about tunnel vision, the new helmets with built-in rear view are worth considering. The Reevu MSX1 reportedly uses an *"... ingenious reflective polycarbonate device that 'bends' the view of the road behind and presents a clear image to the wearer...."* Lastly, the interior of a full face helmet gets hellishly hot in summer. The lining soaks with sweat, and it's worth enquiring about replacement or washable linings if you intend to ride regularly. I line mine with a kitchen wipe. I'm told Rossi uses a sanitary napkin in his, but I've not yet been able to bring myself to try one.

Without a sun-visor, glare is a problem in full face helmets, especially if you wear contact lenses or glasses. There's little room for glasses frames. I find sunglasses with small, flexible plastic or rubber frames the best to fit the limited space. On some you can trim the side-arms, so they sandwich between your face and padding. Tinted visors and liners work well when riding into the sun but note that in some countries such as the UK there are laws on tinted visors. An economical fix is to use tinted industrial cling-film. It clings to your visor and can be re-used. It clings on nicely up to about 70mph (130kph).

Open face helmets come in two types, those with flip up visors and those without. A substantial number of classic riders wear the flip up visor type of helmet because it allows good visibility, ventilation, insect and rain protection and gives the appearance of being a full open face helmet. The original style, open

face helmets require goggles to keep the wind and rain out of the eyes, have little
face protection but have the benefit of looking more authentic.

Neckwear

From the birth of motorcycling, riders used scarves to draft-proof the gap
between head and chest, and protect against flying insects. A white silk scarf, as
worn by Spitfire pilots was prized. On long trips I wrapped one around my face
and on two occasions it saved me from injury. The first happened when a bumblebee
hit, ramming the scarf into my mouth like a large buzzing gag. The second involved
a freak encounter with a seagull, or rather a missile from the seagull. I was half-
blinded by the reeking mess. The scarf saved the day but was dumped.

Boots

David Minton in his *Motorcyclist's Handbook* reckons that 60% of motorcycle
injuries are to legs and feet, so this topic is significant. As with other motorcycling
apparel, there are many boot choices. In the 1960's classic heyday, the choice in
boots was the ex-airforce, fleecy-lined flying boot. Now there are many motorcycle
boot makers. First, let's rule out the motocross, armoured boots, as unsuitable for
road use. Those sexy looking racing boots, made with soft, supple leather can also
be discarded. As with jackets, a heavy, full grain cowhide boot, with good foreleg
and ankle protection is desirable. At the same time, we require a comfortable walking
boot for exploring the places visited on the bike. We need one which will keep our
feet warm, whilst letting us feel for the gear lever and brake pedal. We also need a
solid instep, to cope with the extra load of kick starting, something for which
contemporary motorcycling boots frequently are not designed. Some riders opt
for short, Western-style boots with O-ring protection over each ankle. Others opt
for a traditional calf-length flying boot. Interestingly, feet never seem to overheat
as much as hands on a hot summer ride, so one boot for all seasons is achievable,
unlike gloves. A heavy fleecy lining is therefore worth considering. Other kinds of
boots worth considering are calf-length dress boots and some ex-Army boots.
Equine riding boots are also great for motorcycles. It's worth taking one or two
pairs of heavy socks to try out with the boots that are often on special.

Rainwear

Enduring the worst drought in the Australia's history, it's odd to write about
rainwear. If it rains, we rush out to wash cars in the rain, as it's illegal to hose down
your car. And yet even through this awful drought that is turning Sydney into a
desert, many of us still carry rainwear on long rides. A favourite is the two piece
light-weight nylon oversuit, with reinforced seams. Weighing about 250gms and
taking just a few square inches of storage, it fits anywhere and is also widely used
in the UK. Next up is the one-piece nylon over-suit that can be carried in a backpack or bum-bag. For more serious rain, many of the jacket and trouser textile
composites discussed above are breathable and waterproof. Multi-purpose leather

and textile clothing can be selected with zip-in, zip-out insulated and sometimes waterproof linings and pockets. Heavy-duty waterproof oversuits in composites of nylon, PVC and polyester combine abrasion resistance with dryness. The French Ixon range is a good example. This includes waterproof over-boots and over-mittens for really foul weather (just the kind we wish for downunder!). The same range of textile innovations for controlling moisture and rain have entered the boot market. Waterproof boots lined with Gore-Tex or other breathable waterproof linings are now widely available.

Prostheses

No we're not about to venture into hernia belts and trusses! Yet appliances from the worlds of physiotherapy and Occupational Health and Safety (OH&S) medicine, have entered motorcycling often via racing circles. Some of these are invaluable for rider comfort on long club rides, especially as classic riders transit their 50's and go on into their 60's and 70's.

Back Protectors. These resemble a lifting brace seen on workers in any warehouse (these can also be used). Even if your back is in perfect condition, you'll appreciate the difference on a long ride. It comprises a waist band and shoulder straps attached to an articulated back brace. They're light and magical to use. On long rides it prevents aches and pains. It acts as a 'second spine', taking the load off your spine, and delaying cramps. You wear it under your jacket. They're mandatory for racers, protecting against impacts and hyper-extension injuries to the spine. One twice protected a classic racing friend's back, firstly from a handlebar stabbing into his back and secondly a footrest. He says he'd be a quadriplegic if not for that brace. Interestingly, we're told Barry Sheene invented it. The story goes that back in the late 1970s he wanted some flexible back protection, and tried wiring old helmet visors to a foam backing. It worked well and Dainese took up the idea and introduced commercial versions.

Kidney Belts. I believe these were popularised by speedway riders around the time of WWII. They're a cross between a formal dress cummerbund, a corset and a prizefighter's belt, secured at the front with press-studs. These belts provide useful support to the lumbar spine and help keep the kidneys warm and protected on cold days. They might also help reduce the incidence of cramps and muscle spasms. Originally they were made from a wide leather or elastic band, but now you can find belts made with neoprene banding.

Sheepskin Seat-Covers. I recall in hospitals years ago long-stay patients were given sheepskins to lie on in order to prevent bed-sores. Now the sheepskin helps rider comfort, especially on long rides. I use one and swear to their efficacy. They not only delay aches and pains in your posterior, as they did in hospitals, but provide more shock absorption. On British classics the sheepskin soaks up vibration, which contributes to easier riding. It also serves other duties for example if you break down it becomes a clean place to stack parts at the roadside. If you are camping they make excellent pillows, especially if wrapped in a towel or shirt.

Cramps And Cruise Controls. It's frightening to get a cramp in your right hand on the open road, and dangerous if it forces you to let go the throttle and handlebar without warning. Unfortunately cramps are a part of growing older, and when we re-enter motorcycling, the unaccustomed strain of clenching a twistgrip and steering for several hours, can lead to cramps. Indeed, my first classic bike was sold by a previous owner for this reason. It's worth trying a calcium or magnesium tablet, or a shot of quinine before a day ride, if you're afflicted. Another insurance is to fit a throttle cruise control, as mentioned in Chapter seven. There are several designs about, but the best I've found is a US invention - a simple clip that fits over your throttle grip. It provides a 'heel' on which to rest the base of your hand, letting you relax your grip without losing throttle control. I wouldn't ride a long way without one.

Hydration Packs. As we age, I'm sure our body thermostat doesn't operate as smoothly. Like our appetite satiety centre, I think it cuts in sometimes too early and sometimes too late. For whatever reason, body moisture loss on motorcycles is as big a problem as on Frank Herbert's desert planet Dune. The more we protect ourselves against the sun, rain and chill factor, the more we seem to sweat and dehydrate. I have never seen such orange urine as after a morning's ride in summer and this after regular drinks en route. It's a Catch 22 as if you drink lots of water to delay dehydration, your bladder forces you to pull over and hold up the convoy. Dehydration creeps up on you, slowing reactions, fuzzying perception and judgment, and causing cramps. We're told the average person needs up to four litres of fluid a day. One solution is the range of backpacks with drink reservoirs and feeding tubes. There are several American and Australian ranges, including Camel-Bak, Mountain Designs and Platypus. The models with combined storage and beverage are ideal for classic motorcyclists. The reservoirs can be frozen ahead of the ride, to cool your back. The feed tubes have a chest clip and bite valve, so there's no leakage. They work with all helmet types. Obviously these may not be important in colder, less sunny climes.

Safety Vests. New motorcycle riders are being taught how to stay visible to other road users at many rider training schools. New riders there wear safety vests and learn their value. I hear some older riders protesting they don't want to look like council workers, but on the other hand, everyone wants to return from the ride. Personally, I won't ride without a safety vest, and for several reasons.

As discussed in Chapter seven, car drivers fail to give way because they fail to see us. It's cold comfort being right, if you're injured. The safety vest also acts like a tent flysheet in summer. It covers your black leather back, which is a good heat absorber. I add reflective stickers to my vest, so at night I light up like the proverbial Christmas tree when illuminated by drivers behind me. Some high visibility vests come with pockets that are the easiest place to store road tolls.

There's Leather And There's Leather

I spent twenty years in the hide industry and pass on trade comments for recognising the various kinds of leather. Mammalian skin is divided into two main layers, the outer layer or 'epidermis' and the inner layer or 'dermis'. In the hide industry the dermis is usually called the 'corium' layer. To obtain different thicknesses and characteristics, intact animal hides are split into outer and inner layers by specialised machines that resemble large band saws. The saw blade is an extremely thin, continuously sharpened blade. For some reason the French seem to own the market. The outer layer or 'grain split', is essentially the epidermis. The inner layer or 'corium split' corresponds to the dermis or corium. Here is a quick reference to recognising the types of leather encountered in motorcycling garments and furniture.

Full Grain Leather. This is made from the intact hide, epidermis plus the dermis. It is the preferred base material for motorcycle jackets, providing the best insulation, impact and abrasion resistance. It provides the thickest leather. Naturally, it is also the most expensive.

Recognition. Look on the outside for the natural skin surface, with its irregularities, blemishes, scars etc. that reflect the life of the former owner. It should have no artificial layers stuck to it. It should be at least 1mm thick and preferably two or even three times that. The inside should be the familiar rough suede surface, being almost furry. On edge, you should be able to see the two layers, i.e. the thinner compacted epidermis and the thicker, open dermis or corium layer. No other layers should be visible.

Split Grain Leather. This is the grain-split mentioned above. It is thinner as it lacks much of the corium lining layer. The corium significantly improves the accident performance of the jacket, by cushioning, insulating and resisting penetration.

Recognition. The outside appearance is identical to the above. The inner surface is often smooth, but can be similar to the Full-Grain. It all depends where the knife separated the two layers. The main tell tale is that edge on, the leather is thinner, and the dermis is no longer much thicker than the epidermis. Most of it has been cut away. In motorcycling gear, there's frequently a synthetic layer bonded to the inside to replace the removed corium with a cheaper material. This restores the thickness and feel of full grain leather, as well as some performance. You'll see this clearly inside gloves. Its caveat emptor time. You get what you pay for.

Corium Split Leather. This is composed of most of the inner or corium layer. It has no grain leather.

Recognition. Corium jackets usually have a smooth, machined surface appearance; they can also have a natural suede appearance, like Dennis Hopper's jacket in Easy Rider. Corium split leather is suede or chamois leather. It has an open structure and does not perform as well in spills but it is cheaper than either full grain or split grain leather. It's also the base material for gelatine! The inside has the same rough, hairy appearance as with full grain leather. Processors have a variety of techniques for altering the surface to resemble grain leather. These involve embossing and laminating and are often used for furniture leather. A close inspection will reveal an almost painted surface finish. A small piece of suede is often sewn onto the back of the right glove. This serves as a visor wiper, and it's useful if you get caught in a shower at night.

Illus 8.2 A brace of Triples downunder: a Rocket 3 and a Trident

9 *Maintenance At Home And On The Road*

"Forward facing carburettor air intakes can increase power by up to 3% in a supercharging effect, but only at speeds unreachable by most classic bikes..."
RB

Motorcycle maintenance for classic bikes can be as satisfying as riding them. It can also be scary at first, especially for those returning to motorcycling and riders who like me, judge they lack automotive aptitude. The manufacturers have long closed, and the first question when that 'new' classic bike comes home is who to see for servicing and parts? That apparent difficulty turns out to be one of the unsung advantages of a classic bike. While the makers (and most distributors) have long gone into receivership, the bulk of their service and technical data survives. Even better, much of the intellectual property relating to the old British makes has lapsed, or is unasserted, and has passed into the public domain. The know-how is joyously spread about via magazines, the net and aftermarket guides. Even confidential internal company correspondence, technical bulletins and service notes are now available. Classic riders have more technical and service material available today than was ever accessible to the original riders of these bikes. Idealists in classic clubs collate and publish the data for all riders via reprints, CDs/DVDs and numerous websites. Over the past thirty years or more since classic manufacturing closed, the technical product information for the conservation of these vehicles has grown exponentially. For example, you can surf websites devoted to all popular makes and models and obtain a range of service and technical advice beyond the abilities of all but the largest city dealers in their heyday. And for the purposes of this book, let's assert that classic bikes, like antique furniture are firstly defined by their period, rather than by any supposed merit or stigma associated with any make or model. Thus any British or other motorcycle made between roughly 1946 and 1976 is ipso facto a classic.

Maintenance Information

The first maintenance step for a new owner is to follow the migrating product information to the classic clubs, and be warmly welcomed into the brotherhood. It's worth shopping around before joining a club to ensure there's a member who knows your marque and model, and is happy to answer your calls during the first year of ownership, as you and your bike find your feet. Single marque clubs are often a safer bet in this regard. On the other hand, some riders believe such specialisation dilutes the classic bike community, especially with regard to political representation of classic motorcycling generally. The answer is simple, join a single marque club and another, general club.

Home maintenance is more or less difficult depending on the garage or shed space available, the facilities enclosed, and the toolkit. Many of us start out with no spare space in the shed for the bike(s) and with only a household and car toolkit that's all metric. It's surprising how quickly space can be reallocated for the bike and the workbench. This is easier downunder than in the UK, given the larger antipodean residential section or block size of 600-1000 square meters or more. There houses include a garage with adequate space for a workbench, and often under-floor space to store that growing collection of vital parts, engines and frames. Indeed five minutes ride from here, a friend has his three garages and sheds filled with BSAs in varying stages of restoration. His car, a Rolls Royce, lives in the driveway.

Shopping and fossicking for the imperial toolkit is the first maintenance step, and it's great fun. Downunder, riders are well served by the stock of such tools at second-hand retail outlets and weekend markets often at cheap prices. Fortunately, British bikes, especially the older classics, were designed for ultra-simple maintenance in the typical English garden shed. The starting toolkit can be modest, and extended as you go along. For starters, here's a list to help assemble a basic toolkit for 1950s-1970s British bikes. I recommend good used tools from the better makes purchased from markets as a more cost-effective choice than new, cheap Chinese or Indian etc imperial toolkits carried by hardware outlets. Call me sentimental, but it feels more appropriate working on the bike with period tools.

As riders will be sorting through a lot of boxes putting that toolkit together, it's worth picking out the best brands of tools for the kit. In Table 9.1 below are some premier brands of yesteryear, broken down by country of manufacture.

Table 9.1	Quality Classic Tool Manufacturers
Country	**Manufacturers and Brands**
UK	Armstrong, BriTool, Garrington, Gordon, Lion, Snail, Superslim,
Germany	Dowidat, Elora, Gedore, Heyco, Stahwille, VBW.
USA	Billings, Bonney, Crescent, Fremont, King-Dick, TruFit/Lectrolite, TipCo.
Australia	Sidchrome.
Canada	Gray.
Others	Matador, Nubo.

TIPS

When shopping for used tools at autojumbles, car boot sales and other markets, it's often better to look for quality brands from another country, and brands that are no longer distributed in your own country. Sellers often don't know what exceptional tools they're selling and let them go cheaply. Personally, I look for pre-WWII German Stahwille tools. They were so well made they are often still in virtually new condition around Australia and New Zealand, and well capable of a second service life.

When selecting used tools, it's worth remembering that a lot of force is applied in confined spaces with your eyes right next to the tool. It is important to scrutinise the tools at the point of purchase: beware of ring or open ended spanners that show any sign of forcing or abuse, such as the gape forced open, ring spanners and sockets bent or cracked, strained or welded, hammered etc. Any tools rusted beyond light surface rust should be tossed back. There's plenty of choice! Chromed tools where the plating has worn or cracked off, can give a sloppy fit. Thus unplated versions, while not as sexy, are often the better buy, and even cheaper. It's often cheaper to buy a toolbox with tools in it, than to buy individual pieces. Often you can well, to be candid, assemble the items you want in the toolbox before you buy it, with the seller's forbearance, of course! You're going to collect lots of parts and tools requiring storage, and that extra toolbox will quickly be filled.

For certain key tools, buy them two-up as you'll need a set to leave on your bike for breakdowns on the road - either your own or possibly for others in distress.

The Garage Toolkit

Here's a rough guide to the tools you will require in your garage.

Ring and Open-End Spanners

Whitworth/BSF	For earlier bikes (Whitworth and BSF have different dimensions but use the same standard hex sizes so a Whitworth spanner fits a BSF hex of a different size)
AF	(American Fine or Across the Flats) for some later classics
Size range	A starting spanner size range is $3/_{16}$" to 1" BSF, with the very small and very big spanners harder to find in good used condition for some reason. Certain nuts on certain bikes will require odd size spanners, wheel hub and steering head nuts for example. Bodging these is possible,

say with an 18" top-quality adjustable spanner (Crescent shifter). It's cheaper and preferable to list the odd sized nuts on the bike and take the list to weekend markets with a Vernier to buy the correct spanner. As a guide, open-ended spanners of $1^1/_{16}$, $1^1/_8$, $1^3/_{16}$ and $1^1/_4$" will often handle these odd few nuts. Ring and open-ended combination spanners are preferable as they are more versatile and can tackle those steering head nuts buried under the handlebars.

Socket Spanners

Used sockets at markets are often in poor condition, unlike spanners for some reason. Instead consider buying new Taiwanese (over Chinese) Chrome-Vanadium sockets in sets. As new Imperial tool sets face less retail sales demand than metric tools, the big stores sometimes discount them heavily. It's easy to complement the set with good used German or American sockets in odd sizes. A $^3/_8$" drive is sufficient for most of the work, although the more common $^1/_2$" drive gives more confidence on stubborn nuts. The larger size also allows more choice from a wider range of used sockets which are often cheaper. For the smaller jobs a $^1/_4$" drive is a useful addition for sockets going down to $^7/_{32}$" or so. If, like me you have a heavy spanner hand and seem to strip threads easily, then a $^1/_4$" drive is a good way of preventing excessive force.

The classic makers torque charts ought be read with a generous pinch of salt. The assumptions for such figures appear dubious these days. They usually relate to new, clean nuts and bolts, in mint condition, with no lubricant or thread sealant, and with parts in perfect position. Few of these assumptions are met on aging classics where frames are worn and bent, there is corrosion and plating loss on many parts, and swarf and thread deterioration exist in casting holes. I normally discount the torque figures by 10-20%, use star washers, thread sealant (Loctite or similar) and nyloc nuts, mount everything in rubber, and keep an eye on fixings to see any that may need nipping up. So far touch wood, I've never lost a part due to a nut vibrating loose, even on favourite British singles.

> *TIP: It's worth spying out longer sockets at markets. They help deal with fixings where the stud is sticking up proud of the nut. Around alloy castings and engine fins they also enable the socket handle to stand proud of the surroundings which is enormously helpful when the inevitable slip happens as the longer socket should enable the handle to avoid breaking a fin or gouging a casing. Most sockets are twelve-sided but the hexagonal type, with six flat faces gives a more effective grip on our old nuts.*

Adjustable Spanners

These are useful for holding bolt heads whilst the nut is tightened. Again, a good used brand (see Table 9.1) is a better buy than new, cheap Chinese and Indian makes. The 4", 6" and 8" sizes to start with, maybe doubling up the 4" and 6" for the bike toolkit.

Plug Spanners

Plug spanners or sockets are necessary for both home and bike toolkits. A socket is fine for home, but a tube-spanner is best for the road because it will fit in the toolboxes on classic bikes.

Torque Wrench

A torque wrench is a handy tool, until we regain the 'feel' for what's tight and what's over-tight on classic fixings. It's mandatory for those few nuts that demand precise high or low torque, for example those responsible for holding onto the cylinder head, alternator, main shaft and clutch shaft nuts. If one is not to hand, then simply reducing the shaft length of the driver, spanner or tool, can save stripping threads. On old bikes with compromised threads, the wrench can over-read due to the thread binding. In these cases, a two stage approach is useful. Tigthen with the torque wrench to a minimum reading, and then the rotate the nut say a quarter to a half turn more. Note also that torque settings are far smaller in aluminium than steel and it is ridiculously easy to strip a thread in aluminium, so go easy and use the torque settings as described. A friend of mine learned this the hard way last year, when he stripped his gearbox plug, right before a three-week rally run, and wasted a day dismantling the box to fit an insert.

Screwdrivers

Impact driver	An impact screw driver is nice to have up the sleeve, and cheap for removing those stubborn screws that just won't come out any other way.
Ratchet driver	Instead of expensive screwdrivers, try one of the ratchet sets with a driver and set of hardened tips. These ensure there's always one the right size, and solves the problem of proliferating fixings. For example, Harley-Davidson, assumed to be all AF or Torx, uses some metric fixings that come with OEM assemblies from metric countries.

Allen Keys

A set of imperial Allen keys, preferably with longer handles and a swivel end.

Pliers

Linesman and needle nose pliers, with a set for your bike kit.

Side Cutters

These are useful for clipping wires, cable-ties and bracketry.

Feeler Gauge

An imperial feeler gauge set is mandatory for plug, points and tappet gapping. A flat blade set is fine, even though the wire ones are better, in theory for tappets.

Inspection Devices

A fibre-optic wand that attaches to an AA torch is a must. This is extraordinarily useful for seeing inside the barrel, ports, carburettor, gearbox, chaincase, and casting holes without stripping the engine. It's a low-cost, must-have item for lazy mechanics.

Taps And Dies

A new imperial tap and die set, or even a used set that can clean up butchered threads is very useful. These should include Whitworth, BSC (British Standard Cycle), and BSF threads, or as necessary for the bike.

Voltmeter

A cheap multimeter is indispensable for circuit testing, and earth returns.

Verniers

Indispensable for measuring gaps all over the bike. Get two, a cheap plastic one to take shopping for spanners so it's no loss if left at a swap-meet, and a good digital vernier for the main toolkit. While their housings all look the same, cheaper digital makes don't seem to last.

Vice

A good 100mm (4") engineers vice is vital for the bench, and might be the most expensive single item on it. Some come with a small anvil. Second-hand vices and some new Chinese vices are reasonably priced. A pair of soft jaws made of rubber or fibre is mandatory to hold delicate items. For other jobs, requiring holding power without jaw marks, it's useful to make some alloy jaw liners. If made from scrap right-angle profile, they are self-supporting, and adhesive magnetic tape holds them on.

Power Tools

An electric drill, angle-grinder and bench grinder are so cheap these days, they've become almost disposable items. Likewise a Dremel-type power driver with speed control. (Even air compressors are falling into this category if you're so minded). A couple of sets of good high-speed steel drill bits are also a good idea. A green grit-wheel sharpener ekes out the drill bit life if you are a dab hand at sharpening drills, or buy a drill bit sharpening tool.

Hacksaw

A hacksaw of regular size is needed, along with the mini-size job for fine work.

Files

A selection of good files are needed. Cheap new ones blunten very quickly. Good second-hand ones are again a better bet. Broad and narrow flat bastard jobs are needed, as well as round and half-round files. The one type to buy cheap, are the needle file sets available at markets in rolls. They're invaluable for easing and nibbling holes everywhere, and cheap enough to be disposable.

Wire Brushes

These should be purchased in both steel and brass. The small new sets of brass tooth-brushes are useful, and disposable. It's also worth collecting household toothbrushes for the garage, along with all the cotton-buds the women in every family discard.

Mallets And Hammers

A rubber mallet is very useful for tyres and general persuasion. A hide mallet, or one of the new rubber/plastic headed versions is also very useful not to mention cheaper than the old copper and hide mallets. Short alloy, copper and brass rods to use as punches and drifts will be required (screwdrivers generally damage what the hit!). And finally a normal hammer for use with centrepoints etc.

Engine Stand

An engine stand is very handy, if significant engine rebuilding or major service is to be undertaken. They can be obtained surprisingly cheaply, when shops close down, or from sales, or made up by a mate with a welder. A Triumph engine stand is shown in Illus. 9.1 below.

That is a flying start to the garage toolset, and it will become extended with the passage of time. Turning to the bike's toolset, this is a bit like packing for an overseas holiday. We pack and repack, until all available toolbox space is full. The manufacturers left minimum toolbox space, but it's surprising what can be packed in. The tighter the fit the better, as it stops items chafing, vibrating and moving around. An old-fashioned tool-roll holds things securely. For more tool and gear space, a nice leather Harley-Davidson windshield bag gives a period look to classic bikes. They can be fixed quite easily to the rear grab-rail, or between the forks.

Illus 9.1 A Triumph four-valve head engine in a stand, ready for action

The Bike Toolkit

Here's a rough list of the things likely to be required at some time or another on the bike.

Plug tube-spanner	use a screwdriver for the tommy bar.
Adjustable spanners	4" and a 6"
Pliers	a pair of small adjustable pliers like those packed in the toolkits on Japanese bikes are fine.
Screwdriver	with at least flat and cross-head screwdriver tips.
Cable-ties and wire	amazingly useful.
Insulation or duct tape	possibly the most important item.
Spark plug(s)	a new one (or two) already gapped.
Chain link	a drive chain 'spring' link the right size for your chain.
Bulbs	spare front and rear bulbs, the rear LED type are best as they are less prone to damage from vibration.
Fuses	three, one to diagnose, one to replace and one spare for the rest of the run.
Cable nipples	the screwed kind, to fit at least your clutch, brake and throttle cables.
Inner cable	A spare length of inner Bowden cable and some screw type end fittings correct for your bike, especially if you take very long rides into wild places. Clutch and brake are essential.
WD40	or similar water repellant lubricant.
Emery paper	for points cleaning etc.
Tyre pressure gauge	for tyre pressure.
Tyre pump	mostly for others who don't pack a pump or use a tyre sealant. It's no consolation waiting hours with a mate with a flat tyre, when only you sealed your tyres.

An old friend once had dire need of the toolkit above, but had to make do with much less, in the story of:

The Battle Site Stripper

Vic died recently, but years ago he told me this remarkable story. As a young man in Gisborne NZ, he'd heard rumours about a battle monument dating back to the Maori wars in the 19th century. This monument was a wooden post and sign, well off the road in the Wharerata hills outside Morere. There was, in the 1960s, a track leading miles through rough country to the monument beside a stream, probably the Nuhaka River. Vic successfully rode his Honda scrambler down the trail and late in the day, found the monument. On his way back up the trail, the bike slid out on a turn above the river, and he and the bike dropped down a cliff to the river below. Luckily they came to rest on a small ledge on the river bank. Ken found himself marooned late in the afternoon on the ledge, with an injured leg. The river was too deep to cross, and it was impossible to get the bike up the steep bank to the track. What to do? Vic decided the only way out was to strip the bike on the ledge, drag the chunks up the bank, reassemble it at the top, and ride back to the road. His injured leg wouldn't allow him to walk out, and no one was likely to visit the isolated spot for weeks. The problem was the only tools he had were the few puny ones in the bike's standard kit. He used them to remove the tank, wheels, seat and tinware, and dragged each piece up the bank. With great difficulty he was able to drag the engine and frame up the cliff and reassemble the bike again, to safely ride home. He said to me, "You know Rex, what really scared me was losing that rear chain link. It was the last piece I carried up!" In later life he became a renowned Goldie replica builder. With a cottage industry network in Rotorua, he converted a series of nine, perhaps as many as twelve B33s into Gold Star replicas. At least one of these went to the USA. From the photos he showed me, they were nut and bolt perfect facsimiles.

Top Tasks For Classic Bikes

With the toolkit assembled, let's put it to work. I take approaches to these maintenance tasks that are often different to those in shop manuals and owners guides of the period. Time doesn't stand still, and a great deal of classic know-how not to mention workarounds, have developed over the past thirty years. Why not use them?

Gapping The Tappets

The first task is checking and setting the tappets, or more correctly gapping the rockers at their junction with the pushrods, assuming the bike's a British single or an overhead valve twin. I suppose tappets is an archaic term, reflecting the days of side-valve engines, when it was possible to access the real tappets i.e. the joint between the cam follower and the pushrods. I like the sound of the word, tap...tap...tappets. Some British bikes, especially later ones have lots of upper engine noise from valve operation. Why is this, when other OHV engines don't seem to suffer from it, for example Harley engines? The answer is that the American designers adopted hydraulic tappets some time ago which have the twin virtues of being self-adjusting and very quiet. About the only time you hear valve noise on a Harley V-twin, is on a cold morning before the hydraulic tappets fill up with oil. For those brief moments it sounds like a proper British classic. Before that, Harley engineers and some British ones recommended setting tappets by ear and feel, rather than by some benchmark figures. For example BSA prescribed 'between 8 and 10 thou for all tappets' and that gives appalling valve noise. Why did some British makers like BSA advise such noisy tolerances, when they must have known it would generate customer complaints and affect sales?

Perhaps it was innate conservatism when faced with owners who might never gap their tappets; perhaps they thought it best to let valve recession take up the noisy gaps? Was there a metallurgical change that encouraged greater tolerances? Or was it a reflection of the production-driven hubris that overcame the industry, as one bad strategic decision lead to others? I'd like to think it was a desire to build in a safety margin, i.e. to ensure that no matter what, the situation would never arise when there was no tappet play and valves would burn out. When I worked for a British group, I saw such production-driven thinking in the fastening industry. Our fasteners were conservatively rated to pull out at five times their stated load. A competitor blew us out of the market by introducing the same range of fasteners but rating them as pulling out at only twice their stated load. This increased their apparent holding power by merely moving the goal posts. We refused to change our rating practice and lost the market. Customers perceived the competitor's fasteners as stronger than ours, when they were in fact weaker. Being right didn't help us, and being stubborn lost us the market. It's often said that if you can hear your tappets, there's no risk of valve burnout and this seems plausible, albeit a bit crude. Equally, if there's no free play in the system, then cams, followers, pushrods, rockers and valves are all grinding and hammering away, like that desk accessory with the tapping steel balls on strings. On the other hand, you might argue that closing down free play in the tappets reduces the hammering impact of rockers on valves, leading to increased life for both components. Phil Irving, come back - we need you.

To stimulate a club discussion, try posing the tappet question. When your engine heats up, do your tappet gaps get wider or narrower? While there are arguments either way, on balance it depends on the heat distribution throughout the valve gear, versus the general heating up of barrels, head and rocker boxes. The hottest part is the exhaust valve head, and as this expands, it tends to stand off its seat, opening the exhaust tappet gap. The same goes for the inlet valve, but to a lesser extent, as it's closed during combustion and cooled by the fuel charge. So far then, we seem pretty safe to say the rocker-pushrod gap opens as the classic British engine warms.

After a time however, the unvented rocker boxes heat up and the valve stems start expanding which may reduce the gap again. The rockers and the rocker boxes themselves are also heating up and expanding. Downstairs, as the cam followers and alloy pushrods start heating up, they extend further, tending to narrow the tappet gap. However the barrel and head are also expanding vertically, offsetting growth in the pushrods. If the barrel and/or head are iron, then they probably won't expand to match the pushrod growth exactly. It's hard to generalise but tappet gaps seem to end up roughly the same, or if anything to grow a tad when hot, especially in alloy engines. An infrared thermometer is useful for examining engines. Typical temperatures for a BSA Unit Single are:

Cylinder head	110-130C over exhaust
	95-100C over inlet
Barrel	80-95C
Timing chest	50-60C
Chaincase	40-50C
Gearbox	40C approx

There is an empirical way of judging the best tappet clearance setting and our ears are the best guide. Does the valve gear sound louder when the engine's hot or cold? If it sounds louder when hot, then the bike tappets are opening under heat, and it's safe to narrow them and reduce the din. But beware the totally silent engine: a classic sign of imminent seizure is for the engine to become very quiet. This can mean that the engine is overheating badly, and the piston is starting to nip up. Heat then radiates out through the engine closing up all the tolerances such as the tappets, until the engine finally seizes. This process can last up to half an hour which allows time to stop and check the suspicious silence! (That's why I advocate a temperature gauge kit for classic bikes see Chapter thirteen). A number of riders have successfully used smaller tappet gaps on their bikes. Dave Smith in his excellent Rupert Ratio Unit Single Engine Manual, updates the method used by Harley Davidson and some British makers. The method is simply to ignore the makers instructions, set aside the feeler gauge, and set the tappets by hand, opening the gap from zero untill it's just possible to rotate the pushrods and feel a slight play on your fingers, but no tap-tapping up and down movement. This way you know there's still some slack when cold. This seems to work well on later British bikes, with distinct reductions in valve noise without any discernible accelerated wear. It probably gives an effective gap of 2-5 thou, although the trick is said to be in NOT measuring the gap. I hedge the matter by reducing the gap by a third, say from 10 thou to 7-8 thou and running the bike. If all sounds well, I reduce it again by a third, say down to 5-6 thou. By then, you've achieved a significant reduction in valve noise, while still paying lip service to the makers mark.

Of the various possible ways, the easiest way to set tappets on a classic, say a single, is as follows:-

- Bike on centre stand, remove plugs and rocker hatches and select a gear.
- Watch an inlet rocker. Move the rear wheel back and forth until the valve just closes.
- Check that the exhaust pushrod rotates and adjust the gap then repeat the procedure for the other valve.
- Watch the exhaust valve. Move the rear wheel till its gap just closes up.
- Check and adjust the inlet valve on that cylinder.
- Repeat the process to confirm nothing's moved.

Illus 9.2 Gapping the tappets on a typical OHV engine with screw adjusters.

TIPS

Using a blade feeler gauge, aim for a quite firm fit, and be wary of false readings. If the valve gear is worn, the valve stems may have been dented by the rockers.

Adjustment differs, some bikes have lock-nutted screw adjusters others have eccentric adjusters.

Valve noise isn't all tappets, if there's end play for the rockers to move along, they will do so and inject their own notes into the valve-chorus. Shimming (the fitting of a thin washer so that the play is taken up but the rocker is still free to move on its shaft) is one way to reduce this, should the rocker boxes be removed at some time.

Adjusting The Clutch

While classic motorcycle clutch designs vary, the major marques such as BSA and Triumph employed similar multi-plate clutches designs. The Triumph clutch is said to be superior to the BSA but in everyday riding, I can't detect any difference.

As these two makes comprise the bulk of classic bikes on the road today (see Chapter eleven), we'll focus on their designs. (I confess I never bothered to understand how clutches worked in my earlier days: the fact they worked well enough and rarely needed attention saved studying them further). However, the concept is simple, compact and ingenious. It's really a bit like a friction steering damper, working in reverse. The driving force comes down the chain, through the clutch plates, and out into the gearbox shaft. The acting of pulling in the clutch lever causes the plates to separate, disengaging the drive to the gearbx. There are two types of clutches of this sort - dry clutches and wet clutches. Dry clutches run, well dry like old Harleys; and wet clutches like the Triumph and BSA, are designed to run in an oil-bath. As discussed above, it's ironic that the leading British makers like BSA designed wet clutches and then added chain oilers to their chaincases. This has the disadvantage of emptying the oil from the primary chaincase onto the rear chain, thus ensuring the clutch will run dry unless the owner inspects the oil level every 200 miles. Many did not and still do not. There is no dipstick, and checking involves a bit of fiddling.

In the better clutches, like those fitted to Triumphs and BSAs, there are rubber shock-absorbers built in to the clutch to smooth out power transfer. These are effective compared to the older, drive shaft spring arrangements of the 1950s. For the most part clutches work long and well, unless a previous owner was fond of wheelies, in which case the clutch may show astonishing wear. In extreme cases, new plates and clutch body parts will be needed. Where the chain wheel is badly worn, it may be cost-effective to change to a belt-drive, where a new chain-wheel comes as part of the kit. Today there is a wide choice of plates for classics, from e.g. Barnett, Norman Hyde, Surflex and AP Racing amongst others.

The clutch maintenance challenge then is to set them up, keep them adjusted, and keep them running wet, and with any luck they may never need rebuilding, or even plate changing.

There are really two problems with clutches, slip and drag. Slip is pretty self-explanatory and usually a sign there is inadequate spring tension on the clutch plates to transfer power from engine to gearbox. It's likely the clutch will have gone out of true as the springs tired, and so as you true up the plates, it's worth nipping up the clutch springs to restore operating pressure. Clutch misalignment will also cause drag.

Drag, or the clutch failing to cleanly disengage the drive, can be confused with a gearbox gear selection issue because it makes finding neutral particularly difficult and gear changing much harder and fraught with horrible sounds from the gearbox. It can also be misdiagnosed when riders are unconsciously rushing gear changes by changing gear before fully disengaging the clutch. Retired café racers riding sans clutch, may take note. This is a sure-fire way to experience drag, and it's easy to almost get away with it in these days of forgiving gearboxes and clutches.

There are three points to check on most clutches, the plates' trueness, the operating rod clearance, and the cable gap.

Truing The Plates

This is a bit like a circus juggler twirling a set of china plates on a wand, so they spin smoothly. To achieve this ideal, the outer or pressure plate, needs to spin true. It's possible to get an idea of this without removing your chaincase if you're

lazy and the clutch is otherwise sound. Borrow or buy a dial-gauge, or make up a pointer-gauge and set it against the outer clutch thrust plate, using the clutch adjustment hole in the case, as opposite in Illus. 9.3. By turning over the engine with clutch out, you can often get an idea if the plates are running out of true without any dismantling. If they do have a wobble, and you are experiencing clutch slip or drag, then it's off with the chaincase cover and over to that most useful of classic motorcycle tools - the 'eye-ometer'.

Gazing along the thrust plate as someone turns the engine shows if one side of the plate is wobbling high or low. A dial or pointer gauge does a better job. The three nut Triumph clutch or the four nut BSA ones, give ample adjustment to true the outer plate.

Illus 9.3 Using a Pointer gauge to check a clutch pressure plate, the lazy way.

Clutch Rod Clearance

This, like the chaincase fluid level, is easy to overlook as it's out of sight, and doesn't often make noise. However, if there's no wee gap at the end of this rod, then the clutch will surely slip, as the rod will be ever so slightly holding the plates

apart and not allowing the clutch to properly engage. It's so easy to open the central hatch, loosen the locknut, and screw in the adjuster until it locks up the rod mechanism, then back it off a turn, tighten the locknut, and that's it done. This is something that's worth putting on the 'To Do' list every six months or so, as the clutch plates gradually wear and close up the free play on the operating rod. Holding the screw while tightening the nut can be

Illus 9.4 Checking clearance on the clutch operating rod.

tricky. A small offset ring spanner is ideal, but never to hand when needed. An alternative is shown in 9.4, using a screwdriver through a socket, to hold things.

Clutch Cable Gap

This is really the same argument as for the operating rod. There needs to be just a little slack in the system, to enable the whole thing to operate as intended. A $^1/_{16}$" gap at the clutch lever is typical, although more or less doesn't seem to make much difference - as long as there is some. This is shown opposite. John Favill, who reportedly designed the diaphragm spring clutch for the Norton Commando, moved on to Harley-Davidson and introduced it on to the Sportster in 1984. They still use it.

Illus 9.5 That vital $^1/_{16}$" gap at the clutch lever.

Wheel Alignment And Balancing

With that newly purchased classic bike, one of the first checks to run, is a string-line down the wheels, to check both wheel and frame alignment. The English owner's manuals of the time, helpfully recommended lengths of timber to lay alongside the wheels to measure alignment. Did trees grow straighter in classic days? These days finding a straight two meter length of timber is nearly impossible. More effective and cheaper is the string-line, using the best garden twine, a couple of shelf-brackets and two bricks to hold them in place. Run the string-line from the back wheel, up one side of the bike at about eight inches off the deck; around the front wheel, (lodging the string in a convenient tread with masking tape), and back down the other side; dodging the stand to get a straight run. Once in place, the string-to-tyre gaps are easily compared, either side of the tyres to assess wheel alignment. We can stand back and true up the steering beforehand. Once done, we can also use the string-line as a datum point for our eye-ometer to estimate the trueness of the frame and wheels. Now this doesn't compare with the trueness of an engineers table, but who has one of those?

Illus 9.6 Wheel aligning with a string line.

Proper wheel balancing spoke acorns are a low-cost item, though slices of lead flashing do just as well. Wheel balancing is so well known and documented that it's hard to find a fresh angle on it. But there is one point to watch out for. The new generation of specific motorcycle anti-puncture compounds, i.e. the fibrous, slime products squirted into tyres, can make a difference. I've tested these products and after 6,000 miles (10,000kms) they are still fluid and the tubes are in perfect shape. The stuff flows around the tube or tyre, and centrifugal force smoothes out any imbalance, as you ride along. Now the story is so appealing, you just want it to be true. The only downside is the stuff pools and if your bikes have been laid up, the wheels can be very unbalanced at first until the material flows again. Equally, if you forget it and static balance your wheels you can get a shock, until you spin them a few times.

Caring For Chains

Having trued up the wheels, we can set up those drive chains. Only the right chains, aligned and tensioned, will transmit those 25-40 great British horses to the rear wheels without excessive loss. In most cases we can assume the gearbox and rear wheel sprockets are in good alignment. If in doubt, then a straight-edge can check this. In unit engines, any slight deviation is possibly due to frame distortion, or the engine mounting spacers being omitted. The latter commonly twists the engine in it's mounts, and disturbs the alignment of the rear chain. It's easily fixed with washers or E-clips, and judicious force applied to the engine-frame joints. In pre-unit and semi-unit engines, the alignments of engine and gearboxes also need to be checked.

While elder classics sometimes have a third magneto/dynamo chain, most later classics on the road these days have just the primary and secondary chain. Magneto and dynamo chains are frequently set with $1/4$" slack. Elder, pre-unit classics require separate adjustment of primary and secondary chains, first relocating the gearbox in the frame, to tension the primary, and then moving the rear wheel to adjust the rear chain. If in doubt, Renold advised $3/8$" slack in primary chains. It's mandatory to check both chains when you adjust either. Primary chains on later classics are usually endless and owner maintenance is limited to tension adjustment using a slipper. Triumph like Harley-Davidson, have a nifty primary chain slipper adjuster you can screw-adjust from beneath, without removing the primary chaincase. Why didn't BSA adopt this simple, friendly innovation? Tensioning to the factory manual setting is smart as a too-tight chain puts great loads on the bearings and bushes at each end of the chaincase, while often emitting a moaning sound at speed, as the chain and bushes slowly self-destruct. Too loose and, given the tiny pathway allowed for the chain to travel, a bit like the Columbia's earth re-entry trajectory, then it will start chewing into the chaincase bolt bosses, liberating chunks of alloy that delight in getting into the clutch plates and alternator. On the other hand though, factory advice on such matters was rarely immutable.

Factories often told their customers one thing and did another in their plants and distributors. For example BSA may specify $1/_8$-$1/_4$" for primary chains tension, but internal reports showed they actually used $1/_2$". Why they did this isn't clear. Occam's Razor suggests they liked to minimise rewrites in their owners' guides, and to allow themselves greater tolerances than prescribed to owners. Renold advised to err on the slack side, avoiding over-tightening.

The secondary chain receives all the attention as it's in plain sight and when grey turns to red, it's overdue for oil. Given it's open to the weather, it wears faster than the primary, no matter how well it is looked after. When acquiring a classic bike, it's worth checking the secondary chain maker: the brand is on the side plates.

The cheapest and most common chains are from Asia and Japan. The Asian chains can be quite heavy, with slightly thicker side-plates. D.I.D. is a good example - a well-made, cost-effective chain, but carrying a burden of weight and width, given those thick side-plates that look so reassuringly strong. On the classic bike, the extra width can place the chain perilously close to engine and chaincases, stand tangs, guides etc. The extra inertia in a heavier chain also saps power from the engine, while adding perhaps greater chain-mileage. However, on club runs chain mileage is usually not a

Illus 9.7 Checking rear chain tension with a ruler.

consideration. Over the long term, as conservationists of these machines, the choice of a lighter, thinner chain similar to the original Renolds chain, can make a lot of sense.

Chain tension should be an easy matter, but frequently the British makers left some little challenges along the way. For example, on the last of the Triumph (and BSA) Unit singles, there is a choice of rear chain tensions, depending on what Manual you read. The 1971 Triumph Owners manual says flatly 1". The Haynes says helpfully $1^1/_8$", $1^3/_4$" or even $2^1/_2$". If you turn to BSA Unit single sources, you find $1^1/_8$" being advised. Renold said $3/_4$" with a rider aboard. What is the answer? Well, there is no clinching answer, so you turn to classic websites and look for a contemporary solution. There you find fresh answers, for example *"With bike on centre stand, use a truck strap or similar to load down the rear shocks until the gearbox sprocket centre, swing arm centre and rear wheel centre, are all aligned. This is the tightest alignment for the chain. Above and below this point, the chain slackens. The trick then, is to adjust a small amount of slack in the chain, at it's tightest spot, with the bike held at this 'apposition point'. We can then be confident, that everywhere else in it's travel arc, the tension will be OK."*

This shows how the growing data availability enables riders to resolve confusing factory directions and aftermarket manuals. Apropos this point, there's a 1971 service note from Johnson Motors, the US Triumph agent, recommending a shift from 1" to $1^3/_4$" tension in Triumph rear chains to handle the higher weight loadings with pillions. This was causing strain failure in chains leading to claims on distributors. It's hard to imagine a pillion on a Triumph T25, as the pillion footrests attach to the swing arm, and the pillion's legs are constantly bouncing up and a down, like a chicken walk! We can sympathise with those US distributors, maintaining customer service to the last, as the British manufacturing industry foundered. In Table 9.2 below is a 'rule of thumb' summary of chain tensions.

Table 9.2	**Quick Chain Tension Guide**
Chain	**Typical Tension**
Dynamo/Magneto	$^1/_4$"
Primary	$^1/_2$"
Secondary	1"

Perhaps the last piece of this 'chic-chainery', is to deal with lubrication. If the bike has no rear chain oiler (or if it has been blanked off) there will be no lubrication of the rear chain.

How to correct this? There are plenty of solutions about. Firstly, by redirecting the oil tank breather out over the chain beside the sprocket, where it drips onto the chain. Secondly, terminating any engine breathers over the chain and whilst that involves a mixture of (good) oil and (putrid) blow-by gas, on balance it's a plus for the chain. Beyond that, there's the excellent Scot-Oiler system, requiring the rider fiddle with the engine intake manifold. It's also possible to make up a chain-oiler using a small flask with a screw metering device or a wick wiping feed.

Given much classic riding is on club outings these days, a prophylactic chain lubing before the run, seems sufficient. While the original British makers suggested engine oil, this flings oil over the rear end. Better alternatives are the traditional products like Linkelyfe, an expensive tacky formula that resists oil-fling, and keeps the rear end dry. A cheaper, high-tackiness alternative is chainsaw boom oil.

Carburettor Care

Most British classic bikes specified an Amal carburettor, or one of it's progenitors, an Amac etc. Earlier road classics used the Amal Monobloc, and this was superseded by the Amal Concentric range for later road classics. These two carburettor series outsold any other. Amal is still in production with both series available, as well as a full range of spares at reasonable prices. Early on, Amal and Mikuni formed an alliance, and Mikuni carburettors are a popular replacement for the Amal at much the same price. The Mikuni products are often fitted to early and late Triumph and Norton twins, and BSA/Triumph Triples, where it's claimed they give better idling, fuel consumption and less stiction from chromed brass slides. Still most classics on club runs use Amals and we'll focus on these, though the tuning principles are similar for other modern carburettors.

Of all the classic engine systems, carburation seems to provide owners with more challenges than any other, save the electrical system. Often, this reflects previous experiments to lift performance, or fitting replacement units with incorrect jetting. As the units are made with soft metal, it's easy to damage joint surfaces and distort the bodies by overtightening. Amal issues clear operating and tuning product advice. It's freely available on the net, so there's no point in taking up space here to reproduce that basic product information. Instead, this section looks at innovative ways of repairing, optimising and tuning Amal carburettors, ways that are not in the factory manual. The focus is more on the Concentric, as that's had a much longer production run than the Monobloc, and will suit more readers. However much of the coverage applies to either model. Really, the Concentric is a more compact form of the Monobloc - introduced we're told, to better fit the later classic twin designs.

Is It Worth Keeping At All?

The first thing to be said, is given the price of a new Amal, it's only worth persevering with repairs and parts replacement to a certain point. Sometimes it's more cost-effective to replace the unit. The old one can always be sold on EBay or Trademe, to subsidise the new purchase. There's a surprisingly brisk market in used Amals. If you can't bear to see your old one junked, it can be renovated by sleeving. Small specialists offer this service for about one fifth the new price.

What Is The Build State?

In troubleshooting the carburettor, it's best to double check the correct build state for the bike model. The details are in nearly every classic manual. They were also stamped by the factory on the side of each unit, near the Amal model number. Today, the build number is only useful to check against the parts list. If the numbers tally, then it may be the original carburettor but, by now quite worn. Mostly, there will either be no build number, or an incorrect one as the carburettor will have been changed along the way.

Does It Match Factory Specification?

Next, strip it down and confirm the unit really does conform with the factory specification. In this, it's prudent to cross-check two or three source documents until quite sure you have the correct specification for the bike. Makers sometimes changed their carburettor build state year by year, for the same model. Thus it's unwise to rely on an aftermarket manual like Haynes, that strips down one bike for each book; unless the bike and year exactly match the manual. Even so, validating the Haynes settings with say, a Chilton, Clymers or a factory workshop or parts manual, can avoid angst later.

The items to check include the body size, throttle slide, main jet, needle jet, and the needle itself. If the main jet appears to be wrong, it's worth noting some classic mechanics recommend going up a main jet size i.e. 10, to try and account for the different petrol qualities these days. Also, if the bike has been living at a high altitude, it may have been jetted down. With 30-60 year old machines, there's usually a lot of wear and tear and parts substitution, especially of other parts that affect the carburettor settings such as the silencer and pipes.

The best starting point is to take the bike back to the maker's original build state. That makes a stable platform on which to base later testing and carburettor tuning. Frequently, having re-established the bike's original build state, all the carburation problems disappear.

Check The Joint Surfaces

While the carburettor is apart, it's worth beginning by checking all three joints for burrs and distortion. These are the body and float bowl jointing surfaces and the engine-side flange. The latter is always noted in the literature as bowing after over-tightening, causing an air leak that upsets the mixture. I find it hard to see the bowing and try the joint out on a sheet of fine wet and dry paper on an old mirror. A light rub soon discloses any bowing, and a bit more circular rubbing, first one way then the other, sees it gone. Similar treatment of the other two surfaces deals with most joint air-leak issues.

Illus 9.9 Truing up the flange joint by rubbing on emery paper on a flat surface such as glass, to air-proof the carburetter

Internal Scan And A Probe

Next is a look at all the internal galleries that Amal build into their units. For this, a small fibre-optic wand that attaches to a small AA torch is indispensable. They're cheap and really the only way to get the job done. This lets you see inside nearly every jet and gallery for blockages. After removing any dirt, insects etc, it's worth probing any of the fine holes, especially the pilot air jet and the two wee holes in the chamber floor close to the flange. The pundits say not to do this, but with care and using fuse-wire or better, soft brass wire (a single strand of picture hanging wire is ideal) then it'll cause no harm. It's also worth blowing these jets through, either with a bike pump or a plastic tube and lung power..

Illus 9.10   Wanding the galleries in a carburetter for blockages and insects.

What Parts Need Replacing?

Gaskets and O-rings.	A kit of these is cheaper than checking the old ones.
Needle	Replace if it looks at all worn, scratched or bent, or is the incorrect type.
Needle jet	If it looks oval rather than circular, or you are changing the needle, fit a new one.
Throttle valve (slide)	Replace if it's the wrong size, or badly worn.
Filter	Worn or brittle, then fit a new one.
Banjo washer	There will be one in the washer kit but it's worth adding one just in case.
Flange O-ring	Some riders remove this ring for a better seal. I don't...ever.
Tickler	If the tickler is plain, fit an optional cover kit that keeps your glove dry.
Float needle	Change any white nylon ones for the brass/viton version.
Air slide kit	Great for tuning.

Is The Body In Good Shape?

If the slide valve is very tight at the top the body can be sleeved. A quick fix is to use a brake hone to restore the bore. Usually, the distortion and valve binding are up near the top, and this area can be gently honed, without interfering with the airflow down the bottom, or causing air leaks. A more desperate remedy is to sand away at the valve, until it fits better in the oval bore. I've tried that approach, once.

If the binding is minor, it's worth trying an old distributor's trick and spraying the valve with lubricant. Silicone spray seems to work well. Distributors used a molybdenum spray in the old days. It's a toss-up with lubricating the valve as this can create a dirty film on the slide which can lead to more binding. I find silicone spray seems to avoid that film build-up. However, if the valve is a sloppy fit in the bore, and it has side-movement at the bottom, then it'll randomly vary the airflow into the engine, causing idling that's impossible to stabilise. In the worst case, it'll be rattling at idle, sounding like valve noise. There are three choices. Buy a new valve and hope it takes up the slack, resleeve it, or discard it.

Illus 9.11 Using a brake hone to restore a carburetter bore.

> TIP: *With a few bikes and a collection of used parts, it's worth picking up used carburettors cheaply at markets and swapmeets and combining restored parts to make up your own.*

Refitting The Carburettor

It's worth closely following the factory notes for joining the carburettor to the engine, to avoid air leaks that can ruin tuning. Any paper gaskets, spacers and Tufnol gaskets (the thick grey ones) must be in situ. Having trued up any body distortion, it's good to do the flange nuts up only finger tight, adding star and plain washers to a locknut or stiff nut, even if originally they weren't fitted. Then, it's just a little nip up with your smallest spanner. Only 5-7 ft lbs tension is required, not much more than a toothpaste tube. After all there's no great load on those studs. To doubly insure against air leaks, run around the joint with blue liquid Hylomar sealant. When next the engine runs, the Hylomar draws down and fills any little fissures. As an aside, current Harley dealer directions are to run around the joint with an LPG bottle hose, and the engine running. If the engine suddenly races, you know there's a leak. I prefer a less flammable approach.

Monobloc And Concentric Issues

One advantage of the Concentric over the Monobloc is the absence of a threaded top cover. That's the one that always seems to get cross-threaded! The main top end problem with the Concentric is that some of it's caps are designed for push-in cable ends, and some for cables with screw-adjusters. Sod's law means the favourite throttle cable always has the wrong end fitting. Also, the Concentric top end is not as weatherproof as the Monobloc design. The problem can best be seen on classic bikes re-exported from the USA, with small fuel tanks. Water runs down the back of the tank and onto the carburettor cables. It tracks down the cables onto the top cap of the carburettor, or simply drops there. The Monobloc has a steeply ridged cap that sheds water. The Concentric cap is flat and allows water down into the body more easily. The units with the plain cable end, and a rebate in the cap, are worst. A solution is to insert flashing under the tank, on the top frame, to divert water away from the carburettor. Another is to wind tape around the cable entries on top. This also helps reduce air and dust entry around the cables, another cause of lean running. It's an old scrambles trick. Self-amalgamating electronics tape is ideal for this.

Tuning An Amal Carburettor

Amal's basic tuning advice is clear and should work if the factory settings are restored and other things are equal. If there's still a bad mixture, then it's time for road-testing and plug-pulling, or resort to Colortune plug testing. Perhaps the most original, independent Amal tuning advice is also in Dave Smith's, Rupert Ratio Guide. His advice on marking throttle openings on the twistgrip is very

Illus 9.12 Lazy tuning using an air lever and twistgrip gradations

useful. His other Amal tips are so good, it's worth buying his book even if you don't have a BSA Unit single! For lazy, simple, non-invasive mixture testing, I recommend the approach summarised below and in Table 9.1.

- Fit an air slide to your carburettor as a diagnostic tool. If you have a twin, either swap the slide over or buy two. They're cheap enough, and they help cold starting.
- Mark the $1/4$, $1/2$, $3/4$ and WOT (wide open throttle) openings on your twistgrip, following Rupert Ratio's advice. (See Illus. 9.12)
- Road test by operating the air slide at these four throttle stages shown below. If the engine runs more smoothly at a stage with the air-slide

engaged, you can estimate the corresponding jet, screw, needle setting or throttle slide is too lean. If the engine runs rough with the slide engaged, you can judge the mixture setting is either optimal or too rich to start with. Changing the relevant setting as per Table 9.1, and re-testing the bike will prove which.

Table 9.1	Lazy Tuning With the Air Lever		
Throttle Opening	**Carburettor Using**	**Air Lever Test Result**	
		Runs Rougher?	**Runs Smoother?**
$0 - \frac{1}{8}$	Pilot Jet/Pilot Air Screw	Weaken mixture Unscrew pilot	Richen mixture Screw in pilot
$\frac{1}{8} - \frac{1}{4}$	Throttle Slide Valve	Change up	Change Down
$\frac{1}{4} - \frac{3}{4}$	Needle Position	Down a Notch	Up a Notch
$\frac{3}{4} - $ WOT	Main Jet	Drop a size	Increase a size

NB Change all settings by minimum increments: for example turn the pilot airscrew by $\frac{1}{8}$ to $\frac{1}{4}$ turn.

Troubleshooting A Persistent Carburettor Problem

If the above regime fails to optimise a bike's running, and it should be running pretty well perfectly from idle to 4,000 rpm or more, then it's wise to broaden the checking, as in:

The Case Of The Missing Jet

Ken and his old single were running rough on the ride. Eventually she conked out miles from anywhere in Central NSW. Ken was a very good classic mechanic and correctly diagnosed a fuel problem. After undoing the float bowl, even he was surprised to see the buildup of water, dirt and rust clogging up the bottom of his M21 bowl. He abruptly flung the contents of the float bowl over the fence into a paddock of long grass, and reassembled the carburettor. The problem was now worse and she wouldn't start at all. Puzzled, he again ran through the usual suspects then took the carburettor apart, and found to his horror, that the main jet was now missing. It must have come adrift from the jet holder, and sunk into the debris in the float bowl. He'd flung it into the paddock along with the debris! Ken eventually found the missing jet in the paddock, but it took him an hour on hands and knees, combing the paddock for it, before he could ride home.

Assuming all the jets are in place and correct, then the two remaining likely culprits are the air cleaner and the exhaust.

Air Cleaner Checks

Removing an air cleaner or otherwise increasing air-flow, gives a leaner mixture. It's best to restore the original filter and housing, especially if an airbox is involved. If the air filter is clogged with dirt or oil, perhaps from a crankcase breather misguidedly connected there, then remove it and clean the filter, to correct the rich running that will otherwise occur.

Exhaust Checks

Air leaks across exhaust joints can result in rough and lean running. If it's a push-in header pipe joint, then expect it to be loose. These joints are easily sealed by smearing some high-temperature silicone sealant around the head port rebate, before sliding in the pipe. Frankly, I find the regular-grade (e.g. Permatex RTV Blue) engine silicones are up to the task and only half the price. The 'neutral-cure' silicone building sealants also withstand high temperatures, and could be used here as they're cheaper and in many riders' sheds already for gutter repairs. Avoid the 'acetic-acid' (vinegar) curing building silicones, as they're unsuitable for some metals. I remember the dramatic 1979 trade demonstrations given to plumbers by the silicone companies, as they weaned plumbers off soldering guttering, in favour of pop rivets and silicone sealant. The demonstrator alternately soldered and silicone'd flat-head nails under a piece of rain-water guttering. He then played a gas torch along the top of the metal. Every other nail dropped off, as the solder melted, while every silicone'd nail hung on, the silicone withstood the fierce heat.

If the exhaust pipe is non-standard, say if it's larger, then it may change the amount of gas evacuated on the exhaust stroke. This can affect carburation by altering in turn, the next intake charge. Also any exhaust wave-form scavenging planned into the exhaust system by the maker may be disturbed, further interfering with cylinder charging, and performance suffers.

If the silencer (muffler) is non-standard, and often they will have fewer baffles than the original, it's likely to be have an effect on the carburettor. Lean running is more likely, if only because more cylinder scavenging occurs on the exhaust stroke, with more cylinder space made available for later induction strokes. Also, engine performance may unpredictably alter as the waveforms shuttling around the system, are pushed further out of whack. Lastly, it's worth checking all pipe-muffler joints and blocking these up if they appear leaky. When these aspects are locked down, the carburettor problems are more likely to have resolved themselves.

Fuel Additives And Valve Seat Recession (VSR)

After researching this, I'm dubious about there being any generalised risk to classic British bikes. In theory, iron heads on older classics at lower compression should be fine. Newer classics with high compression alloy heads, might benefit from hardened seats or added protection. Yet what happens inside engines doesn't follow only one theory, and every engine build and tune state can be different. There are opposing views on VSR, and little evidence either way. To be safe, and as it's a low-cost item, a lead replacement product is used by many riders which provide some evidence of reduced VSR. and it shouldn't do any harm. It may postpone a rebuild, and offer side benefits.

What Fuel To Run In Classic Bikes?

This is another complex, slippery decision area for classic riders, who are not helped by inadequate disclosure from the oil companies. There are some technical anchors on which a decision may be based, at least with Australian fuels.

- Pump fuels 91, 95, and 98 octane produce a similar amount of heat.
- Octane ratings indicate the rate of combustion.
- The higher the compression, the faster the burn.
- The faster the burn, the higher the risk of detonation.
- A higher octane gives a slower burn.
- The slower the burn, the higher the risk of overheating and burnt exhaust valves.
- 98 fuels should not be used on classic bikes.
- Brands differ - Shell has more friction/viscosity modifiers and injector cleaner, and runs richer.
- Sulphur and benzene levels were reduced in 2006, for clean running.
- If a fuel change gives a rich mixture, a hotter plug and pilot airscrew tuning may be needed.
- There is no rule for fuel and compression ratio, except 91 octane up to approx 8:1 CR.
- Fuel selection is empirical for each engine, e.g. relating octane to abscence of pinking.
- For early pre-lead fuel classics, a 10-20% blend of lighter fluid (e.g. Shellite or Shell X55) with an octane rating of 40, and 91 octane, may be worth trying according to some writers.

Fuel choice seems to boil down to selecting a fuel with a burn-rate that suits the engine timing, compression etc. A 'sweet-spot' can be empirically found with an engine temperature gauge. It's determined as lying between engine pinking (from too low octane) and engine overheating (from too high octane) slowing the burn.

Oil Filtering

As classic bikes enter their second century, too many still lack an effective oil filter. For this reason, I've covered the installation of oil filters as a special project in Chapter 13. British makers provided mesh oil screens as an advance on felts. It could be argued these matched the low-tech oils of the time, when solids in the oil settled out in the tank or sump. Modern oils keep solids suspended. Metal particles slip through mesh screens and wear into bearings every time the bike is started. The solution is simple. Fit a modern paper filter that matches modern oils. These stop solids down to 15-20 microns, and extend engine life. There are several bike kits available. The most common downunder is the Norton kit.

It is also worth placing magnets in the oil tank and sump plate to capture ferrous swarf of 1-15 micron size. Rare-earth

Illus 9.13 Norton oil filter installation on a BSA, with rare earth magnet and cooler ring.

magnets collect far more and fix on the end of the oil filter, adding powerful magnetic filtration. They also fit to the gearbox and chaincase drain plugs. Adding an oil filter also boosts oil volume by up to a pint with the extra hoses. This expanded volume helps reduce peak oil temperatures in summer. If riding in the tropics, it's worth considering an 'oil cooling ring' for the filter. These are or were a Harley-Davidson part. Stocks of the ring are always on EBay. It's a finned alloy cylinder, split so it can cling to the oil filter cartridge, and form a push on fit. The Norton filter may need to be shimmed for a snug fit in the cooler ring - a piece of copper sheet is ideal as it also transfers heat to the ring. It's claimed to reduce engine oil temperatures by 10^0C or more.

There's no doubt an oil filter postpones oil changes and helps pay for itself. It also postpones major engine maintenance and is a potent conservation aid for every classic bike. If you take only one idea from this book, please make it this one.

Air And Fuel Filtering

The conservation arguments for oil filtration hold also for air and fuel filtration. The case for air filtration is clearly based on preventing airborne abrasive materials entering the cylinder and accelerating wear.

For road going classics, the latest filters, for example those provided by K&N, outperform the usual classic filters and allow more airflow and hence power development. Using these can alter the mixture and nudging the throttle needle up a notch may be necessary. An airbox is also worth considering to assist airflow, by

Illus 9.14 A typical sintered fuel filter in the line.

acting as a surge tank. A rule of thumb is a 1-3 litre airbox should assist air intake and mid-range power on a classic 500-650cc bike. It's interesting to reflect that BSA replaced their pancake air filters in 1971 with an airbox. While on assisted breathing, it's also worth recalling the original exhaust breakthrough, the Brooklands silencer. This silencer found an expansion chamber ten times engine capacity reduced exhaust noise without power loss. It makes you wonder about the tiny, noisy silencers fitted to some bikes. Are they missing the point?

Fuel filtering is also worth considering. As classic fuel tanks age, corrosion occurs unless some form of tank sealer is used (Examples are Red, White & Blue, Petseal, POR15 etc). Rust fragments easily migrate to the carburettor and block jets and filters. The excellent and cost-effective range of motorcycle fuel filters available prevents this, and some such as the sintered metal types, are also said to prevent water reaching the carburettor. For a few pounds or dollars it's cheap insurance.

Keeping Nuts And Bolts In Place

This can be straightforward, even on vibratory British singles. Good practice includes the following:

- Using the correct size bolt for the hole, allowing that some installations call for shanked bolts to fit properly such as some engine mounts.

- Using spring washers on everything, and particularly either kind of the star spring washers. They hold better than the slash-cut type.

- Fitting a plain washer with a star washer. Some riders always put them one way or the other. I put the star washer on top of the plain washer.

- Buying a mixed lot of Nyloc or 'stiff-nuts', for any fitting that may vibrate...and that's nearly everything!

- For plain nuts or fixings screwed in threaded holes, a dob of thread sealant (Loctite or similar).

- Inspecting casing screw holes with a fibre-optic wand, and cleaning up threads with a tap. The wife's used cotton buds are perfect for extracting metal rubbish from such holes.

- Switching the most used sizes to stainless nuts and bolts. Eke out the budget by changing only the nut or bolt, depending on which part is on show.

- Stainless socket heads seem to look better than hex heads on some parts, for example handlebar caps, even if they're not an original part.

Cable Care

When young and immortal, I neglected cables and didn't ever oil them until they seized. These days, I'm atoning for that with thorough cable care. Some key points include the following

- **Lined Cables.** Switching to the Venhill nylon or Teflon lined cables that never need oiling. These are expensive but for clutches they're a must, especially if you suffer from arthritis in your hands or finger cramping.

- **Regular Cable Lubrication.** The days of plasticine dams, balloons and rubber bands have been replaced by that new cheap 'Cable Luber' device. It's essentially a rubber lined clamp that grips the cable outer and bridges the gap to the inner, enabling lubricant to be injected down the cable bore. A Teflon spray from the bicycle shop can be used with it and gives excellent results (see Illus 9.15)

Illus 9.15 The Cable-Luber in action with a Teflon spray

- **Lever Care.** Cables operate best if the brake or clutch lever pivot is lubricated, and the cable nipple holders are greased. Lubrication is maintained far longer if the lever pivots are covered from rain and grime with slip-on

Illus 9.16 Leather lever covers keep out the rain and Aussie grasshoppers

rubber covers. If they're not available, they can be scissored from scrap leather, cut in a boomerang shape to fit (see illus 9.16).

If arthritis makes clutch work a pain, the Ezi-Pull clutch device is also worth a look. This is a popular Harley-Davidson aftermarket part, and available through most bike catalogues. It changes the fulcrum point of the lever to give greater leverage with less effort.

- **Soldering.** One of the best bits of advice I was given recently, was for soldering nipples on cables. The trick is to drill a hole in wood so that it neatly accommodates the nipple. Then fill the hole with molten solder, enrobing the nipple. This ensures the solder gets into all the wee cracks around the cable and makes a sound bond. The nipple cleans up with a file. It requires no skill and interestingly, the wood never burns.

- **Reusing Cables.** If you're a lazy, cheap mechanic like me, you can buy used cables and also recycled cables. Cables are often discarded simply because the plastic outer covering is chewed up by pinching and chafing. Some black heat-shrink tubing from the electronics store will slide over the nipple and cover the chewed outer. Heating with the wife's hair dryer shrinks it down over the damage and makes the cable as new. NOS British cables are often on sale downunder, and it's wise to lay in a stock while they last at these silly prices.

- **Long Runs.** Some riders double up cables just in case. A simpler alternative is to take a length of inner Bowden cable, and some screw-on nipples. Usually it's an inner that gives way. You can either screw on a new nipple or, if the inner is broken, thread in a new inner down the old outer and fix new nipples at each end.

Some air lever designs can do with improvement, as a friend of Ed's found at a Snowy Rally years ago in the yarn about:

The Last Man At The Rally

Ed and a mate went to a Snowy Rally years ago in Australia. It rained that last night, but the boys weren't concerned for their bikes, as they'd brought bike covers. The last morning of the rally, Ed's mate's B33 was uncharacteristically slow to start. He kicked and kicked but she wouldn't fire. The plug and spark were fine. Ed said sagely, "you've got rain in your tank, mate". "Rubbish", said his mate, "The bikes been under the tarp all night, she's bone dry. It must be something else". An hour later, came the time they were the last two riders at the site, and still she wouldn't start. They drained the tank and added fresh fuel but still she wouldn't fire. Eventually, Eddy overrode his mate's protests and undid the carb drain plug. Out gushed fresh water. What had occurred, under the tarp? After much head-scratching, the boys worked out one handlebar had poked out a bit from the tarp the night before. Water must have entered the choke cable inside the air lever, and passed down into the carburettor, filling up the float bowl overnight. She started next kick. After hearing this yarn, I now fit a short rubber boot over any suspicious air lever cable entries.

Tyres

Tyre technologies are a quantum jump ahead of classic days, with today's compounds offering improved dry and wet roadholding, along with wider choice. The permutations of make, model, compound, grip, mileage, cost, tread pattern etc mean the best way to make an informed choice is to borrow the local shop catalogue and bone up on the range available. After that it's worth getting feedback from owners of the popular choices. For typical classic club riding, brands and even tyre models do not appear to be a make or break matter. More important considerations are the dangers from all new tyres, i.e. from the mould release film and in older tyres from case hardening and the resulting poor adhesion.

Classic Oils, Greases And Fluids

This is another contentious area where many classic riders use proven favourites. It is possible to pick up a golden thread from classic days to now, with regard to classic bike engine lubrication. From WWII to the close of the classic period, there were significant advances in oil technology around the middle of each decade, and mineral oils ruled. Lubricating oil technology advances go hand in hand with longer service intervals and modern engine longevity. Let's consider engine oils first. The first question is whether to go Mineral, Vegetable or Synthetic. In Table 9.2 I invite criticism with a Good, Better, Best summary of oil choice.

Table 9.2 Oil Choices - Good, Better, Best?							
Oil Type	Lubricity	Load Bearing	Flow	Cooling	Deposits	Service Life	Cost
Monograde	Good	Best	Good	Good	Good	Better	Better
Multigrade	Better	Good	Better	Better	Better	Best	Best
Vegetable	Best	Best	Best	Best	Good	Good	Good
Synthetic	Best	Better	Best	Best	Best	Best	Good

Most downunder classic riders I know use a 20-50 engine multigrade, one formulated for older car engines, or a premium monograde. Classic high-viscosity monograde oils are once again available, specially formulated by Shell, Castrol, Penrite, Millers etc. These recipes are claimed to be more friendly to older bikes. It's nice to have a choice to suit the budget. Typical mainstream multigrade car products include Castrol GTX, Havoline, Valvoline and Mobil oils that were originally specified, although doubtless are now formulated differently. Penrite and Pennzoil products are used by those looking for something different. The major oil brands for new motorcycles such as Motul, Spectro, Silkolene, Harley-Davidson, Screaming Eagle etc seem less used on classics whether in their mineral or synthetic forms. The Silkolene Titan Formula is one exception. Personally I use whatever 20-50 multigrade is on special and bump up it's hot viscosity with an oil stabiliser.

One classic product deserving a plug is Lucas Oil Stabiliser or the Moreys equivalent. It's a tacky oil product that's claimed to stabilise and maintain oil-films and viscosity in mineral and synthetic oils, and even ATF oil. The main benefits are said to be from a persisting tacky oil film that reduces cold-start wear and blow-by, while increasing oil service life and oil-film integrity at high temperatures. This translates into reduced oil consumption and smoking in worn engines. Under high engine temperatures and pressures, it seems to maintain a better oil film even than SAE50 monogrades. It's good for a bike ridden occasionally. Lucas Oil Stabiliser is said to help keep an oil film on internal surfaces over storage. Certainly it's tackiness is impressive. In worn gearboxes it improves gear change (shifting) performance.

For gearboxes, most riders seem to use mineral hypoid GL5 gear oils of approximately SAE 75-90. The hypoid and Lucas combination is a cost-effective recipe for easier gear changing. Synthetic gearbox oils are also being found more commonly in classic boxes, but their price limits adoption.

Chaincases are a different story. Multigrades containing friction modifiers are a no-no. Many riders stick to a traditional SAE30 monograde, or a 10-30 or 10-40 multigrade with no modifiers. The use of ATF (Automatic Transmission Fluid) oil in chaincases is also popular.

For forks, ATF products are being displaced by specialised SAE 5-20 synthetic and semi-synthetic anti-foaming fork oils. As springs age and weaken, the heavier synthetic grades maintain suspension performance.

Classic riders are well served with greases. A number of the original greases are still formulated, for example Castrol LM for wheel bearings, and they work as well as ever. As with oils, there is a proliferation of products for specialised applications. My shed contains,

Graphite grease, for gasket sealing,

MoS2 jointing compound, for anti-seize use.

High pressure grease for wheel bearings.

Copper grease for spark plugs

Castor grease for brake seals etc.

Vaseline....for chapped hands.

Engine Oil

The pundits still say to run the engine before draining the oil. Why, when modern oils suspend the rubbish in the oil film, and the filter holds the rest? I never work on a bike when it's hot. Fixings tighten up in their threads, and even if you run it briefly, you still burn your hand on the exhaust. It's prudent to change drain plug washers routinely, especially if they're fibrous or copper. Alloy jobs seem to be good to reuse once or twice, if they're reversed. Metal filters and screens in tank or sump should be washed in petrol. This point is often laboured, but given blowby is 70% unburnt fuel, I figure an extra tad on a sump screen isn't going to be noticed. Some older classics use fabric oil filters and these can be recycled using paraffin (kerosene), as can fabric air filters and some paper oil filters.

Gasket Sealing

A lot of classic riders no longer use gasket cements for gaskets on oil-bearing structures, and instead use graphite grease or anti-seize molybdenum compound. This seals voids and is so gentle on gaskets they can be reused.

Oil Priming

Priming the engine after an oil-change, is one area the early manual writers tended to overlook. If started up straight after an oil change, the bike may have a dry sump and dry lines to the oil pump. Some bikes have in-line anti-wetsumping devices. These may need priming to assure safe operation, especially with worn oil pumps. Ideally, the oil pipe between tank and pump is primed before starting up. It's prudent to dump a little oil into the sump via a timing plug, rocker cover or spark plug hole, to prime the scavenge side. Any oil-line taps are also easy to forget during an oil change.

Wet Sumping

Aging classic bikes seem to wet-sump easily with modern oils, especially when they're ridden infrequently. BSAs and Velocettes have ball and spring oil valves that often malfunction. This coupled with aging geared oil pumps that don't hold against gravity, contributes to wet sumping. A lazy solution to wet sumping is pushing the bike round the yard with the plugs out. This saves removing the sump plate, and dumping oil. A much riskier solution which is sometimes advocated by others is an in-line oil tap. A gas-fitting chrome ball-valve is ideal for this, and the red handle helps reminds you to switch your oil on before riding. I have only once forgotten to turn mine on, thanks to the red sticker on my speedo and a start-up mnemonic. That one time was a short run in the garage to check a breather for 30 seconds. I was lucky. Providing you follow a start-up sequence you should never forget, but the consequences of forgetting are horrendous. *So the advice is, do not make this change unless you fit some method of preventing the engine starting with the oil tap in the off position (see Chapter 13 for some suggestions).*

Equally important is the post-oil change level check. With more riders adding accessory oil filters and coolers, it's surprising how the oil level can drop after the engine is first started. It is also easy to overfill the tank if you add the usual amount from memory and overlook that the filter's not been changed. In this case, a spray over the rear of the bike from the oil tank vent is a reminder.

On Breaking Down

The best advice is 'Don't Panic'! The best way to cope is to analyse. Here's a handy checklist.

Five Break-Down Steps

1. Review what happened, as you broke down.
2. Stop and think, before acting.
3. Think of likely causes to explain the breakdown.
4. Run through fixes for the cause.
5. Try out the fixes, one by one, till she starts.

Most likely you're on a club run and surrounded by an army of keen mechanics, all anxious to demonstrate their skills and show off the tools secreted round their bikes. Peter 'The Bear' Thoeming is the best known Australian motorcycling author and one of the small band who've ridden round the world on lightweights. He reminds us that a bike responds to logic, if only because our classics are really 2,000 parts bolted together. Peter troubleshoots a breakdown under four systems - tyres, fuel, electrical and mechanical - and so shall we. Lets assume we've come to a halt on the roadside miles from anywhere.

It's Up To You, Doctor!

After getting through the panic stage, let's borrow some of our family doctor's diagnostic tricks. Diagnosing a kidney stone in five minutes in a surgery is similar to roadside diagnosis of a fuel blockage. The GP plays the probabilities, like a poker player. He starts by asking a few questions. These show which body system is involved. He asks a couple more questions on symptoms. He thinks of probable causes and forms a hunch, comparing the symptoms with common illnesses. He challenges his hunch by sorting the symptoms along a range of possible illnesses, from the 'worst fit' to the 'best fit'. He picks out the top two or three illnesses that match. Then he goes with his hunch, or changes to one of those two. This goes by the elegant medical term of the 'differential diagnosis', but it's really about picking winners. He writes a prescription, and this is still part of his diagnosis. He knows that if his first pick fails, you'll be back to try his second pick. His success rate is about 80% on the first pick (if he's any good). He increases that to about 90% on his second attempt. That's why I never play cards with doctors anymore. The same medical approach can be used at the roadside. David Minton in his fine 1981 *Motorcyclist's Handbook* reckons that half of all breakdowns are electrical, followed by tyres, fuel, cables and chains, so lets start with the electrics.

Electrical System Breakdowns

Assuming the bike is stalled by the roadside, then the most likely cause is electrical. It stops more classic bikes than the other three systems combined. In principle the electrical system is like the fuel system. Both have a flow of stuff down pipes. The odd thing with electricity, is that no one seems sure which way it flows, i.e. + to -, or vice versa. Roy Bacon, who usually simplifies everything, says it's positive to negative. Earlier writers say the reverse. What complicates it is that in the vintage era, great-grandfather's bikes were 'negative to earth'. In the 1950s our grandfathers switched to 'positive to earth' circuits. In the 1970s our fathers switched back to negative to earth. The only reason I can find in the literature for these changes, is to achieve better earthing, and reduce galvanic corrosion.

At the roadside, the best thing is to review the symptoms as you broke down. If, as happened to me recently, the bike misfires and eventually conks out, that's a vital sign your GP would note, as he diagnoses a flat battery. If it conks out in an instant, that's also important . Most electrical problems turn out to be physical ones and therefore easier to find. For example, bullet connectors vibrating out of their connectors, earthing wires loosening, short circuits due to components rubbing insulation off wires etc.

As with the fuel system, the first thing to check is - is the stuff flowing? The electrical system has two sub-systems, the low tension (LT) and high-tension (HT) systems. Our family GP on the job, would first pull out Occam's Razor and check the Kill switch, in case it's on or malfunctioning. Ditto the ignition switch, where a spray of WD40 never goes astray. Next is the LT side by checking lights and accessories and then the fuse, if one is fitted. If its blown and you are carrying at least two spares, it's worth popping a new one in, just in case age, vibration or surge has done for the old one. If that blows too, then it's time to look for a short circuit, most likely due to vibration. A good start is the battery terminals, and working along the visible harness looking for something that doesn't feel right. Rubbed wires and blown bulbs or suchlike. The other likely cause is an earth return failing, so opening the circuit. Prevention is the best approach here. On all classics it's worth running at least two fat earth wires back to the main frame. One runs from the headlight or yokes, and one from the rear guard. These are two regions of the bike that are rich in electrical gear, and where the earth return is likely to fail, if left to run through paint, bolts and greasy bearings.

Next, turn to the HT side by removing a spark plug and resting it on the engine, to check the spark while turning the engine. If there is a spark, especially a nice blue one, then we can tick off the plug, coil and the HT side. If not, then whip out that spare, gapped plug, as it's surprising how many newish plugs develop faults. If there is still no spark, then it's time to backtrack up the HT lead to the coil, although that seems unlikely, unless a coil lead has pulled away. If you have a test lead-light with you, then connecting it across the points, and checking for light when the points open is a useful test of the LT-HT interface. Back to the breaker points, it's worth seeing they open and close as usual, and their cam is operating normally. If they really spark when opening, then suspect a dud condenser. It's worth checking the gap is roughly right and passing a points file through (or a bank note works well) to check there's no dirt. I have never seen a Boyer or similar sealed electronic systems break down so you shouldn't be stranded in the first place.If it does there is nothing to check but if it was a wet day, lightly spray it with WD40, before giving up and calling the club salvage vehicle or breakdown service.

Fuel System Breakdowns

Fuel issues mean problems with the Concentric or Monobloc, or upstream or downstream from it. The first question is, did the bike just cut out or did it fade away or run unevenly? Sudden stops or cut-outs sort the problem along the 'illness range' to the electrical system. Misfiring and fading away point to the fuel system, generally. Four fuel possibilities exist. The fuel-air mix has badly changed, the carburettor is flooded, dry or there's a blockage.

Fuel-Air Mix Has Changed Suddenly

The most likely cause is an air lever left closed for some miles. Blockages in the carb are unlikely but could be caused by one of the four Amal metering stages being disrupted by some fine tank rust or other dirt blocking a jet. It's also worth checking for a sticking throttle slide, by hearing it bottom out in the body when the twist grip is closed. The main or needle jet may have loosened, but this is unlikely. If it seems to be running lean, try your air lever as described earlier or cup a hand over the air intake. Also check the inlet and exhaust for any loose joints. If it's rich, take off the air cleaner and see if it makes a difference.

Flooding

This is unlikely but could be due to a leaking float, a stuck float or a faulty bowl needle, especially if a viton needle is not fitted. If drying the plug and clearing the cylinder of fuel don't help, then it's time to strip and check the bowl. Sometimes it's just worth waiting a while, and trying again.

Fuel Blockage

If there is fuel in the tank, that points to a blockage. If there's a clear plastic fuel filter in the line then you can see if fuel is clearing the tank and reaching the carburettor. Otherwise just undo a fuel line and see if fuel runs out. If there's a wait before it does, there may be a vapour lock in the line - a problem more likey to be encountered in summer downunder than in northern climes, or if you're riding an iron head sidevalver or a Sunbeam. A blocked tank cap breather is an outside pick but does happen. Also check the carb inlet filter is clear, especially if the tank hasn't been sealed. It's worth assuring the carb is clean, the jets are correct and the fuel is fresh and not out of an old watery drum. NB: It's always worth kicking over after every step, as some issues are subtle and may solve themselves.

Next step is to undo the bowl. On a concentric, undo the drainplug with a coin. Water in the bowl may be the cause and draining the fuel will fix this. If she still won't start, sniffing up the exhaust pipe will disclose whether fuel is reaching the cylinder and being pumped out the back. If you can smell raw fuel, it's time to stand back and give the fuel system a probable tick.

Mechanical System Breakdowns

Less common are outright mechanical problems, unless they're caused by accident. It is chastening to watch the accident statistics for older and born-again riders. Fortunately classic riders don't seem to figure in these statistics as much as BABs riding new and more powerful bikes. Maybe that makes us more responsible riders than we see ourselves?

Chains and cables are the common mechanical breakdowns on club runs, so let's deal with them first. The effects of a primary chain break aren't pretty. Likewise magneto chains unless you're lucky and they coil up tidily at the compartment bottom. Rear chain breaks are however more common. On a recent Rotorua Classic Club run two of us broke rear chains. Frankly it's a lottery when this happens, and you hope the chain uncoils behind you on the road. The nasty scenario is it wraps around one or both sprockets, pitching you off and/or damaging sprockets and/or cases. For simpler breaks, a spare spring link may get you home especially as the spring link is the most likely part of the chain to break. If there's no salvage vehicle and no spares, then a chain can be jury-rigged by a bolt or even nails substituting for a missing rivet. Wire can cover for a spring link for those few, gentle miles home.

Cables are easier to provide for, as discussed under tool kits. Some screw-on nipples and a length of inner cable deal with just about any break.

Tyre Breakdowns

With tyres, prevention is the best policy. Using a fibrous tyre sealant in every tyre works wonders. NeverFlat is one proven brand among several others. Some say such products harden in the tyre, lose efficacy and cause balance problems. That may be true of car sealants used in bike tyres. It doesn't happen with the correct sealant. A mate once picked up a nail in a sealed tyre in Melbourne. The tyre stayed up and he only noticed the nail as it went round banging on the frame. He pulled it out, the tyre self-sealed, and he rode home to Sydney. I rode round Australia with a sealant. Afterwards, I pulled out the tube to check and found the sealant in good condition. It's more or less essential on a Harley-Davidson with no centre stand. It is also prudent to ride with a tyre pump and repair outfit, and on long runs, to pack tyre levers. Having prevented punctures, there's not much to do at the roadside for the remaining issues, such as multiple broken spokes, shredded or burst tyres, major pothole rim damage etc. The mobile phone (cell phone) or CB radio is the best recourse.

Listening To The Engine

Recognising the sounds a classic engine emits can save a lot of worry and enables preventative maintenance to be taken before a catastrophe strikes. On the other hand, we've all got a tendency to read medical texts and imagine we have all the symptoms, so this section may cause distress, as well as relieve it. To become conversant with engine sounds, it's worth buying an auto stethoscope with a metal rod tip. They're available from auto outlets and electronics retailers (for example Jaycar in Australia) and they give better sound quality than the traditional mechanics' screwdriver. It's entrancing to hear the tremendous range of sounds an engines makes as it turns over. It's almost like being inside. The medical stethoscope is also fine, and can sometimes be picked up cheaply at boot sales.

Stethoscopes magnify sound. It's easy to be deafened, and preferable to first listen by turning the bike over by hand. If it's still too loud, then medical stethoscopes usually have a second or 'bell' head. Still too loud? Pinch off the main tube with a clothes peg, till the volume is right. The head can be removed and replaced with a short length of copper tube. Here are sounds to listen for:-

Tappets

The trick here is to isolate the noise to the rocker box region, simple with the stethoscope, but be careful of leaving the diaphragm on the hot engine! If you have a tachometer or rev-counter, you can hear the tappet noise at half the speed of the engine beat, but see below as that's still twice the exhaust beat on a single. It sounds a bit like a bunch of dwarves beating hammers inside a can, or very noisy cicadas.

False Tappet Noise

This sounds like a high-pitched rattle on idle, very much like valve noise. If it fades as engine revs increase, it may be a worn air valve in

Illus 9.17 Using a stethoscope to listen for a clicking alternator rotor

the carburettor. It's easy to check by removing the air cleaner and holding the throttle slide with a finger. If the sound stops, the cause is clear.

Knocks And Noises

Knocks and engine noises are said to occur 'at engine speed' or at 'half engine speed' or at least thats what the manuals say. How can we associate an anonymous knock in the hidden bowels of the engine, with something called 'engine speed'? And what is engine speed - the exhaust note or RPM or something else entirely?

Engine speed surely can only be counted from the beat of the engine which is what happens everytime the exhaust opens: the resultant 'bang' is what we actually hear.. In a four stroke engine the exhaust operates once every two revolutions and therefore the engine is running at twice the speed you hear from the exhaust note. Most riders, if asked would simply equate engine speed to revs per minute. For myself, I think I'll stick to RPM, as there's surely no question about counting how often the crankshaft revolves.

So when pundits say to 'beware a big end knocking at engine speed', all they can mean is that the rapidity of the knock increases with the 'engine speed' which for all practical purposes can be either RPM or the exhaust note.

There are two main 'knocks', the big-end and the little-end. Hearing the difference, more or less regardless of the engine speed makes them easy to diagnose.

Big End Knocking

If the big-end knock is caused by bearing play on the crankshaft, then it bangs once each time the piston changes direction, and it's probably louder on the combustion stroke, as the piston is fired down the barrel, to rebound up on the exhaust stroke.

So take the stethoscope and listen to that big end. If the 'scope has the narrow funnel-shaped end, as well as a flat face, apply the narrow end to the crankcase near the bearing, that is to the front or bottom of the cases.

With a friend to hold the bike on the stand, blip the throttle and listen for the knock to appear and then fade as the load comes on and then off the big end, as the revs go up and then down. You may even imagine a pattern in the knocking, if you listen long enough and get into the engine sounds. They can become hypnotic.

Now the characteristic sound of the big-end knock often presents as a cross between a low-pitched knocking note and a deep, rattling percussive sound. It's caused by the plain big end bearing surfaces breaking down, allowing free-play for the conrod to fling itself around the crankshaft. It's lower pitched than the small end note, and seems to be coming from lower in the engine than the small end sounds. It's nature is different to the main bearing basso profundo grumbling discussed below, which is more continuous. Often the big end shells are comparatively thin, and it's wise to pull over having identified this as a continuous sound, to avoid an engine write-off.

Little End Knock

The little end knock is another percussive sound higher in note than the big end, given it's a smaller assembly, and has no echo-chamber around it to magnify the sound, like the big end down inside the bass drum chamber of the crankcase. The little end is often just a bush, not a bearing. The key difference to the big end knock is that it's louder when the load is off the engine i.e. when coasting or over-running, and correlates with RPM. That's the thing to listen for, along with the higher pitched knock It's also usually quieter than the big end, wear for wear.

Gudgeon Pin Knock

this is very similar to little end knock but more audible when idling, when it makes a kind of 'guitar riff' of little knocks.

False Big-End Knock

One of the ways in which a stethoscope pays for itself is in distinguishing this sound. It's another loud rattling, clicking sound from the bottom end; one that can easily be misdiagnosed as an expensive big end. in fact it is likely to be the alternator rotor loose on it's shaft. It's a time-based wear item and rotors that have been spinning for 30 years are now loosening up on their shafts. It's the flexing, syncopated motion imparted to the rotor, out there on the end of the mainshaft, that gives the clicking sound. It starts quietly enough but if overlooked can get frighteningly loud, and was often overlooked by the early writers, as the problem really didn't present before the industry closed down. The Trident and Rocket 3 were perhaps the first bikes to widely exhibit the problem, and it was mostly dealt with by dealers. Now it's something every rider with an alternator ought keep in mind, when the subject of odd engine sounds is canvassed. Fortunately it's easy to remove the chain case and stator and give the rotor a heave-ho for any looseness. It's easier and cheaper than a big end! Replacement rotors are available, either NOS Lucas, or the Sparx jobs with rare earth magnets that out-perform the Lucas. While it's possible to repair the rotor by refixing it to it's shaft, who would bother with the ready availability of new pattern parts? The consequences of a rotor that loosens enough to collide with it's stator, and create havoc in a chain case, plus the likely shaft damage makes it worth investing in a new rotor.

Bottom End Grumbles

Whereas the big end gives a clear knocking sound, the main bearings and their journals give a characteristic low grumbling or rumbling sound when they're tired. The two or three main bearing assemblies are close together so the stethoscope is of limited use in localising the sound. However the big end and main bearing sounds are fortunately so different, they're almost unmistakable once heard. Also the mains have a harsher, vibratory note compared to the big end, that can often sound like quite a soft knock. An early sign is extra vibration before the sound is heard. You may feel the mains going as a more or less continuous grumbling from down there, sort of like a very upset tummy after bad prawns. The only good thing is there's a lot of metal in the bearing and you can expect to ride home, minimising load on that bearing.

Pinking/Pinging

This sound of pre-ignition was part and parcel of vintage and early classic motorcycling, and a reminder that the spark advance lever was too far advanced. With the advent of better fuels and oils and better designed engines in the classic years, it is not now a common classic problem, unless the bike's carburation or ignition is badly out, or the plug is way too hot or only finger tight. It's different to detonation but is related. It's that sonar-like pinging from the top end when the engine is struggling up hills, and there's 91 octane fuel in a 10.5:1 engine that should be on 95; and the main jet is 20-30 under size. The solutions can be that simple.

Piston Slap

A degree of piston Slap, is very common in aging classic bikes, especially when starting up on cold mornings, and where they're run less often so that the oil film on the cylinder decays. If it's a few thousand miles on from the last rebore and you ride in Winter, then most likely you'll hear what sounds like a big end on it's way out when the bike is first started. It's just innocent movement of the piston in the barrel, and disappears as soon as the engine warms up. On hot starts you never hear it. Adding Lucas oil stabiliser further controls the noise.

Grumbles And Whines

An unnoticed grumbling sort of vibration through your left footrest, can sometimes be traced to one of two or three causes, and none of them are a big end.

Primary Chain. An overly tight primary chain might give rise to a whining sound. If it's just after a service, then it's wise to check chain tension again, (at the tight spot). A tight chain does bad things for all bushes and bearings involved.

Gearbox Bearing. It could be a gearbox shaft bearing on the way out. Check the gearbox drain plug

Dry Primary Chain Case. Probably the most common cause of this noise is that the clutch and alternator are running dry and objecting. If there's still a chain oiler operating from the chain case, this becomes a prime suspect as it will empty the chaincase over the rear chain as it was designed to do.

BSA and Triumph, the two leaders of the UK industry, jointly stuck to chain oilers long after they ought to have jettisoned them. In BSA's case they continued building them until 1970-1971. There's pressure on the innocent restorer, encouraging us to install the kosher chain oiler fittings, of which plenty are still available. I wonder why? Before doing so, its worth reviewing the problems BSA and Triumph experienced in the USA market, caused by dry chain cases. As early as 1968, Triumph USA was directing all distributors to either blank off the oilers, by soldering if necessary, or to direct customers to refill their chain cases every 200 miles, as the oiler would drain the case within that time. Still BSA continued selling bikes with this redundant assembly for another two years, presumably out of old comfortable habit, and with no regard to their customers.

Slack Primary Chain. This causes a clicking sound that comes and goes caused by a too-loose chain, that is occasionally fouling either a screw boss in the primary chaincase, or the rear chain tipping part of the rear suspension or a centre stand tang.

Clutch Problems. An aging clutch can provide an ensemble of clatters, clicks, vibrations, knicks and knocks. Given the number of components and with many classic clutches dowsed in corrosive blowby gas from poorly designed BSA and Triumph engine breathers, it's not surprising the chaincase is a fruitful source of engine sounds.

Broken Rings And Sticking Valves. Both of these can give rise to a 'clicketty clacking' sound from the engine.

Camshaft And Cams. These can give rise to loud whirring sounds from low down in the engine. Unless the sound can be traced elsewhere, it may be time to strip down and inspect.

Fin Ringing. A mysterious ringing in the ears (no, it's not just tinnitus), it's possibly those alloy barrel fins tuning up a chorus. Fin ringing is pervasive. It's a high-pitched well, 'ringing sound' as you go down the road, a bit like a kangaroo whistle if you ride in Australia. (What's a kangaroo whistle? It's no joke, but a device fitted to the bike to warn kangaroos you're coming, and to keep them from hopping out onto your bike!) At certain engine speeds the fin harmonics are such that the fins can start ringing. It was only in 1971 that BSA introduced vertical ridges linking the fins, and so finally stopped their engines fin-ringing. Now we fit 'Roo Whistles' to produce the same ringing sound. Funny that. It's easy to fashion rubber tabs between the fins to stop this engine noise. Honda used to make such high-temperature tabs, and some dealers have old stock.

10 *Wherever Your Classic Bike Takes You*

"Near the NSW border the road fell into disrepair. Here lay the worst trap of the 8,000km trip. It was a long, invisible depression in the tar, at least a foot deep. At 95kph, it bottomed the front forks and then the rear shocks just as the far lip of the hole booted the Sportster front end into the air. Next, I and the back end of the bike were catapulted into the air. I recall doing a Rossi in mid-air looking down on the bike, which was also airborne. Somehow we landed, with my tackle as a shock absorber. Ouch. We groaned across the border into NSW and the road improved, as if the Queensland government left that bit as 'no mans land'..." RB 2005 Uluru Rally

Some of the keenest classic clubmen don't ride. It's true. Some guys get such a kick out of classic club life, restoring, haunting swapmeets and collecting parts, that they never get around to actually riding a bike. Others slip out of the habit of riding, whether due to age, family pressure, illness or lifestyle change. Those exceptions aside, it seems obvious to try and match a classic bike purchase with the types of riding that will follow. There's a catch-22 here for first time buyers though, because until a bike has been owned and ridden, it's often impossible to predict what kinds of riding will be undertaken. In any case riders have little idea of the capabilities of their first bike until much later perhaps even after they have sold it!.

There is one more uncharted group of classic riders who are never mentioned in the literature, but to whom the choice of first bike is absolutely vital. This group ride classic bikes, but usually only the one. They are often well educated. They love to talk about bikes and are the first to get involved in new runs or club escapades. What distinguishes them is that they evince no interest in things mechanical. This is such an article of faith for most classic bikers that this paradox can make others feel uncomfortable. It's not that these riders are inept or in any way unable to wield a spanner, they just have no interest in this aspect of classic bikery. For them, the classic attraction is compelling, but they seem to feed the passion in different ways to other riders. I know several riders who fit this mould, and respect them for their different approach. Here is a group of riders who are perhaps in love with the 'idea' of classic motorcycling versus the 'reality'. If you will, these riders may be best described as romantics. They romanticise motorcycling, and can achieve great things for the benefit of their colleagues, except when it comes to maintenance and breakdowns, then they are forced to depend on their clubmates for all assistance. If they are lucky, they find a tolerant spannerman, who doesn't mind helping out, and helping out some more. Some fairly 'odd couples' can form as a result. For these riders, it's even more important to choose a bike that complements their interests and it would make sense to seek out a bike notorious for it's reliability, paying a premium price for an outstanding restoration. Oh, and to take a good mate with them for the pre-purchase check. It's a good way also of recruiting the future mechanic cum ride partner!

In this chapter we'll take an overview of the major branches of classic bike riding, beginning with classic clubs.

The Classic Club Scene

Nearly every classic rider will belong to a classic club, and often to several clubs. Even riders who dislike riding in groups and rarely come to meetings, can value the support network, newsletters and cheap registration (in some parts of the world) that clubs offer. I'd guess the ratio of inactive but financial members to active riders and meeting attendees is about 3:1 or even 4:1 in some clubs. Club committees sometimes misread this and can feel threatened by the apparent disinterest. Some clubs attempt to legislate it out of their clubs by demanding minimum attendance frequencies, points schemes and suchlike. In the long run however, such negative incentives rarely work, especially with ornery bikers.

Classic clubs fall into two types, single marque clubs and those welcoming all makes and riders. How did so many single marque clubs come about? Some are easy to explain e.g. the Vincent and the Velocette marque clubs. These are high-value vehicles produced in small numbers, a very long time ago. They now require specialised parts and maintenance. Over fifty years have elapsed since the Vincent plant closed, and spare parts manufacture ceased in about 1975. The marque owners club then formed a company to supply spares and this has offered improved parts supply to Vincent owners internationally. This business model has been followed by other clubs to varying extents. Sometimes, single marque clubs break off from the general classic clubs because of the personalities involved or the perceived bureaucracy of the larger multi-marque classic clubs. Motorcycle riders can be an undisciplined, rebellious lot for whom club administration is such a low priority after riding that it fails to get even the minimum attention required.

Perhaps the underlying motivation is simply that marque riders have more in common with other riders of that marque, make and model, than they do with other marques. Given the typical classic owner's high priority on maintenance, improvements and restoration there is no substitute for having an experienced group of old hands on call for the particular model and year.

Club runs, rallies and 'Annual Days' provide a variety of riding experiences, with an automatic common interest for the mainly male riders. This helps overcome the social isolation men often feel, especially older men and those without a workplace affiliation. A classic club can meet the tribal need for men to congregate in an environment where there is a shared focus and all men on the floor are equal. For many men, a dose of this once or twice a month is sufficient to meet their socialising needs. In Chapter five the available research into just what attracts men into classic motorcycling was explored.

Illus 10.1 Lunch stop at a summer club run downunder, this one to Broke, NSW.

Some classic club runs are becoming shorter as the bikes age. This reduces wear and tear along with the breakdown risk, and ensures riders aren't far from home if the worst happens. The shortest runs tend to be the best attended. This is also true for those riding modern bikes. For example, my local Ulysses club musters 40-50 riders (a 50% turnout) every Saturday morning at a local coffee bar, where members stand around for an hour or two swapping yarns and coffee and inspecting the latest acquisitions. Often there's an ad hoc ride organised to, say the Road Warrior Cafe or Pie in the Sky on the Northern outskirts of Sydney, so as to be home by early afternoon. It's a very congenial life in clubs.

Solo Riding

In the city, it's better to ride in a group, or at least with a friend. You increase your silhouette, double the sound and become the fore and aft of a single larger vehicle. In the country however, from the accident point of view, I believe riders are safer riding alone. Riding in a group means riding to a set of rules. It therefore raises stress levels, as it also forces riders to take responsibility or at least account of those in front and behind. For some riders it somehow dilutes the enjoyment of the ride. It's distracting and that can be dangerous.

Riding in groups repays these negatives by providing comfort and backup for breakdowns and 'laydowns'. On those classic bikes which are shall we say, less well maintained this can be a comfort for that rider when he breaks down, even as it inconveniences those who prepared better for the ride.

Group riding also provides an audience and entertainment at breaks. Many ordinarily taciturn bikers become unstoppably garrulous after a morning's ride. Others retard their conversation as they enjoy the afterglow of the ride. Groups usually find an equilibrium, and sometimes a pecking order. They also tend to encapsulate riders. The group is a 24/7 thing, often to the detriment of meeting interesting new people along the way. A group of leather clad bikers tends to meet mainly service station and fast food staff. In that way it's like a guided tour on a bus, efficient but formulaic. Solo riding helps overcome this and the rider will meet more new people.

Illus 10.2 A good reason to ride alone! 1,200 bikes wait an hour for fuel, in 30C heat at Eridunda, near Alice Springs, Australia.

Motorcycling, like bungee-jumping, is a thrilling activity designed to be carried out alone. The main difference with a bike is that you can change your mind about the route as you go along. Such freedom can only be enjoyed on solo rides, as on group rides, the route is ordained. Solo riding allows riders to concentrate on the road and the bike and the time. Many riders find the best 'flow' when riding alone, reason enough for many riders to prefer it.

Rallies

What is it about Classic Motorcycle Rallies? The memory of my first rally is still waiting to be filed. We started on the 1,000km drive/ride to the All British Rally (the biggest British-only rally downunder, attracting 1000+ riders in 2006) at 10pm one Friday night. We arrived at 11.30am the next day on the rally site. This is in an old stock holding area and, along with hundreds of other happy campers we pitched our tents over a carpet of sheep droppings, amongst gum trees notorious for dropping boughs without warning. It was a bad drought and for the first 500kms we had seen no green thing along the roads. After driving all night we were now weary and after a quick look around, lay down for a nap. We woke up at dusk, and started socialising with neighbours. Soon the big bonfires started up and the R&B band on the semi-trailer wound up their guitars and Marshalls. The good ladies in the food section kept up the supply of bacon & egg sandwiches all evening. The beer tent kept the queues short. The one shower was surprisingly empty. I've since noticed the amazing tolerance amongst motorcyclists (self included) towards dirt and malodorous clothing. The chill evening passed in a syncopated blur of beer, sandwiches and earnest conversations about old bikes and regalia. I made a batch of mulled wine over a camp cooker that pleased my colleagues. More experienced companions systematically worked the rally ground, from campfire to campfire, bike to bike, all evening and long into the middle reaches of the night. Occasionally a bike would roar into life as pumped up riders ignored the rally rules about riding after dark. Men, women and children sat around log fires in the encampment. Sons brought fathers. There was nary a Japanese bike or Harley to be seen.

By midnight the band was ground shaking, the temperature well down into single figures and the evening became quite surreal. The Victoria bitter beer forced me out of my sleeping bag at 4am, and I trudged through a chill and motionless landscape. Every tree sheltered sleeping hobbits amongst the roots. It was like ground zero. There were fires burning everywhere, with the flames the only movement. Figures lay around them in leathers, passed out on the cold ground. No need for sleeping bags or tents here. The scene reminded me of Hunter Thompson's description of the Hell's Angels 1965 Bass Lake run, at the same hour.

On Sunday morning it was early to rise, and extraordinary figures emerged. Family units were interspersed with feral figures in the backs of trucks. Everyone was moving again. I never saw a raised voice that weekend except in laughter or song. All drunkenness was benign. It was like Woodstock with leathers, and without rain. A truly filthy unkempt, bearded wild man crawled out of the back of a matching truck, and rolled an immaculate AJS single down a plank to win the major prize. He then rolled it back up again and drove off. The contrast between man and bike was so pronounced I wondered if there was some transference process that goes on amongst the very best restorers. A sort of Dorian Gray process where restorers invest so much of themselves in their concours winning bikes, that they diminish themselves in the process. A process where the 'dishabille' of the basket case transfers to the owner, as the bike again takes pristine shape. Something like this is known in Japanese salarymen, who invest so much time in their career, that when retirement comes they are unknown to their family and christened 'Grey Ghosts' as they flit about their unfamiliar house, without purpose. I notice myself dressing less well since I started restoring bikes, and my wardrobe is migrating into the garage as the need for rags increases, so I may be at risk.

Illus 10.4   A nice Vincent and it's owner still abed at a rally downunder.

The only official rally event we actually saw was the prize giving where one of our members won the furthest traveled for his 1,300km odd journey on an original A65. He strapped the big trophy in it's box onto his pillion seat, raising the question... why do they award such bulky rally trophies, especially for the furthest traveled? They must know he had no space on the bike. He set off back on those 1300 kms, much later arriving home on one cylinder; with the last set of his original points frozen shut. But he made it. Seemingly just as we were settling in we packed up, having been at the rally barely 24 hours. Another 1,000km drive in the old van and a night on the club president's floor at Walla Walla and we were home from that first rally.

The next year, I missed it for some plausible reason. The team that went had a great and terrible time, with a series of damaged tyres stretching their run. After the second puncture they found the bikes had shifted on the trailer, and an errant M20 stand tang was abrading the left tyre. They'd holed their last spare tyre before noticing the cause, so had to wait four hours for the NRMA (RAC equivalent in Australia) to bring out a third tyre. They finally arrived at the Rally site just as dusk was falling on Saturday. They were so tired they lay down for a nap, and woke up on Sunday morning, missing the rally altogether. Still they said they had a good time. I wonder what it is about rallies.

Concours

Some riders have no interest in concours events, while others love winning prizes. There's no single right way. My first two restorations won trophies. To be honest, this illustrates the tactical value in choosing to restore unpopular bikes such as small BSA Unit singles. Still, on both occasions I felt like I'd graduated again, only better because my peers knew more about what they were awarding and what I'd done to get there. It's a transparent process, that adds to it's emotional impact.

Real concours bikes call for real money and are often rarely ridden. I guess that underlies the trend towards multiple ownership of classic bikes. If the best bike is too valuable to risk riding, riders have to buy something else that can be ridden. The second bike is developed to a similar build state, and the process goes on till there's a stable of unridable bikes. Fortunately there are sufficient classic bikes available to meet the need for both applications.

Illus 10.5 A pristine Indian at beautiful Lake Okataina in NZ; the best Rally site I visited, and they even carved a hot glazed ham for dinner!

Illus 10.6 Voted 'Best Bike' at a recent Kiwi rally, a lovely twin-port BSA.

Illus 10.7 A beautiful Triple-Triton at a rally in NZ last year.

Offroad Riding And The VMX Scene

Australia and New Zealand are ideal countries for taking classic motorcycles off-road. The climate, size, sparse population and strong motorcycling traditions of both countries ensures plenty of prime dirt track, and motocross circuits are placed within reach of major population centres. Dirt-biking with old and new machines is extremely popular with all age groups and demographics. One can stand at the entrance to any Australian city at the weekend and count the number of bike trailers with off-road bikes two and four-up, heading for a favoured piece of farmland or wilderness. Not surprisingly, there is a growing scrambles and vintage motocross movement in most Australian states and around New Zealand. It's developed to the point where it warrants its own book.

The first question is, what's the difference between scrambling, trials and vintage motocross (VMX)? To an observer the differences may not be obvious. All involve older, very dirty machines and riders careering around some fairly rough tracks or courses. Scrambling is an older term for the sport. Motocross partly superseded it during the 1970s-1980s although in both countries downunder, there are scrambles clubs and motocross clubs today. The line is somewhat blurry. Scrambling caters more specifically to an earlier time in motorcycling with classes for bikes made prior to, and during the period 1960-1975. Vintage Motocross tends to kick off later and deals with bikes made during in the 1980s and '90s. To this extent, scrambles are more likely to feature classic British bikes. Scrambling sees itself as not quite so competitive as VMX, defining itself as being 'the great fun of [vintage] motocross without the hassles of having to be serious'. Trials on the other hand, are not about racing. It's just the rider pitted against 'an obstacle course of boulders, streams, huge hill climbs, logs, drop offs, and nearly anything else they can find...'

according to Trials aficionados. There are estimated to be a thousand or more active trials riders round Australia, with classes for Classic and Post-Classic bikes. A useful entree is via www.trials.com.au for downunder riders.

In Australia, the local VMX clubs and offroad sections of motorcycle clubs are grouped under state clubs or registers. In NSW, the main club is Heaven. In Victoria it's VIPER, the Victorian Pre-1980 Evolution Motocross Register, who represent twelve or more clubs in that state alone. Western Australia has a new club in 2006, the EVOMXWA. Tasmania has the Tassie Scramble Club. Probably a hundred VMX events are staged around Australia annually under the auspices of Motorcycling Australia. VMX has its own machine categories in Australia and the Victorian VIPER categories are shown below, by way of an example.

Pre 1978   All mx/trail/enduro motorcycles manufactured prior to the January 1,1978 and designated 1977 models or earlier.

Pre 1980   All mx/trail/enduro motorcycles manufactured prior to the January 1, 1980 and designated 1979 models or earlier (excludes pre 1975).

Pre 1985   All mx/trail/enduro motorcycles manufactured prior to the January 1, 1985 and designated 1984 models or earlier (excludes pre 1980).

Pre 1990   All mx/trail/enduro motorcycles manufactured prior to the January 1, 1990 and designated 1989 models or earlier (excludes pre 1985).

Evolution   All mx/trail/enduro motorcycles that were 'originally' manufactured with air cooled engines, drum brakes, and non linkage suspension. No later components, e.g. powervalve cylinders, upside down or cartridge forks etc, can be adapted. There are no travel limits, year cut offs, or performance indexing.

The category clustering around the 1970-1990 period is no accident. Enthusiasts see it as a period of rapid advances in off-road bike technology, one that underpins today's motocross machines. As well as the supply of machines available for restoration, they point to innovations such as mono-shock suspension, water cooling, disc brakes and power valves during the period. The same motivations drive these restorers along with restorers of classic British and Japanese road bikes. There's the added appeal of working on a race bike that may have a provenance, rather than a generic road touring machine. Their meetings are characterised by bold, aggressive competition along with that familiar dose of sentiment encountered in other riding experiences. There are usually events for Clubman, Intermediate, and Expert Riders and races are often short three lappers. Events are normally held at weekends on authentically designed motocross tracks.

The sport is extremely well coordinated via local and state clubs and registers via the national OZ VMX Website www.ozvmx.com. The sport is also fortunate in having the premier world vintage motocross magazine 'VMX' headquartered in Sydney and on the web at www.vmxmag.com.au. This very classy bound magazine appears to have hit on the right recipe, format and positioning to attract reader and advertising support from around the globe. It's distinguished by it's heavy paper stock, contributing to astonishing photographic standards, and it's board stock covers, unmatched by any classic bike magazine. VMX magazine draws on a large stable of writers to fashion a mix of technical, race reporting and sentimental journey stories, and readers regard each issue as collectors' items. Production costs are clearly high, and the magazine is premium priced by nearly a third. It is a model other classic bike magazines might study, and it prospers where other downunder classic bike mags have come and gone.

In New Zealand, given its preeminent position in classic motorcycling, we'd expect a healthy off-road scene and indeed there is. The Classic Scrambles Club has been organizing meetings since about 1989. The younger Kiwi Vintage Motocross movement has grown quickly to more than a dozen clubs all over the country, with the aim of promoting '...the restoration and riding of vintage, pre 1980 (evolution class) & pre 1985 motocross bikes in New Zealand....'. In March 2006, the New Zealanders held their inaugural British Bike Dirt Day at a town called Marton. Organiser Rob Cochrane, (moonlighting from his other job at the BSAOCNZ), capped his masterly work organising the BSA centenary celebrations the year before, by assembling some rare and exciting offroad machines. These included a brand new 1964 Cheney 500 Triumph, the 1965 Cheney DBD34 GoldStar - one of only three produced, and the 1968 G85

Illus 10.8 1964 Cheney Triumph 500 at Marton VMX, NZ. Picture courtesy of R Cochrane

Illus 10.9 Cheney Goldstar at Marton VMX, NZ. Picture courtesy of R Cochrane

Illus 10.10 1968 Rickman Metisse at Marton VMX, NZ. Picture courtesy of R Cochrane

powered Rickman Metisse. This later machine was the last British Bike to win the NZ MX Title circa 1970. These bikes are pictured above.

The aim of the British Bike Dirt Day was to display the machines in the pits at a major VMX event, assemble the owners and show off some machines in action. The race track was judged unsuitable for old bikes on the day, but the BSA A65MX, B44 and B50 riders enjoyed themselves along with the Trackmaster, Matchless and Rickman riders. The day was so well attended it's being repeated with the 2007 British Bike Dirt Day 'Grand National' at Wanganui on Sunday March 4th. The 2007 event, will take place as this book goes to press, and is to include grass/dirt, flat-track and TT racing plus a Classic Trial. This event forms a 'classic trifecta' with the Circuit racing at Pukekohe and Street racing at Paeroa. This trifecta should attract even more overseas visitors downunder to the land of the Long White Cloud. I confess my only intentional off-road riding was confined to a more informal sort of race:

My Off-Road Racing Resume

In 1965 I rode my Ariel to a Guy Fawkes party at the Teachers Training College outside Auckland. It was an exuberant time and David, another young man there from Napier had a Vincent 1000. As young men do, we stoutly defended our marques and, probably due to some fomentation by third parties, we agreed to settle the matter by a chicken run through a large bonfire, with pillions aboard to add interest and increase the stakes.

We lined up about fifty yards away from the blaze amid the crowd of cheering drunken student-teachers. At age seventeen, it felt great to be the centre of attention. Dodging revelers as they silhouetted against the roaring fire, we raced towards the flames. We were neck and neck at full throttle in second gear, over the rough grass. I was on the outside, to the left of the Vincent. He faced squarely, and unwisely at the fire's centre. The Ariel accelerated with the Vincent, but only just. As we neared the fire, reality started to dawn. From the corner of my right eye I suddenly saw the Vincent drop short of the fire and guessed the rider had chickened out and laid her down, or his pillion had leapt clear and caused the drop. In that last second, I decided I'd won, and joined his discretion by veering left, passing through the edge of the flames, and coming to a halt just before we hit a dormitory building. My pillion was very relieved, and the bike unharmed, save for a smell of burnt rubber.

Circuit And Road Racing 2006: A Classic Racing Season Downunder

I find the idea of racing a classic bike intensely appealing, and only two things are holding me back. Firstly, I don't like to ride fast, and secondly, I don't like riding in a crowd. When they invent events to cater for such riders, please sign me up. Meantime why not review the 2006 classic racing season downunder?

There are more than a dozen classic motorcycle clubs in New Zealand and this is no surprise, given the enormous density of classic bikes conserved there. The annual, three-day Classic Festival at Pukekohe circuit south of Auckland, is the ideal choice for that first club run of the year in February. Now in it's 27th consecutive year, the racing draws entries from every classic country around the world. Over 300 riders competed in 42 races in 2006 and over 400 in 2007.

Club riders converge from all over New Zealand, ferrying their bikes across Cook Strait in a similar fashion to British riders and their seaborne leg to the Isle of Man. Wily campaigners send an advance party up early on the Friday practice day to secure a front row camping site. The Hill Stand area is favoured as this

Illus 10.11 (Left) Graeme Cole and No. 9 at Pukekohe. His favourite from the ten or so 350cc classic racers he's built from Triumph 3TA bikes, virtually creating his own class.

Illus 10.12 (Right) A Brace of Pukekohe racers, 1929 Harley Peashooter and Velocette KNS

Illus 10.13 (Left) In the Pukekohe Pits with the Scott Owners Club

overlooks the pits and the start/finish line. On a Saturday night, it's as noisy as the Mountain at Mount Panorama in Bathurst Australia used to be in the 1980s, till the police cracked down on the fun. To be fair though, I've not heard of riders towing logs and drunken mates around the Pukekohe carpark at night, nor blowing up the toilets, nor the traditional assault on the police compound at sunset on the Saturday, as at Bathurst.

The New Zealand organisers correctly christen it a festival, as it's much more that a race meeting. Stretching over three full days and nights, it includes a range of satellite activities. This year for example, it celebrated the sixth British marque centenary, that of BSA. A marquee loaded with the full range of classic Beezas, and a unique educational exhibit drew visitors and families all weekend. Rob Cochrane, Bill Dempster and other enthusiasts from the BSAOCNZ, entertained visitors with the achievements of the marque, while Gold and other Stars thundered past outside.

Illus 10.14 Hugh Anderson, Rob Cochrane and the author at the BSA
Centenary Marquee at Pukekohe, New Zealand.

The 'Sidecar Spectacular' was for many, the highlight of the weekend. Some forty-two outfits competed, including Australian and British machines. The NZCMRR Sidecar Section is one of the keys to the success of the Festival, being a huge spectator draw. It also negotiates sponsorships to support the overseas outfits at the meeting. It is noteworthy their numbers have grown by a third in twenty years, and even back then they were considered a big, successful group. They're fast as well, just 4 seconds behind the best solos on that famous 2.8km circuit.

Illus 10.15 The 'Fast Lady', David White's very quick Vincent Outfit.

Special classic machines are part of the prescription and this year it was a world-class mix. Sunday demonstration laps by Norman White on the Peter Williams John Player Norton, followed Peter's entertaining presentation the evening before. Four other John Player Nortons living in New Zealand joined the parade, with one lucky rider enjoying a ride aboard the Williams machine. A Mike Hailwood 1967 Honda 500, a Britten, an Imola Ducati and the current Kiwi world record outfit holder at 272kph (169mph) were there, along with the Trials Register display, and a smallish trade area. Perhaps the only thing missing was a full swapmeet.

For me though, one rider and his bike best summed up the attraction of classic motorcycling for us all. I snapped him on his BSA Sloper in racing trim, leading the muster for the BSA Centenary Parade. He was too much in the moment to disturb for an interview. I learned later he had just turned 90 years of age and was riding the bike he'd owned most of his life. He inspired every rider around him, and it's all there, in the gleam of his eye in the photo below.

Illus 10.16 That classic gleam in the eye.

Street Racing

Like most countries, Australia long-ago banned motorcycle street racing on safety grounds. Downunder, Paeroa's Hacksaw circuit and Wanganui in New Zealand's North Island keep the memories alive, and healthy. At the perhaps better known Paeroa event last summer, some 182 bikes thrashed the narrow town streets, reaching 250-275kmh (155 mph plus) down Belmont Road, the town's usual main street. A number of riders backed up from Pukekohe the week before. The risks of road versus race circuits were typified on the day by the variable road surfaces encountered by riders. At key points on the Paeroa circuit, e.g. at the entrance to Dunlop Straight, the tar had unaccountably been freshly patched. The fresh wet asphalt finish soon became dodgy on the S-Bend exit. A large section of it sloughed away during the hot day, forcing riders to alter their line, or fishtail wildly as they accelerated through the gooey mess up Dunlop Straight.

Illus 10.17 Paul Dobbs' Goldstar among the crowds at Paeroa

Illus 10.18 Honda closes Jawa 350 at Paeroa 2006

The close racing between for example Andrew Stroud and Craig Shirriffs gave downunder riders a good feel for the Isle of Man, as Paeroa is a small town surrounded by farming country. Contributing to the feel was the ability to stand at a friendly bar on the main straight with a great Kiwi beer, and watch the riders at full chat almost close enough to touch. This all delighted the huge crowds, some said over 20,000 spectators attended this year. Looking at the thousands of parked bikes, and the crowd of curious riders surrounding my own smart little Triumph T25SS, I could believe it! For older spectators, it was a gas to see Ginger Molloy back on the card, with his fast Bultaco. Paul Dobbs, an international and a current UK champion on a very quick 1960 Goldie and an earlier 500 BSA made us close our eyes and remember our youth, as that Castrol 'R' aroma spread around the course.

The Paeroa event triangulates the month-long Australasian racing series. This had started with the New Zealand Classic Motorcycle Racing Register's 27th meeting at Pukekohe the week before. Paeroa was closely followed by the Post-Classic Racing Association of NSW's meeting at Eastern Creek circuit outside Sydney, Australia just three weeks later. Where else in the world can you see three international classic race meetings within four weeks, over a great mix of circuits, and all within a couple of hours fly-riding time? Travel agents ought to begin offering packages for Northern Hemisphere tourists on this one, especially given so many British riders come down-under for it already.

After Paeroa there's time to head for the third trans-Tasman leg, in 2006 at Sydney's Eastern Creek, for the Post Classic Racing Association of NSW's 'Barry Sheene Memorial Meeting'. Still enthused by the classic racing at Pukekohe and Paeroa, I fired up the BSA B44SS and joined a Ulysses run to the meeting in 30 degree heat. The Eastern Creek circuit is similar in design to Pukekohe, although a kilometer longer. If you imagine Pukekohe with a long sweeper replacing Castrol Corner, and the pit area being pushed out around a low hill, into a cloverleaf shape, then that's Eastern Creek. The traffic goes anti- clockwise, which is handier for classic singles with low-mounted right-side megaphones. Unlike Pukekohe, (where the traffic is clockwise with 75% right-hand turns), fully half the Creek bends are left turns - even Harley-Davidsons can race there!

The classic event classification is a lot different here than in New Zealand, with a classic being defined as something pre-1968, and with a category for pre-1950 bikes. There are categories also for BEARs, Forgotten Era, Class C, and New Era 1 & 2 - all very confusing but great fun with some Kiwi riders coming over from Pukekohe such as Dave Cole. Paul Smart was also down on the list of 42 races.

It was hot and sweaty work that morning as for many clubmen, the racing took second priority to the swap-meet in the carpark. The swap-meet and a 'Show and Shine' competition were included in the £6 fee. To give UK/US readers a taste of parts and prices downunder, here is my tally for the morning.

A box of NOS BSA Unit Single parts for £19. This contained ex-RAAF parts in original wrappers stored for over 30 years. The last military BSA B40 was auctioned off and replaced by Suzukis sometime around 1976. In the box were over 120 different parts including bearing and shaft bushes, thrust washers, chaincase & crankcase plugs, condensers, footrests, engine steadies, bearings, and even a nice big end. It seemed a bargain, providing I could get it all in my backpack!

A pair of good narrow, chrome shock absorber shrouds £6,

An 'as new' boxed Moore & Wright 0-2" micrometer with spare anvils £9,

Heaps of UK classic magazines, including Classic Mechanics. 3 for £2, and that's all I could carry in my backpack.

Race spectators are well served at Eastern Creek which has a suspended concrete deck on top of the pits. This is right over the starting grid and opposite good covered stands. The circuit swings back in close to the back of the pits, and spectators cross to the rear of the deck to watch the action along the rear of the circuit. That's a big plus, as from here you can survey, I guess nearly three quarters of the circuit.

Illus 10.19 McMillan's quick Esobed at the Creek

About 130 bikes raced that weekend, less than half the field at Pukekohe. There was great pit access and many racers were happy to stop and give you the history of their machines. Among the terrific machinery, Fraser McMillan's 'Esobed' caught my eye. This is a very nice Norton ES2 engine in a featherbed frame, hence ES-O-Bed. It was fast too, chasing down Matchless G50's and Manx Nortons for a third place in the main event. Replica machines were about, and in one pit I came across several boxes of Matchless case and barrel castings ready for assembly into new racers. If you're coming to Sydney I recommend staying on for this weekend in mid-March to catch Eastern Creek, and it's less than an hours drive from the airport.

Every racer I interviewed said the same thing, they race for the fun of it. They say it cannot be compared with any other road riding, or even track days and the intensity of the experience is what brings them back to the circuits. Interestingly, most of the racers were close to, or over retiring age and the hot day was taking a physical toll despite the drink coolers and the blower fans. Yet every last one of them was happy to answer questions about their creations and let strangers wander around their works. Age is no drawback as among the eldest I interviewed were the most overtly competitive. Questions of expense and of value or prudent budgeting were dismissed with the counter that on a comparative basis to say car or boat racing, their outlay was small and the payoff gained just as substantial. Speed is surprisingly often not the prime consideration. Each race I saw, contained several different types of racer. Firstly, those at the highest level, with natural ability and significant capital and time to devote to developing their art. These men had a certain quiet gravity, or seriousness, along with their grey chest hair and leathers unzipped to the waist. Such men might have up to £40,000 involved in their pursuit, and for them it is the mainstream of their life in retirement or semi-retirement. They are almost professionals.

Others, often a decade younger, were technically just as capable as the first echelon, but were often with machines that required just a little less capital and time involvement. Such riders often seemed to have other lives requiring their time and capital. They also are accomplished riders and follow the circuits. A third group, often younger again, clearly have family and work commitments and racing is more a hobby, often with distinctive machines that are part of a tribal sub-network. The classic Harley Davidson racing group is a fine example of this. These enthusiasts compete with Harley WLAs from the 1940s and early Sportsters amongst other machines, in the Unlimited Clubman Classic Pre-1968 class. A group of twenty are taking their wonderful old machines to compete at Daytona and a couple of other American circuits in 2007, along with their own cheer-squad. Classic racers with original rather than replica engines, sometimes find their old components finally letting go, as in the story of:

A Seizure Survived

Bill D. took up motorcycle road racing back in the 1950s and really never stopped winning club and regional races until just a couple of years past. His favoured engines were BSA Stars, with frames he adapted from stock BSA frames imported from as far away as Perth. In one of his last races at Pukekohe, he told me how he felt when his engine blew and locked up at 116mph on the main back straight. "the rod came out the left crankcase with a shower of hot metal fragments spraying along behind me. I thought this is really serious, I'll have to walk back and pick up all the parts to put her back together again..." Bill and his Star will race again in 2008. Like Captain Kirk of Star Trek fame, he said he really wasn't scared at all, having a certain feeling that he was never meant to end his life on a race-track. He was able to simply de-clutch and bring her safely to a halt and she's shown resting below in Illus 10.20.

Illus 10.20 The BSA as she finished her last race, with fractured crankcase.

Very Long Distance Riding

Australia is a big country, and long-distance riding, with it's attendant records and their breaking was an early focus for riders. Harley-Davidson and Indian motorcycles and sidecar outfits were initially favoured, laying down a fashion that remains with Australian riders to this day. Harley-Davidsons still feature prominently in Australian classic survival statistics, as do Indians in New Zealand.

Today's Iron Butt Association (www.iron butt.com) follows in this tradition by sanctioning long distance touring. Their 'Saddlesore 1000' requires 1000 documented miles to be ridden within 24 hours. While tiring and hazardous, the pioneers nearly four generations ago had to also address other challenges, beginning with navigation as roads were often absent altogether. A favourite early downunder route was the 'overland' route from West to East across Australia, a distance of approx 3,500 miles (5,600 kms) depending on route. By 1924 the Perth-Sydney overland record stood at 7.5 days, held on an Indian outfit by Ford and Watson. Not all such journeys were for records. In 1926 a group of 16 Perth riders on Harley 10/12 outfits, christened 'the Overlanders', rode the return journey of 7000 miles from Perth to Sydney and back, taking 27 days for the outward leg. They had no major breakdowns, despite traveling in the high summer temperatures. The next year, two of these riders, Cunningham and Cracknell, attempted the transcontinental record on a new 600cc Harley 10/12 outfit. They made the Perth-Sydney run in 6.1 days, lowering the record by 33 hours. Interestingly in those days, the police issued racing permits to riders attempting such rides. Two years later, perhaps the greatest ever Australian motorcycle ride took place. Bowers and Smith made the first circumnavigation of Australia, riding a new Harley-Davidson outfit, in eleven weeks. The distance now on modern roads is about 9000 miles (15,000kms) but they would have traveled a great deal further than that. Such sanctioned rides are history now, but unofficially the bike circumnavigation time is down to under a week.

In New Zealand, the country scale and topography does not lend itself to such long distance riding. Those riders with a yen for long rides tend to do it offshore. One of the most creditable such rides was that by septuagenarians Molloy and Hurdemann, who rode a Panther and a Norton 12,000kms from China to the Netherlands in 2005. Molloy wrote a delightful book about their extraordinary ride. (His *The Last Hurrah* is coincidentally also published by Panther Publishing Ltd.) Back in 1930, in New Zealand it took my father four long days and nights riding on his BSA, to cover just 1000kms, as recounted in this extract from the true story of:

The Barrytown Christmas Ride

My father was riding his BSA 250cc 'B' series home for Christmas 1930, from Barrytown, in the South Island to Whakatane in the North Island, passing through the Murchison earthquake zone.

"...The challenge to Lyle for Christmas Eve 1930 was to cover another 440 kms, this would be more than twice the daily mileage he'd achieved over the previous three days. If he'd calculated his average daily mileages so far, he'd have been worried to see he was still 15-20 riding hours from home, and the chances of a fourth straight day without punctures, serious accidents or mechanical breakdown, must have seemed unlikely. While roads in the more populous North Island might be generally in better repair, he still had to tackle some of the island's roughest roads, of which the aptly named 'Desert Road' would be the worst. He would ride through a part of New Zealand that would, seventy years later be chosen as a set for Tolkien's Mordor. It's still easy to see the Emyn Muil and Gorgoroth, embedded in that desert country..." A.C. Bunn Christmas 1930.

Illus 10.21 My mother and the BSA that made the Barrytown Christmas Ride, 1930.

In 2005, I joined a small Ulysses group and signed up for the 2005 Australian HOG Rally to Ayers Rock in Central Australia. This went clockwise from Sydney via Victoria, South Australia, and the Northern Territory to Alice Springs, and thence back through Queensland into NSW. It was mostly on rural highways and secondary tarred roads, including some metal. That 8,000km ride taught me a lot about human nature as well as about riding. I saw two kinds of riders on that trip, firstly those who had no aims other than riding their bike, and the further the better in any direction. The second kind are those who when booked into a Rally, like to know where they're going and also when they might get there. Arranging a lengthy group ride, without recognising these different rider requirements is a recipe for angst along the way. Undertaking such long large-group rides without adequate research and planning simply increases the level of risk for all involved.

As scribe for the trip, here are my trip diary conclusions, to consider for such future long rides.

- Salvage vehicles aren't necessay. They break down more than the bikes.
- Support vehicles need co-drivers. We lost solo drivers to falling asleep.
- Planning /communication/ navigation increase with group size.
- The Ride Leader must ride full-time, or else appoint a Co-Leader.
- Rider Briefings should be held each morning with attendance mandatory.
- A 'Tail End Charlie' must be appointed.
- The vehicles convoy or split into fast and slow groups, to avoid KUFO.
- Waypoints and refuelling stops need to be clearly communicated .
- A navigator must be appointed for research, planning, and briefings.
- Only primary maps are trustedworthy. Secondary maps may have errors.

- The convoy will normally scatter over 50kms of road.
- Mobile phone and CB radio communications will break down.
- Use Despatch Riders as a communications fallback.
- Fatigue, stress and poor leadership fracture even groups of close friends.
- Harley Sportsters make fine long-distance tourers with a few mods.

International Riding

As the world shrinks, more downunder riders are riding in other countries. UK and European riders with land or channel borders have been doing this since Pioneer days. For those in the 'New World' the costs and hurdles have only recently been breached, enabling the start of mass-travel by riders and their bikes. The downunder innovator is Dave Milligan and his 'Get Routed' service between Australia and New Zealand, now in it's ninth year.. Get Routed probably shifts some 500-1,000 Australian bikes and riders annually, going as far as the Isle of Man. That number again would be handled by road and racing club transits across the Tasman Sea, as discussed in chapter four. On top of this are the individuals undertaking longer overseas runs, usually the overland routes between Australia and the UK. These riders traverse the same routes their parents did in the 1960s, when the route became popularised with hippies traversing it with Tolkien in hand, sampling botanical preparations along the way. Riders like Marriott, Simon and Thoeming have amply captured the special nature of such riding. Interestingly, Ted Simon of *Jupiter's Travels* fame, wrote a sequel twenty years later called *The Gypsy in Me*. This is not as well read by bikers, as Simon set aside his Triumph for the second trip. He comments, "...while a bike had made me usefully vulnerable to the natural hazards of huge undeveloped continents like Africa and South America, here (in Eastern Europe) it would have the reverse effect. It would shield me from trouble and move me too quickly..." He walked instead. He did return to motorcycling in 2003, when he reprised his first grand trip. That other classic motorcycling icon, Robert Pirsig, also wrote a twenty year sequel to his *Zen and the Art of Motorcycle Maintenance* The sequel *Lila*, is also disappointing for bikers, the only mention of motorcycling is a vignette about a meeting with Robert Redford on the film rights to Zen. Zen defied conversion to a screenplay, despite the attempts of several writers. Ten years on, a lot of options have been sold, but Zen still hasn't made it to screen. We may never see it.

As motorcycling circumnavigations are widely achieved, and the McGregor & Boorman *Long Way Round* epitomises these, what challenges are left for today's classic rider? Perhaps the last great riding challenges remain in Antarctica. For this reason, in September 2006 I founded the ANZACE Expedition, the Australia and New Zealand Auto Cycle Expedition. The objectives for ANZACE include making the first bona fide return transit by motorcycle to the South Pole, and celebrating the 50th anniversary of Sir Edmund Hillary's first automotive transit to the pole in

1957, during the first International Geophysical Year. We plan to retrace the Hillary route, or an alternate route with a small group of motorcycles during the second International Geophysical Year, over 2007-2008. Planning is already underway. The are a couple of motorcycling precedents in the Antarctic. In 1948 Gilchrist first rode an Indian down a plank onto the shore of Heard Island, and bounced briefly up the beach, before falling off. He properly claimed to be the first to ride a bike in Antarctica, albeit briefly and not actually on the continent. In 1991 Kazama claimed to have ridden a Yamaha to the South Pole. This claim was self-reported. Recent correspondence from the ground-force at the time indicates the claim might more accurately have been for the first motorcycle to be carried on a sled, by skidoo to the South Pole. The challenge to actually ride the first motorcycle all the way, unaided to the South Pole and back appears still unachieved at this time. Preliminary research and expedition planning, as well as advice from leading long-distance riders and explorers, indicates that the ride, while hazardous is also feasible. Anyway, it couldn't be more dangerous for motorcyclists than Thailand during the Songkran Festival week as recounted in the story:

Ride-Water-Die

The Songkran or Water festival in Thailand is terrific fun, but it's also the biggest single motorcycling road kill event in the world. Every April, hundreds of motorcyclists die during the festival week. In 2002 when I last visited, 800 riders were declared dead during the week. In 2006, it was 400, with twice that many injured. As Thailand is a 'top five' world motorcycle producer, it must be difficult for the government to regulate this event. The accident causes include water, alcohol, no helmet, the week-long party and running into cars from behind, often at only 50kmh. Most riders carry a pillion bearing a large water-blaster. Everyone is excited, distracted and soaked in mud and water from water pistols, buckets and anything else that can hold water.

Another small but growing international riding service is the Harley Ride-Fly program, with around a dozen countries available. Beyond this are two options becoming increasingly popular. Firstly, the buy-and-sell approach, much practiced among the VW Combi travellers from the 1960s forward in Europe. This is growing and predicted to grow, being driven by a number of favourable trends. Firstly the easy sale and purchase of near new Japanese and US motorcycles in many countries through well developed factory distribution and service channels. Secondly the reliability of modern bikes and the pervasiveness of dealer logbook servicing, reduces the risk in buying and selling. Thirdly, the steep price drops on near-new bikes, coupled with the increasing warranty periods, enables riders to buy an 18 month old Harley, tour with it under warranty for two or three months, and then sell it, still under warranty for not much less than the purchase price.

The other approach is being quietly practiced by another growing number of riders, who for a variety of reasons haven't been noticed by the motorcycle media.

This group buys motorcycles in other countries and stores them against the times they visit those countries, on say business trips for example. The bikes take up little storage space, and can be lodged with friends, relatives or business associates. The owner now has the key to unlimited, low-cost travel on another continent. Such riders can develop this ownership via 'arbitrage gains' e.g. by buying classic bikes cheaply in less developed bike markets. Keen riders can then add value to them over successive trips by maintenance and restoration work. Once completed, they can then enjoy the unique pleasure of riding their own restored bike in strange lands. This approach has the added benefits of having a bike that's set up exactly for the rider and in a known condition, versus a rented bike. When compared to the costs of shipping your bike overseas using a proprietary service, the costs of buying a nice classic bike in another country can be comparable. The owner also now has an appreciating asset, one that can possibly be repatriated home in pieces if desired. There are few exotic pleasures to match the feeling of riding your own bike in another country, as Des Molloy recounts in *The Last Hurrah*. In some countries it might also give a taste of time travel.

Illus 10.22 BSAs take over Pukekohe. NZ Centenary. Pic R.Cochrane

11 *Classic Motorcycle Survival*

"Between 1893 and 1942, some 396 brands of Australian motorcycles were offered for public sale." R.Saward, 1996

To riders, the classic bike scene is important for more than just riding bikes. The riders in a real sense are the investors and stakeholders of the 'Classic Motorcycle Industry'. As in any industry, investors and everyone else involved need to know the answers to these questions. How big is the industry? Is it growing or declining and by how much? Where are the big chunks of the industry located? How are prices and profits? Are they going up or down? What is the outlook?

Apart from the Buyers Guide in *Classic Bike* 1993-1994, these questions have largely gone unanswered in the classic bike literature, whether in magazines or in the many books published on classic bikes. In this chapter, a variety of statistical modelling techniques have been used to estimate the global population of surviving classic motorcycles. These techniques are explained in the methodology section (page 225) at the end of this chapter for those who would like to know how the estimates were derived. Here detailed country breakdowns of surviving classic bikes are provided for the United Kingdom, Australia and New Zealand, the key classic countries. This section also provides a picture of the British industry's exports to provide a better understanding of where they went and so where they might be found now. In the next chapter we will look into the past, present and future values of these survivors.

United Kingdom Survivors

The United Kingdom is seen by many riders as the ancestral home of most classic motorcycle marques, so it seems appropriate to examine the British scene first. Table 11.1 gives an estimate of the numbers of bikes surviving that were manufactured before 1979. These figures are based on a survey of bikes for sale in auctions and classic bike magazines. The table includes makes of motorcycle sold in the UK during the classic period of 1946 to 1979. Thus Honda is included given it's considerable UK sales up to 1979 the closing date for this research.

As can be seen, the surviving classic motorcycles in the UK number approximately 136,000. This number is supported by published UK figures and I'm sure it will surprise some readers, and be criticised as being either too low or too high. Please note the survey includes estimates of complete bikes

Table 11.1   UK Classic Bike Survival Estimates

Make	Number in Sample	Sample as % of Total	Total UK Survivors
AJS	87	3.5	4,720
Ariel	77	3.1	4,180
BMW	59	2.4	3,200
Brough	2	0.1	110
BSA	402	16.0	21,830
Bultaco	3	0.1	160
Coventry	2	0.1	110
Douglas	9	0.4	490
Ducati	36	1.4	1,950
Enfield	94	3.8	5,100
Excelsior	3	0.1	160
Francis-Barnett	15	0.6	810
Gilera	7	0.3	380
Greeves	4	0.2	220
Harley-Davidson	22	0.9	1,190
Honda	168	6.7	9,120
Indian	6	0.2	330
James	16	0.6	870
Jawa	7	0.3	380
Kawasaki	60	2.4	3,260
Laverda	21	0.8	1,140
Levis	2	0.1	110
Matchless	91	3.6	4,940
Moto-Guzzi	40	1.6	2,170
New Imperial	4	0.2	220
Norman	1	0.0	50
Norton	178	7.1	9,660
OK	3	0.1	160
Panther	13	0.5	710
Rickman	9	0.4	490
Rudge	6	0.2	330
Scott	2	0.1	110
Sunbeam	48	1.9	2,610
Suzuki	50	2.0	2,720
Triton	20	0.8	1,090
Triumph	623	24.9	33,820
Velocette	96	3.8	5,210
Vincent	18	0.7	980
Yamaha	37	1.5	2,010
Other 2 Stroke	19	0.8	1,030
Other Italian	31	1.2	1,680
Others	114	4.6	6,190
Total	**2,505**	**100.0**	**136,000**

Sample sourced from: Classic Bike 05/06, Classic Bike Guide 05, Old Bike Mart 06, Auctions 05/06.

only and excludes basket cases and rusting wrecks in barns. Also excluded were racers and off-road bikes, those ordinarily not ridden on the roads and also scooters and mopeds. Obviously these categories would inflate the national figures. Unsurprisingly, Triumph motorcycles topped the survey, with nearly 34,000 models estimated to be on British roads, or at least being reasonably roadworthy. Meriden Triumphs represent one quarter of all Veteran, Vintage and Classic motorcycles in the UK. Equally unsurprisingly, BSA models are in runner-up position, with a 16% share of UK classic bike stocks or nearly 22,000 Beezas still on the roads thirty-three years after the factory closed. The smaller marques are naturally far more difficult to estimate, and the numbers given in table 11.1 cannot have the same accuracy as those for the major brands.

Rank	Marque	Estimated UK Numbers	Estimated Market Share
\multicolumn{4}{l}{**Table 11.2** **Top Ten Surviving Marques in the UK**}
1	Triumph	33,820	24.9%
2	BSA	21,830	16.0%
3	Norton	9,660	7.1%
4	Honda	9,120	6.7%
5	Velocette	5,210	3.8%
6	Royal Enfield	5,100	3.8%
7	Matchless	4,940	3.6%
8	AJS	4,720	3.5%
9	Ariel	4,180	3.1%
10	Kawasaki	3,260	2.4%
Totals		**101,840**	**74.9%**

The marques in Table 11.2 above, comprise some three quarters of all classic bikes in the UK. It would be nice to think the original UK 'Top Ten' manufacturer rankings for production volumes would form a similar ranking to the above. This would imply that all manufacturers' designs have lasted equally well down the decades. I'm fairly sure this would be so for the first three manufacturers, Triumph, BSA and Norton. For Velocette, Royal Enfield, Matchless, AJS and Ariel, we can't be sure without complete factory production and domestic sales records and these only seem to be available for Velocette. It's possible those medium and small marques with perhaps better frame and engine design, and higher values, have survived better pro-rata than marques that sold more, cheaper models with perhaps less inbuilt longevity. Of course the periods of production differ and it's really unfair to compare the surviving Velocette fleet, with say the Norton fleet, when Norton kept manufacturing for another twenty years and had access to new technologies, materials and computer aided design. It's satisfying at last to put some survival numbers against these classic makers but this research is very much at the beginning and further efforts may shine more light on the numbers now surviving.

Australian Survivors

The classic motorcycle scene is different for each country, and Australia is typically different. Table 11.3, shows the the Australian survivors. In the Australian table, I estimate that some 42,000 classic bikes survive around the six Australian states and two territories. Similarly to the UK, this data will doubtless disappoint some readers by over- or under-stating the population of some makes compared to readers' long-held hunches, or that I understate the rank of their favourite marque. (If you are for example a Norman-fancier, and feel strongly about this, I invite you to try replicating this research, or perhaps consider buying a Triumph!)

The Australian classic bike estate differs in important ways from that in the UK. Firstly, there was an Australian motorcycle manufacturing industry, over the 1893-1948 period as Robert Saward records in his seminal *A-Z of Australian -Made Motorcycles*. Few of the makes were made in large numbers, and very few of these survive. The longest production run was for the Waratah marque from 1914 to 1948. Like a lot of other small local brands they used Villiers engines and other British components.

It is interesting to note that almost as many classic bikes survive downunder per capita as survive in the UK, after adjusting for the different population size. Overall, Australia is perhaps even more pro-motorcycling than the UK. The current ratios for the number of all motorcycles (not just classics) per thousand population are 1.2 motorcycles per 1,000 people for the UK and 2.1 per 1,000 for Australia. This probably reflects the attractive Australian climate enabling all-year riding in dry weather compared to the UK. It is also true that the dry air helps classic bike longevity and survival. On the other hand, riding downunder at dusk or at night risks sharing your tank with a kangaroo, and a scrapped bike.

The first finding is that nearly all marques detected in the UK survey are also surviving in Australia. No OK bikes were found, but that doesn't preclude a few existing out there somewhere. That is the only exception. However the distribution of marque numbers in Australia varies from the UK in interesting and unexpected ways. Triumph motorcycles topped the survey as in the UK, with nearly 7,000 models estimated to be on roads downunder. Triumphs represent 16% (25% in the UK) of total veteran, vintage and classic motorcycles in Australia. BSA models are estimated at 12.2% (UK16%), and are pushed down the rankings by classic Harley-Davidsons, which number some 5,400 against an estimated 5,100 BSAs.

Table 11.3   Australian Classic Bike Survival Estimates*

Make	Number in Sample	Sample as % of Total	Total Australian Survivors
AJS	41	1.9	806
Ariel	47	2.2	924
BMW	77	3.6	1,514
Brough	2	0.1	39
BSA	264	12.4	5,191
Bultaco	13	0.6	256
Coventry	1	0.0	20
Douglas	15	0.7	295
Ducati	57	2.7	1,121
Enfield	15	0.7	295
Excelsior	7	0.3	138
Francis-Barnett	2	0.1	39
Gilera	5	0.2	98
Greeves	2	0.1	39
Harley-Davidson	262	12.3	5,152
Honda	244	11.4	4,798
Indian	38	1.8	747
James	6	0.3	118
Jawa	7	0.3	138
Kawasaki	83	3.9	1,632
Laverda	12	0.6	236
Levis	4	0.2	79
Matchless	43	2.0	846
Moto-Guzzi	23	1.1	452
New Imperial	2	0.1	39
Norman	1	0.0	20
Norton	136	6.4	2,674
OK	0	0.0	0
Panther	11	0.5	216
Rickman	1	0.0	20
Rudge	5	0.2	98
Scott	1	0.0	20
Sunbeam	4	0.2	79
Suzuki	124	5.8	2,438
Triton	5	0.2	98
Triumph	345	16.2	6,784
Velocette	33	1.5	649
Vincent	19	0.9	374
Yamaha	128	6.0	2,517
Other 2 Stroke	17	0.8	334
Other Italian	11	0.5	216
Others	23	1.1	452
Total	**2,136**	**100.0**	**42,000**

Sources: Just Bikes 03-06, Australian Motorcycle Trader, Trading Post, EBay.
* *Manufactured prior to 1980*

Table 11.4		Top Ten Surviving Marques in Australia	
Rank	**Marque**	**Estimated Australian Numbers**	**Estimated Market Share**
1	Triumph	6,780	16.1%
2	Harley-Davidson	5,360	12.8%
3	BSA	5,120	12.2%
4	Honda	4,460	10.6%
5	Norton	2,760	6.6%
6	Yamaha	2,720	6.5%
7	Suzuki	2,420	5.8%
8	BMW	1,570	3.7%
9	Kawasaki	1,420	3.4%
10	Ducati	1,130	2.7%
Totals		**33,740**	**80.3%**

The leading ten marques are summarised in Table 11.4. The top ten marques comprise four fifths of all classic bikes in Australia. The comparable figure for the UK is three quarters, illustrating that the assortment of classic bikes downunder is somewhat narrower than in the UK. It is also the case that the composition of the classic bike estate is far more international than might have been expected when viewed against the traditional British marques in a British Commonwealth country. The early adoption as far back as the 1920s of Harley-Davidson motorcycles in Australia shines through these figures with an estimated 5,360 Harleys comprising 12.8% of the total compared with just 0.9% in the UK. The early, burgeoning market share for Japanese bikes is also clear in Table 11.4 (and please note that scooters and mopeds are excluded from these data). The 'Big Four' Japanese plants were already climbing the rankings by 1979, with a combined 26.3% market share versus a 'Big Three' UK share of 34.9%. Interestingly Ducati with a 2.7% market share (versus 0.9% in the UK) takes the tenth position. I don't recall seeing Ducati's about in such large numbers downunder, and must keep an eye out for them on future runs.

New Zealand Survivors

It quickly became clear that a relatively greater percentage of New Zealand classic bikes apparently are not registered or licensed, or have never been registered or licensed compared with the UK or Australia. This, coupled with a fair bit of 'plate-swapping', may account for a few suprises in the New Zealand statistics.

New Zealand can fairly claim, on a per capita basis, to be the leading classic motorcycling country on the planet. The country is a storehouse of classic

Table 11.5   NZ Classic Bike Survival Estimates

Make	Number in Sample	Sample as % of Total	Total NZ Survivors
AJS	105	3.2%	473
Ariel	79	2.4%	356
BMW	151	4.5%	681
Brough	2	0.1%	9
BSA	380	11.4%	1,713
Bultaco	1	0.0%	5
Coventry	0	0.0%	0
Douglas	12	0.4%	54
Ducati	63	1.9%	284
Enfield	34	1.0%	153
Excelsior	2	0.1%	9
Francis-Barnett	5	0.2%	23
Gilera	1	0.0%	5
Greeves	0	0.0%	0
Harley-Davidson	173	5.2%	780
Honda	323	9.7%	1,456
Indian	100	3.0%	451
James	10	0.3%	45
Jawa	11	0.3%	50
Kawasaki	79	2.4%	356
Laverda	9	0.3%	41
Levis	0	0.0%	0
Matchless	132	4.0%	595
Moto-Guzzi	66	2.0%	297
New Imperial	0	0.0%	0
Norman	0	0.0%	0
Norton	354	10.6%	1,596
OK	0	0.0%	0
Other 2 Stroke	5	0.2%	23
Other Italian	11	0.3%	50
Others	21	0.6%	95
Panther	8	0.2%	36
Rickman	0	0.0%	0
Rudge	6	0.2%	27
Scott	8	0.2%	36
Sunbeam	13	0.4%	59
Suzuki	127	3.8%	572
Triton	1	0.0%	5
Triumph	803	24.1%	3,619
Velocette	72	2.2%	325
Vincent	24	0.7%	108
Yamaha	137	4.1%	617
Total	**3,328**	**100.0%**	**15,000**

Sources: LTNZ, MMP, Clubs, Registers

motorcycles, particularly of British makes. Naturally, countries like China, Greece and Italy, and many Asian countries, would take the title based upon total motorcycling numbers, but purely for classics, New Zealand takes the cake. It is the 'Classic Bike Capital of the World'. The classic motorcycle scene there is vibrant, with a dozen active classic cubs, plus the vintage and off-road scene. Many towns have an active classic club. The Rotorua Classic Motorcycle Club is the oldest club in New Zealand, founded in 1976, just as the classic scene was emerging in England. As discussed in chapter ten, there's a very successful Classic Racing Register, fielding some of the best classic road and circuit racing to be seen anywhere. That Register was founded by the present patron, Hugh Anderson, who was New Zealand's first World Champion Grand Prix rider, back in 1963. He backed up and won world titles again in 1964 and 1965, and is warmly remembered in the UK and honoured in his own country. I am fortunate to share this book with him, as he kindly agreed to handle the foreword, placing us all in safe hands.

In New Zealand, Table 11.5, some 15,000 classic bikes are estimated to survive throughout that magic motorcycling country. This is more than one third of the bikes in Australia - in a country just one fifth the size. On a per capita basis New Zealand has about 50% more classic bikes that either Australia or the UK. British marques, especially the middle-ranking makes are better represented here than in Australia. It isn't a thoroughly British bike scene however. Many Indians were imported and the Indian barely missed a Top Ten position, there being 300-400 or perhaps more still about. Many of these were WWII vintage US army bikes. Indeed, I can remember such Indians in unopened crates being sold in the 1960s in New Zealand for £30. They sat there for years unsold, as no one wanted to buy an outdated bike with girder forks, even if it was half the price of a used British twin! The Henderson and many Harley-Davidsons were imported from the 1920s on, and Harley-Davidson remains a popular import today. During the 1960s and 1970s as the traditional suppliers folded, the statistics show that NZ riders switched not to Japanese bikes, but to German and Italian marques, along with American. This explains both the low Japanese representation today in the NZ 'Top Ten', and the surprising number of BMWs, and especially Moto-Guzzis, everywhere you ride in New Zealand.

In Table 11.6 opposite, the top ten marques comprise some four fifths of all classic bikes in New Zealand. This is comparable to Australia. Both figures are greater than in the UK, illustrating the assortment of classic bikes in these countries is narrower than in the UK. The composition of the classic bike Top Ten, shows five British makes in New Zealand, versus three in Australia and seven in the UK.

Rank	Marque	Estimated NZ Numbers	Estimated Market Share
Table 11.6	**Top Ten Surviving Marques in New Zealand**		
1	Triumph	3,620	24.1%
2	BSA	1,720	11.4%
3	Norton	1,600	10.6%
4	Honda	1,500	9.7%
5	Harley-Davidson	780	5.2%
6	BMW	680	6.5%
7	Yamaha	610	5.8%
8	Matchless	600	3.7%
9	Suzuki	570	3.4%
10	AJS	470	2.7%
Totals		**12,150**	**81%**

Why would there be so many classic motorcycles in New Zealand? On a per-capita basis there appear to be half as many bikes again than in either the UK or Australia. The answer is firstly that New Zealand riders state proudly they have been 'mad keen motorcyclists since veteran days' and secondly, 'we never throw anything away'! Examination of the motorcycle imports for the early and middle of the last century shows a consistently high import level for the country.

The country, as a British dominion naturally preferred to import British bikes. Even in the 1970s with the UK industry in its twilight, bulk shipments of Triumphs, BSA's and Nortons were still being imported, right up to the last gasp of the UK industry.

Analysis of the scrappage (the number of bikes broken up and put in landfill etc) over the 1926-1980 period, yields an average scrappage rate of just 10% per annum. There does seem to be some truth in the NZ claim of never throwing anything away. Those readers in larger countries such as the UK or USA, should allow that compared to their countries, New Zealand is a tiny lifeboat adrift on the Great Southern Ocean. The first rule of survival in a lifeboat is - never throw anything away. New Zealand as a consequence grew to have one of the oldest fleets of vehicles in the western world. It was a uniform tourist comment from about 1960 on, that NZ motor cars belonged in museums, and not on the roads. Perhaps the only comparable country now would be Cuba, where a similarly aged fleet is kept on the roads, and arouses that same comment from every visiting film crew.

The underlying driver for this conservation of what are now, classic cars and bikes in New Zealand, lies in the country's economic experience over the 1960-

1987 period. The country was chronically short of foreign exchange and imposed import restrictions on new vehicles for many years. I recall the draconian foreign exchange deposit requirements in the 1960s for buying a new vehicle. The purchaser had to muster *two thirds* of the price in foreign exchange to qualify for a new vehicle. For most this was impossible and many chose to ride bikes instead of cars, and older British bikes at that, as they were cheaper. The position was similar to that favouring the sidecar boom in the UK after WWII. This practice persisted right up to 1987 when the first grey channel car imports commenced from Japan. Motorcycle registrations dropped immediately by a third. In New Zealand, this meant that motorcycles from the 1940s, 1950s and 1960s were still being ridden daily through the crucial 1960-1985 period, when scrappage rates for classic bikes increased in the UK and Australia, and were as a result conserved. By the time Japanese cars became available in volume in the 1990s, these motorcycles had once again become valuable as classics, and so were not scrapped.

This classic bike conservation was helped further by the relatively small size of the country which limited the average trip mileage of bikes, and contributed to their longevity. For example, I recall the longest journeys I took in New Zealand over the 1950s-1960s were from Auckland to Gisborne, a distance of 330 miles. That was considered a very long journey for the day, one that would be undertaken for some overwhelming family reason, or for the Christmas holidays. That journey solo, took seven or eight hours in the early 1960s. That's a slow pace by today's standards, but was quick for the time as I rode an Ariel Huntmaster quite vigorously. To be fair, more than a quarter of the way was on metal roads, and in Winter the long section through the Waioeka Gorge was often blocked by land slips. I still recall the exhausts of the big Caterpillar bulldozers echoing along the gorge as they crawled miles from their road camp in the middle of the gorge to the slips. It was a welcome sound at 1am on a frosty Saturday morning.

The only time I ever had to be towed home in those classic days, was from a puncture in the middle of that gorge, late one Friday winter evening. I recall the back wheel tracking out on corners in the thick creamy mud, and having to stop in the pitch black of the gorge at about 11pm. I couldn't push the bike off the road as the thick mud jammed under the mudguards. I hadn't seen any traffic since the last town. Fortunately the centre stand found a hard surface under the mud. I waited in the cold dark. It seemed only a short time till the welcome lights of a government bus (NZ Road Services), came through the night: fortunately for me it was running late that night, or I would have waited till the next day. The driver, Mr Wave Legge, a good friend's father, and my best mate, Jim Nicklin happened to be on the bus. Apparently I was so upset as I climbed onto the bus that I announced matter-of-factly, "would you believe my Ariel has a f***** puncture!" Mr Legge kindly overlooked the outburst and took me to Matawai without charging a fare, where the local constable let me stand in his station doorway, out of the biting wind for two hours till my father drove out and trailered me home at dawn. What a trip, and of course on the Sunday, I had to ride back to Auckland.

We can be relatively sure of the figures for New Zealand classics, as the available statistics while incomplete, are more accessible than in other countries. The New Zealand statistics brought to light some of the bias in other countries' classic bike data. One significant source of bias lies in the many bikes remaining outside the licensing and registration system. In New Zealand, there appear to be up to three or even four times as many unregistered classics, as those actually registered and number-plated. This is excluding racers, scooters and offroad bikes. Once imported, many never appear again in official registers until possibly there's a change in ownership, or the bike enters a club or racing register. This illustrates the usefulness of using advertising data to estimate bike numbers, as the data are current, and otherwise invisible bikes can be detected and counted. There is still bias in these advertising data however, as bikes may be retained in a family and perhaps passed down from father to son, so remaining invisible for generations. Some 48% of British classics are reported as being still with their first registered owner which may back this up. I think it's likely the New Zealand data include something of that 'father and son' kind of ownership lineage, as well as reflecting the average age of many classic riders.

World Conservation

Combining the British, Australian and New Zealand survivor estimates indicates roughly 200,000 classic bikes are conserved in these Commonwealth countries. How many more are there scattered about the rest of the world? Given the difficulties encountered with original production and export sales, I re-read the major industry books by senior managers from the British industry including Hopwood, Shilton and Davies etc. It was surprising how little domestic and export sales information was included in those books, especially given Hopwood's general management positions and his evident recourse to company files after leaving the industry. Or was it that the industry left him? For the avoidance of doubt, I'm a Hopwood fan. On the other hand, I worked for a British group, Burmah Oil at the time he wrote his book, and recall sales figures being regarded as confidential. Even the sales force were denied access to their own sales data, which was so vital for their work! Davies gives us tantalising glimpses of sales and export data, and publishing Edward Turner's correspondence, gives us insight into the management of the crucial USA export sales operations.

Based upon these, VMCC support and other secondary data sources, I developed a model of the British industry production and US export sales over the post WWII period. This is included as Table 11.11 page 234. I estimate up to 300,000 bikes were exported to the US between 1946 and 1974.

Table 11.7   World Classic Motorcycle Survival Estimates

Country	No. M/cycles Total 000s	Population Million	No. Owners % popn.	Forecast Min	Max	%
UK	1,176	60.5	1.5	136	136	46
Australia	422	20.2	2.1	35	42	14
NZ	51	4.1	1.2	10	20	7
USA	6,161	297.0	2.1	30	60	20
Canada	417	32.9	1.3	10	20	7
Europe	25,000	335.0	7.5	5	10	3
All Others	n/a	-	>20.0	5	10	3
Total	**n/a**	-	-	**231**	**298**	**100**

Sources: UK 2003 Compendium, Fedstats (USA), Can Stats (Canada), ABS(Australia), NZStats(New Zealand), AISI(Indonesia).

In Table 11.7, the Worldwide Survivors are assembled. It is estimated that up to 300,000 classic road bikes survive throughout the world as indicated in the table above. Coincidentally, this is close to the estimate for British export sales to the USA over the post-war period. Given the large USA population, a fairly high bike ownership, and the decentralized, fifty state-based licensing systems, the choice of motorcycle statistics at the national level is slim. The estimate of the number of US classic motorcycles was checked via correspondence with a number of US classic experts. None could really guess at their national numbers. I estimate that approx. 10-20% of classic bike imports survive in the USA, especially in the higher, drier states. The estimate was tempered by the ongoing re-exports of USA-delivered classics around the world. For example, container loads of US bikes have been imported by the UK, Australia and New Zealand on a regular basis for some years and is ongoing. There is a limit to these exports, and correspondence with US riders would indicate that the supply of popular models such as complete BSA A10s, is drying up. Only basket cases are now being found at autojumbles. Similarly BSA B50s, always popular for racing in the USA, are now scarce, and BSA unit 250cc engines are being remanufactured to meet the demand for B50 crankcases. These estimates were checked by calculating scrappage rates over the 1975-2006 period. (See page 221 for further information on scrappage rates). Assuming a total population of British bikes at 300,000 in 1974, net US re-exports and attrition (eg scrappage) would be expected to have reduced these to approx. 30,000-60,000 bikes by now. Attrition is one fairly hard classic ratio that can sometimes be extracted from country registration data.

Classic Bikes in Other Countries

Returning to the global Table 11.7 above, confidence in the figures lowers as one moves down the table. The data for Canada, Europe and the Rest of World are best described as provisions. Canada's classic bike population was always relatively low, traditionally less than New Zealand's, being just 34,000 by 1961: and that included scooters. However there may be some more surprising caches of classic motorcycles and parts in countries that have been overlooked so far. The International Road Federation (IRF) published a global census of two-wheeled transport back in 1961. This was an important year for classic motorcycling coming immediately after the peak in classic motorcycle sales and production in Western countries over 1959-1960. By examining the smaller countries it may be possible to start zeroing in on any surviving bike or parts stocks overlooked for the past sixty-five years. For example, in 1961 Indonesia reportedly had 116,000 bikes and scooters. Coincidentally, a classic bike register has recently been formed there and small numbers of BSAs and Triumphs were noted on the roads by Australian clubmen in 2005, as shown in the photos below. It's doubtful the classic bikes pictured by the sea would have survived the big tsunami there recently.

Illus 11.1 (Left) A BSA M20 and owner at Pangandaran in Indonesia, taken whilst discussing BSA durability and 'chick magnet' effects with a BSA club visitor. Our BSA member also saw a B40, Ariel Red Hunter and an ES2 Norton, and learnt of their Classic Vehicle register.

Illus 11.2 (Right) This M20 was chased by our member's Honda 50, for the interview. Sadly, some coastal classics in Indonesia were lost in the Asian Tsunami.

Japan has an active classic movement for their own classics and also for British bikes and Harleys, as Harley-Davidson had significant exports from before WWII. However, I doubt it's worth looking there for undiscovered classics. Elsewhere around South Asia, the older British Raj countries such as Burma (IRF 6,620 bikes), Singapore (IRF 17,244 bikes), and Hong Kong (IRF 3,322 bikes), would have had significant numbers of classic British bikes by 1961. These were frequently for army and police use. These countries now seem to have relatively few classics surviving. A pattern of re-export from the 1970s until recently was common due to departing servicemen repatriating bikes to Australia, New Zealand and doubtless the UK. This is noticeable with military bikes such as the BSA B40. Many ex-Singapore service bikes were vacuumed up into RAAF and RNZAF Bristol Freighters and Hercules aircraft for repatriation downunder. Similarly the survivors of the eighty BSA A7s shipped to the Burmese army in 1968, still pop up in Australia. These bikes often show evidence of what happens to classic bikes after years in the monsoon shadow across Asia. Frame and chrome corrosion is often marked when compared to bikes from a dry country like Australia. During the height of the 1987-1990 classic bike boom, when auctions were at their peak in Australia, shipments of classic bikes were imported from Singapore. However, their condition was very poor, and so were the prices realised. After the decline in prices in the early 1990's both classic auctions and Asian lot imports have become infrequent. However, basket cases in significant numbers may still exist there. Table 11.8 below, summarises countries where fossicking for classic British bikes may yet repay your effort. Given even modest assumptions about attrition, re-export and scrappage rates, then probably only those countries with the larger starting populations are realistic prospects; but who really knows? Naturally the drier, higher-elevation countries and those outside the monsoon shadow, should offer the best pickings. If I was to take my choice, I'd follow Che Guevara and his Motorcycle Diaries and look first around parts of South America for La Poderosa III.

From personal experience over 1984-2001, when I traveled to many Asian countries regularly, I cannot recall seeing or hearing many classic British bikes on the roads in Hong Kong, Southern China, Thailand, South Korea, Indonesia, Malaysia, Taiwan, Philippines, or Japan. India of course is the exception, where Royal Enfields, old and new were all about. On the other hand, perhaps in other Asian countries they went unnoticed in the sea of locally made lightweights, or were only about at weekends, as in Western countries, when I was usually in transit to the next country.

Looking at the world breakdown in Table 11.8 above, it can be estimated that roughly half of all classic bikes remain in the UK. Australasia and the USA account for a further fifth each, with the balance probably scattered around the world. More insight can be teased from these data, by comparing the overall motorcycle ownership rates with the forecast ownership rate for classics. They should be different within a country, if only because of the different demographics etc.

However looking at international comparisons might give further insight into the rightness or otherwise of the classic estimates. The ratios of classic ownership to total motorcycle ownership are summarised in Table 11.9 below.

Table 11.8	Target Countries for Classic Bike Hunters		
Country	**1961 Bike Population**	**Country**	**1961 Bike Population**
Africa		**Asia**	
Congo	3,000	Burma	6,620
Egypt	20,952	Cambodia	26,978
Kenya	3,800	India	67,186
Libya	19,000	Indonesia	116,000
Morocco	14,322	Malaysia	39,255
Nigeria	5,019	Pakistan	14,000
South Africa	75,000	Sri Lanka	14,944
Tanganyika	4,450	**South America**	
Tunisia	70,000	Argentina	130,000
Uganda	7,863	Brazil	111,282
Zimbabwe	5,687	Chile	14,358
Middle East		Peru	20,609
Iran	8,426	Uruguay	10,000
Israel	19,500	Venezuela	12,325

Source: IRF 1961. NB: statistics include mopeds and scooters.

Table 11.9	Classic Motorcycle Ownership Ratios		
Country	**Total M'C Owners % population**	**Classic M'C Owners % population**	**Classic : Total Owner Ratios**
New Zealand	1.2	0.36	0.30
United Kingdom	1.5	0.23	0.15
Australia	2.1	0.21	0.10
Canada	1.3	0.06	0.05
USA	2.1	0.02	0.01
Other Europe	7.5	0.003	n/a
Rest of World	<=20	n/a	

Sources: UK 2003 Compendium, Fedstats USA, Can Stats, ABS, NZBS, AISI.

The main interest in Table 11.9 lies in the right hand column. This shows the ratio of classic owners to total motorcycle owners in each country. It can only be a very rough ranking and nothing much more can be read into the numbers, than to rank the countries. This table therefore represents a measure of the overall popularity of classic motorcycling among the major classic countries. It will come as little surprise now to see that New Zealand heads the list as proportionately the most enthusiastic classic motorcycling country on the planet, leaving the UK and Australia well behind in second and third place.

Basket Cases

Of central importance to bike survival and future bike supply, is the position of so-called 'basket-cases', i.e. bikes in pieces, or even large pieces of bike, anything that might form the start of a restoration for a dedicated restorer. There is a continuing flow of such bikes into the market across all the countries surveyed: indeed it's a major plank in meeting the growth in consumer demand for classic bikes. At some point, this flow will taper off, with possible damaging effects on the classic bike scene. How and when will this occur? One has to look again at demographics and housing patterns for guidance as to how and when this is likely to occur. Most of these basket-cases were presumably consigned to their under-house or barn resting places by their owners and families. It's now over thirty years (or one and a half generations), since the end of the classic period in about 1979. Given the high house ownership patterns over that period, we can assume many basket-cases are still in the care of the same owner. The UK 'keeper' data, supports that assumption. This fascinating research was published in a 2004 UK DFT study, the *Compendium of Motorcycling Statistics*. The research shows that a remarkable 47% of classic motorcycles i.e those first registered before 1979, were still in the hands of their first owner or keeper. Even more remarkably, 64% of all registered classic bikes at that time were with either their first or second owner. If we further assume the average age of these owners was say 30-40 years in 1979, then today they are 77-87 years old. Now it's not commonly appreciated that if you survive long enough, your life expectancy actually increases! Our hardy group of aging, motorcycling basket-casers have a life expectancy of another five to ten years yet. After that time however, during 2011-2016 their houses and farms will all be sold and the new owners should unearth the last significant caches of basket-cases, releasing them to the market. So then, how many more basket cases might there be? Frankly, one can only guesstimate this, in a way akin to the survival models, starting with a few assumptions.

We can expect the relative numbers of basket cases to follow the original import patterns of the brands. Thus there should be more Triumph baskets than other makes. Two stroke engines might be over-represented, given their expectedly greater internal oil filming. Smaller capacity bikes may be under-represented, due to their greater wear and tear, and accident damage often by learner riders. Dry countries like Australia should have better condition basket cases, other things equal, than say New Zealand due to climatic advantages. Some marque communities for example Vincent, appear to have a high degree of awareness of basket cases. Some dealers with established client networks know where basket cases are, and wait patiently for the years and mortality to provide access. Marque clubs advise that fresh basket cases of their marque continue to surface on an almost weekly basis. Given assumptions about scrappage, I guess that undiscovered basket cases may comprise up to 25% of current bike numbers, or perhaps more depending on the country.

Your Motorcycling HALE?

While on actuarial matters, there's another milestone here for every classic motorcyclist, and that's the 'HALE' or Healthy Life Expectancy age. This measures the life expectancy we all have during which we're sufficiently healthy to kick start and ride most classic British motorcycles. (The HALE age for Harley-Davidson owners may be somewhat lower, given their weight and mass.) As an aside, it's not surprising to see the growth in the Trike market in the USA and downunder - they effectively extend one's 'HALE' age. The current HALEs are as follows

UK	69.1 years
USA	67.2
Australia	70.9
NZ	69.5

The HALE age is generally about 90% of total life expectancy. So there's plenty of time available to buy and restore that next basket case, and enjoy some more good riding years! There are a number of riders around Australia in their eighth decade, including the founder of the Ulysses Club, Stephen Dearnley, who rode a Burgman scooter round Australia at age 79 in 2002, and only hung up his gloves in late 2006. In the UK Len Vale-Onslow was still riding his SOS motorcycles at 100 years of age. Sadly Len Vale-Onslow died in 2004.

A Note On Scrappage

Scrappage is synonymous with attrition or the writing out of motor vehicles from national motor registries. It's possible to generate a scrappage rate for classic bikes for specific time periods in some countries. First we need to obtain the total national registrations and another series of annual new motorcycle registrations for the same time period. We can then move forward through the total registration series, adding in new registrations annually to the previous years total, and then calculating the difference between that figure and the published total for that year. That difference is the estimated scrappage rate for the country, in that year.

Few countries publish scrappage rates on motorcycles outside Asia. The Asian interest is driven by the extreme air pollution from older, not classic, and two stroke motorcycles. Government policies in the worst affected countries e.g. China, Thailand and Indonesia, are aimed at boosting the scrappage rate for these bikes. Incentives are offered for riders to scrap their old bikes in the public interest. Some Chinese cities are also reported to be considering banning some motorcycles. Naturally, this also coincides with the commercial interests of motorcycle manufacturers in those countries. In this regard, it's worth noting that the leading motorcycle manufacturing countries in the world are all Asian...and Japan is no longer leading the list. The leading three countries recently were China, India, and Japan, closely followed by Indonesia, Thailand and Malaysia. Now to be fair, a number of the plants involved are joint ventures with the big four Japanese makers.

In the UK there are well documented scrappage rates available from the National Statistics Office. The UK motorcycle scrappage rate in recent years is approx 60% per year. This seems high. The rate has reportedly exceeded 100% in earlier years, implying an absolute drop in the total number of bikes in the UK in those years.

No Australian bike scrappage data have been collected and published by authorities. The inter-census comparisons in Chart 11.10, appear to show scrappage but the decline in numbers shown there has more to do with migration to historic vehicle registration, not to mention the inadequacies of the vehicle census method. Car scrappage is running at 3-5% pa in Australia.

In New Zealand there was some available data to enable the classic bike scrappage rate from 1926-1986 to be calculated. The rate averaged just 10% per year over that sixty year period. Even today it is barely 15%. This is a very low rate, and possibly among the lowest rate in the classic motorcycle world. It helps explain the estimates of a relatively high classic bike population in New Zealand. In fact, given the keen restoration scene there at present, the scrappage figures could even become positive!

Applying the scrappage concept to the important USA population gives more insight into the estimates. Assuming there were say, 300,000 US classic bikes in 1974, then at the NZ scrappage rate of 10% per annum, the population would have decreased to some 10,000 bikes by 2006, or even less allowing for continuing exports from the USA. For interest, I halved the scrappage rate to just 5% pa. This seems a very conservative figure with just five bikes out of each hundred being scrapped, written off, lost, or otherwise disappearing each year. At 5% scrappage the 300,000 US classics starting from 1974, declined to 38,000 by 2006. This figure is within the forecast of 30-60,000 bikes calculated here, and thus provides a degree of confirmation. Supporting this is the relative under-use by US owners, with very low annual mileages. Some additional information on this is provided by the estimates in the *Rupert Ratio Unit Single Engine Manual*, on the survival of BSA Unit singles. Ratio cites original production volumes of approximately 140,000 bikes. This was a popular range in the USA. He estimated that 'over 10,000 survive'. This is a survival rate of some 7% or more. If we apply his '7% or more' survival ratio to the 1974 US figure of 300,000 then this gives 21,000 or more surviving classic US bikes today. This is pleasingly close to the indicative range of 30-60,000 surviving US bikes. Useful archival work by the VMCC librarian in the UK, showed mean total US exports through the 1950s was only 8,000 bikes per annum. If this had persisted through the 1960s, then the 1974 starting population would be only 200,000. Therefore the 300,000 figure looks generous if anything. However, more research is needed to sharpen up the US population estimates as it has implications for all other classic motorcycling countries. As the last great repository of low mileage and often dry-stored classic motorcycles, coupled with prices and availability that encourage re-export, US survivors support the continuing resurgence of classic motorcycling in the UK, and downunder. Even more importantly, the large parts stores in the US are vital in keeping the existing world fleet of classic British bikes on the roads. Should that US parts supply dwindle, then the retail and direct parts distribution channels downunder and perhaps elsewhere, would quickly show the impact. I hope the suppliers are planning ahead to cope with this event. And this is another good reason why statistical analyses of the kind in this book are so important - with this information suppliers can anticipate future parts supply channel shifts, enabling them to tailor the supply of pattern parts to fill any projected decline in supply of new old stock parts.

A DIY Guide For Classic Bikes In Any Country

This section provides interested readers with a 'step-by-step guide' to working out classic bike numbers in any country.

1. Find suitable magazines, papers or auctions including EBay, to harvest ads.
2. Decide on sample parameters, i.e., what to include and exclude.
3. Collect as many bike ads as you can - at least 2000, spread over 2-3 years or more. Try to leave a gap of 2-3 months between monthly samples, to avoid counting the same bike twice.
4. Tally the ads by make either manually with graph paper, or on a laptop.
5. Establish a 'Projection Factor' (see page 228) and thereby the estimated national population of classics. This will be a process of canvassing your national statistician, net searches, club and register enquiries, number crunching, lots of dead-ends and judgment calls, and cross-checking against other information sources. Eventually, you'll come up with a factor that passes your validations.
6. Apply the Projection Factor and examine the resulting marque projections against any known marque registers or international data from similar countries.

7. Challenge and validate your findings by seeking some census or population tallies for one or more marques. Ideally three or more club registers giving a mix of large and small marques should fall in and around your model forecasts in a sort of triangulation process.

8. Accept your findings, unless or until further information arrives that lets you refine your model.

NB: This simple approach is made more difficult, by government statisticians' disinterest in motorcycles. An example was the Australian Statistician excusing himself several years ago, when he announced they were ceasing the analysis of motorcycle registration statistics because 'motorcycles comprise less than 5% of the Australian vehicle fleet'. The funds going into motorcycle crash statistics, of course continued. Unsurprisingly, just a few years later motorcycles are the fastest growing segment of the country's transport fleet with 31.5% growth. A key section of transport statistics are now going under-reported. No wonder motorcyclists are unhappy with government agencies.

Illus 11.3 A NZ Rudge-Whitworth ca 1926

Methodology Used In The Classic Bike Survival Model

When we buy the family car two questions we always ask are, first, is it a 'popular' model, or an orphan where parts are hard to get? And second, what's a 'fair market price' for it, both now and when we sell it?

For classic motorcycle buyers, neither question has been easy to answer. Apart from the summary 1993 Buyers Guide in Classic Bike, I found neither question covered in the classic bike literature, whether in magazines or in the hundreds of books examined in writing this one. On the first question of 'popularity', later Triumphs, BSAs and Nortons are plentiful, or at least often advertised. For many of these bikes, parts are indeed still available and backup through marque clubs offers help. For other marques and models the situation is less clear, and it becomes quite opaque for smaller and less familiar marques. On the second question, of 'fair market prices'; establishing a fair market price partly depends on the market i.e. retail shop, auction or private sale. It also depends on the bike brand, model and condition, and on the market knowledge of the parties involved. Again, for smaller and less familiar marques, it's hard to estimate a fair market value, because so few turn up for sale at the same time.

For all makes and models, there has really been no research to guide riders on the question of the future resale value of classic bikes. These issues demanded answers and applying statistics to map the industry was the only way riders were going to get them. Going back to our original question of 'popularity', this could be answered if we knew how many classic motorcycles and makes survive around the world today, and especially in our own country. This knowledge would guide us into market conditions i.e. to popularity, range of bike choice, new and used parts supply, technical literature, existence of clubs and support circles etc . The second issue of 'prices and values', really called for a sort of 'Consumer Price Index' for classic motorcycles, and of course such a thing has never been done. So I tackled both.

At the end of the day, what matters is not the analysis, but the answers they give classic riders. These charts and tables let riders see their favourite pursuit from fresh angles and in ways that have never been offered to riders before. Even so, the 'sizzle is more important than the sausage', so all the boring stuff on methods, details etc, is taken out into this appendix. First, I'll roughly sketch out what was done and what it showed, and then pull apart the interesting bits to answer some fundamental questions about our favourite pastime.

Background - How Many Bikes Survive?

This simple question took me months to even get to the start line. My phone and internet bills went through the roof, and libraries became familiar places to spend the days. Initially, the best approach seemed to be to access the original British industry production statistics, and/or company sales and export records, then trace the original bike exports to countries of interest, finally working forward with marque club registers to count and/or estimate the approximate numbers surviving. The lack of all marques' production data availability knocked this approach out early on and a further reason for doing so is that subsequent re-exports and bike migration between countries would stymie such a line of research. As well, the data were just.... well...really old. Clearly, using old data would not do. The answer had to lie with more recent records of classic bikes, but where were they? Licensing bodies in most countries seem to have overlooked the existence of motorcycles until quite recently, except for in depth measures of motorcycle accidents, and endless papers on helmet research.

Even in the UK, the ancestral home of classic motorcycling, the first real motorcycle industry statistical analysis didn't occur till 2003, and classic bikes weren't properly explored in that. In the USA the federal-based system is admirably detailed for every form of human transport, except for motorcycles. I considered working through each of the fifty US state registries, but realised it would take a call-centre team months to handle the communications, and the data may not be accessible from all registries. Another dead end. Another promising genealogical line of research was to collect the number of previous owners of classic bikes, the 'keepers' and use that to work forward to an estimate of surviving classics. This proved another dead-end, as only the UK seems to go to this trouble.

Finally, after poring over the Classic Bike Buyers Guides from 1993-1994, I realised the truth in Tolkien's hobbit-saying '..you can see through a brick wall in time...'. The obvious source of recent information about classic bikes was...recent For Sale advertisements. How simple! I'd ignored one of Fred Hoyle's 'Rules of Forecasting', i.e. to 'look for the obvious things, as they're the ones most people overlook...'

The Research Approach Develops

Initially in the UK and then in Australia, I qualified advertising sources and harvested many thousands of classic bikes via ads from a mix of magazines, papers, and auctions. This sampling approach, with entry criteria to weed out e.g. specials, racers, mopeds etc, produced a workable platform of some forty classic marques, from AJS to Zundapp. The sampling plan was piloted, pre-tested, checked and validated with marque clubs. A projection factor was developed to bring the sample numbers up the estimated national tallies of the forty-two sample categories. This is a standard industrial research approach, used by government, business and academic statisticians, as well as by market researchers. The projection factors were formed from data series available from regulatory authorities' archives. These data derive from bike licensing and registration information. The projection factors were validated, with marque clubs and classic riders having a good grasp of their country marque stocks. When completed, the country studies were compared one to another for any obvious discrepancy. This chapter's tables and charts summarise the findings from that research and consultation. It is pioneering stuff, and I expect it will trigger other classic riders to try and replicate my findings, and extend them to further states and countries, especially in the Asia-Pacific region, and in North and South America.

Country Survival Model Statistical Notes

"...any hacker can run data series through a PC...much of the expertise in forecasting is based upon the 'art' employed in the forecasting process...' Dick Berry, Business Forecaster

Dick Berry could well have had classic motorcycles in mind. Researching this section of the book showed how necessary it is to combine statistical and classic bike know-how, to produce meaningful results. While some readers won't bother with this section, there will be many others who want to delve behind the summary statistics presented. Still others may be stimulated by the research in the book and take my models to begin classic research in their own country. If you fall into this category, I'm sure your fellow riders will welcome your efforts. I'm happy to assist any such research efforts with advice to help you get underway. You can email me on *rexhunn@bigpond.com* or via Panther Publishing in the UK. To all those interested in the research details and modus operandum...welcome to the hunt!

Sampling Plan

The sampling plan called for quota sampling of classic motorcycle advertisements in the UK. After consultation with UK riders, I selected the following magazines for the sample: Classic Bike issues from 2004-2005-2006, together with Classic Motorcycle and the Old Bike Mart issues from the period. Auction results were from Bonhams. The criteria for inclusion included road bike ads that gave a clear description of at least Year, Make, Model and some description of condition. Ads for racers, choppers, hybrids (except Tritons et al, of course), scooters, mopeds and specials were excluded. Basket cases and incomplete bikes 'suitable for restoration' were also excluded. Also excluded were bikes that were advertised from outside the UK, and bikes that were freshly landed in the UK. This was necessary to preserve the integrity of the sampling. The essence of the sampling approach was that advertised bikes represented in important ways, the balance of the population of similar UK bikes that were not up for sale that year. Thus freshly landed bikes could not meaningfully be said to represent similar bikes that were originally sold and delivered in UK and had remained there.

The strengths of this approach is that it uses the very latest data on classics and in very large numbers, but also potentially contains a source of bias. This lies in the assumption that the retention of bikes from different marques is approximately similar. Putting this another away, I had to assume that any Triumph Bonneville say, was just as likely as any Matchless, to be offered for sale by the owner during the years I monitored. Being conscious of this from the outset, I extended my sampling from 2006 back into 2005 and later back into 2004, to help account for any different propensity to list different marques at differing frequencies. The concern is real as the sketchy national data available on classic bike retention tends to support what we see around us at club level, i.e. that classic owners hang onto their bikes for a longer time than riders of modern motorcycles. These data need to be interpreted however, given the way licensing authorities collect and record their data. They certainly don't design their records for insight into classic motorcycling!

Bikes registered some years after manufacture, but for the first time in a country, may pop up in such figures as older bikes that have never been resold. Nevertheless it may be that using current for sale ads still fails to detect bikes that haven't been sold more than once. For the major marques this isn't a problem as the numbers of bikes involved are so large that the 'law of large numbers' is on our side. We can safely assume the range of say Triumph models, kept off the market for 30-40 years, is consistent with the range of Triumphs that have and are being offered for sale. Partly this is a question of sample size, and the selection of a 2% sample size, (as used by UK transport statisticians) was deliberate to help the control of these aspects. It's interesting to speculate however, that if there is a sizable number of classic bikes still held by their first UK owner, then that owner group must be nearly ready to fall off their perch! In that case, we may look for a spike in bikes offered for sale over the next few years, irrespective of price and market shifts. This will show whether this aspect is significant or not. On the other hand, the aging owners may do as my sons are demanding i.e. that I hand my bikes down to the next generation. Thus, I suppose it's possible some classic bikes will never be sold more than once!

For the majority of classic makes and models, I believe we are portraying the state of play with reasonable accuracy. As mine seems to be the first such study, then it is up to those who follow to improve on my research model.

Sample Size Considerations

The sample size was set at approx 2% for the UK and Australia, following the sample sizes normally used for such transport surveys in the UK, e.g. surveys for National Statistics, the DVLA and MoT. The 'sampling power' of a 2% quota sample seems to give meaningful results, certainly for the major marques. Equally, for a number of the smaller marques, e.g. Norman, OK, Excelsior, Brough etc. such an approach cannot be held to give accurate projections of the total UK population, down to the last bike. That is simply unachievable. This method should however, give reasonable insight into the relative numbers of the smaller marques, even if not the absolute numbers. The small total number of survivors, coupled with their rate of turnover, reduces the probability of 'capture' in a survey approach of this type. Increasing the sample size would not necessarily give more accuracy to these marque projections. Indeed for the very smallest marque survivors, a better approach may be to perform field research among the marque clubs and attempt to count each surviving bike. Therefore all we can properly say about the marques that comprise the lower half of the rankings, is that we're now sure... that there are not many about!

This in itself is valuable information, where for example, a reader is considering purchasing such a bike. Armed with these survey results he may temper his enthusiasm with the knowledge that bikes, parts and back-up may be a real issue for future ownership. On the other hand, these smaller marques contain some of the most valuable of classic British motorcycles e.g. Brough, Vincent and Rudge. For these marques, peer support is probably greater than for most other makes, including the larger ones. Tallying them may well be practicable.

There was an opportunity to validate the model in New Zealand where some historical data on classic bike registrations by year and make became available for research. This data was qualified and a 22% sample formed, excluding scooters and off-road bikes. New Zealand advertising data were compared and the two sampling approaches compared well. I've used registration data in this instance as it enabled a larger sample size, and also disclosed important aspects of classic bike sampling in other countries.

Projection Factors

There are several types of Projection Factor that you can choose. The 'sample survey coupled with a projection factor' approach is widely used in commercial market research and is a valid approach to difficult problems. In a number of industries including the pharmaceutical industry, it has provided most companies around the world with their basic market research into sales and share for more than forty years. In our case, the choice of a Projection Factor was made easier in countries where archival data could be extracted and massaged, and a factor developed.

Other ways of computing a projection factor include taking a 'vertical marque tally', if you like, and coupling it with the horizontal sampling approach taken here. For example, sampling horizontally first to give the percentage shares of the forty makes; then using a reliable and known country population of bikes such as Vincents or Velocettes or perhaps Indians, and calculating a projection factor to bring the sample Velocette numbers up to the total register population. In this approach, one has to allow for bikes outside the register, but marque members will usually have a good feel of these numbers, or at least some ratio you can use. With a projection factor established for say Velocettes, you could apply this to all makes to assemble the estimated national population for all classic makes in your selected country. This approach is less preferable than the more broadly-based approach used here, as sampling errors in the Velocette tally, will be exaggerated in the final population estimates and worse, spread across all the other marques.

Depending on the country circumstances, and if neither of the above approaches is workable, then researchers could always undertake a smaller 'field survey' to establish a projection factor. This would involve taking a defined geographic area, one that was representative of the national classic scene, and undertaking field research to try and count every last classic bike in that area. Using population and demographic data, we could then scale up the findings to represent the national scene in the country. Providing the sample area is representative of the demographics of the rest of the country, then the approach should work.

Data series from country registrations can sometimes be accessed to break out the bikes by the 'year of manufacture' coding. This can allow the generation of estimates for say pre-1979 or pre-1985 registered bikes. In the latter case, our data series will be biased by it's mixture of two distinct epochs in motorcycle history, i.e. the end of the first British era (somewhere between 1974 and 1976) and the flowering of the Japanese bike era (starting between 1976 and 1980). In such cases, we will need to dissect out the earlier period, to avoid bias. It is possible to do this by 'data bridging', if you like to term it that. Such data series are often presented by government authorities as grouped into five year lumps. By taking the percentage changes period by period, and then averaging the percentage change, we may be able to work back and dissect out the beginning of the Japanese period from the end of the British period. The arithmetic is pretty straightforward and if you're comfortable with percentages and averages, anyone can do it. If handy with Excel spreadsheet, then a few more high-powered tools such as geometric means etc can be used.

Registration Hurdles

These country registration data can be slippery, as they are sometimes not particularly geared to our survey category. Other types of vehicles may be included as for example in certain Australian states where farm tractors, mopeds and ATV's (all terrain vehicles) are misleadingly included. More importantly, where historic vehicle registration schemes exist, these enable discounted, concessional or conditional registration of classic, vintage and veteran bikes. Such categories of bikes may be miscoded, excluded, miscounted, or relegated from any mainstream census. For example in the 1995 Australian census, South Australia omitted to code 17,173 bikes. This sort of situation reflects a widespread disinterest in motorcycle ownership statistics at government levels in many countries. This disinterest generates anomalies in the national vehicle census and devalues the census into some sort of biased, large sample. It's no longer an authentic vehicle census for any statistician. These difficulties are best summed up by a recent conversation I had with a government statistician about vehicle census data. He was surprised to find his published census omitted significant groups of vehicles, and admitted he had no idea of scrappage rates, numbers of unlicensed bikes on the road, or the population of scooters vs motorcycles, nor any idea of the national census of classic bikes on club plates. He even had no idea of the distinction between veteran, vintage and classic vehicles! Where do we begin to correct all this?

Classic bikes under conditional plates in most, but not all Australian states are coded using an insurance code. This code is a grab-bag type of code which includes other vehicle types, and is incompatible with the national statisticians (ABS) codings. Rightly, the ABS reject such data as 'out of scope', but publish the partial data anyway. This is no solution. It injects systematic bias into the so-called census figures because classic bikes are increasingly migrating across to conditional plates. The census figures report this as a decline in the number of classic bikes in the country. It is plainly wrong - see table 11.10 below. Also using official sources can overlook bikes that may be unlicensed temporarily or usually, but are roadworthy, and may be being ridden regularly. This practice is somewhat of a grey area, ranging from occasional road testing of restorations all the way to outright licence evasion. It's more often seen in countries where either license plate testing hurdles are high or unsympathetic, and/or licensing fees and insurance are unduly high, thus encouraging unlicensed use. In the UK the SORN, or free of charge licensing of pre-1973 bikes, reduces that source of potential bias in the recent data. Plate-swapping can still occur, where perhaps bikes have failed an MoT or where the owners build-state isn't acceptable to authorities even if it is to the owner. This is perhaps more likely where owners possess a collection of classics,with some plated and others not, and the plates simply changed around for the 'bike of the day'. (NB this is an illegal practice and may invalidate insurance not to mention involving a heavy fine should the owner be caught) For example, I own six classics but only three are ever plated.

This practice may be reducing in the UK but is still prevalent in some countries, New Zealand for example, where classics are fully taxed until they are 40 years old. Here classics made between 1966 and 1976 fall into this category, and owners face an unfair licensing charge and thus temptation. It's perhaps not surprising that in New Zealand, a typical owner may have three bikes and the regulatory authorities say its not unknown for owners to switch a single plate around up to six bikes. This is a silly and an iniquitous situation for classics, exceeded only by the historically exorbitant costs of motorcycle licences in NSW in Australia. Here, license fees were once ramped up to car rates, allegedly to assist an ailing car industry. New South Wales bike registrations plummeted, and remained there. To this day, NSW has only two thirds of the per capita motorcycle riders it once had, and riders are still paying inflated licence fees. In Victoria, riders are being charged £20 per annum for a 'safety levy' that has aroused many riders anger.

Here, as in other countries, you hear the same complaints and demands for a single transferable license as in computer software, i.e. one that's legally transferable to whatever bike from your collection that you elect to ride on the day. This argument of course, rests on the reasonable claim, that one can only ride one bike at a time. Hard to deny that one.

Projection Factor Validation

This is necessary, if only to force ourselves to set aside our views and challenge the findings by comparing them against someone else's. I was able to do this for the Australian Model, by locating some census figures from the ABS, and working through the bias in the data. These were data from 1995 and 2005 that broke down classic motorcycle registrations by year of manufacture (YoM) and even brand. The validation is shown in Table 11.10 below

	Survival	1995 Census*	2005 Census*
Table 11.10 Model vs Census Validation for Marques, Pre-1979			
Marque	**Estimates**	**Make by YoM**	**Make by YoM**
BMW	1,570	1,688 (-7.5%)	1,691 (-7.2%)
Ducati	1,130	1,287 (-13.8%)	1,171 (-3.5%)
Harley-Davidson	5,360	4,521 (+15.6%)	4,186 (-28.0%)
Others	n/a	5,162 (n/a)	n/a n/a
Total	8,060	7,496 (+6.9%)	n/a n/a

* includes scooters, excludes Qld, SA, WA, NT, ACT, Tas club plates.
NB: *Most states introduced conditional plating schemes over 2002-2003.*

The 1995 MVC [motor vehicle census] report included eight Pre-1979 marques. The 2005 census included more. Comparison of the eight marques' raw data, totalling 26,000 bikes or over half the population indicated an average 4% variance between model and census. However encouraging this might appear, this illustrates Dick Berry's axiom above on the danger of using raw data. I excluded the four Japanese makers as their figures included a large number of mopeds and scooters that would bias any pure motorcycle comparison. Scooters were of course, excluded from the Survival Model. The marques above were not noted for moped sales during the validation period. Triumph were also held aside but for a different reason. The 1995 census showed 3,108 Triumphs on the road, versus the 2006 model forecast of 6,780 on the road now. Why the difference? The answer lies in the pattern of Triumph imports from the USA over the years since 1995. The gap of 3,500 bikes is partly explained by the containers of Triumphs landing in Australia over that ten year period. Doubtless those containers also included Harleys, which help to explain some of that variance also. The marques above comprise nearly 20% of classic bikes in Australia, which is an adequate validation sample.

It's worth noting also that the 1995 census failed to allocate 15% of the bikes to a brand, so understating most or all brands, and perhaps explaining some more variance. This was due to a known ABS coding failure in Adelaide. We can control for this by pro-rating the 'Others' category across the validation marques, assuming that the ABS omissions are distributed consistently across the marques. This seems reasonable for what were clerical omissions.

Allocating the omitted bikes to the total validation sample brings that to 8,255 census bikes versus the 8,060 bikes predicted by the Survival Model. The difference overall is then just 2.4%.

Now for avoidance of doubt, I'm not claiming that degree of accuracy for the Survival Model, especially for the smaller marques. I think it's more likely that a +/-10% overall level of accuracy is achievable with models of this type, and then only for those medium and larger-sized marques, and for year on year trends. This should be sufficient for riders to use the model to grasp market trends with a fair degree of confidence. However, for overall validation purposes, that 2.4% variance is reassuring.

On balance, I think the validation points to the Australian classic population being, if anything, less than the existing model projects. I anticipate the next generation of the Survival Model will better assess scrappage against new classics entering the market, more accurately dissect out scooter, mopeds, power-cycles etc, better capture club bikes, and better cope with the inbuilt census bias. On balance I expect it may assess the 2006 population at less than 42,000. If so it may be coincidentally closer to the 37,580 bikes counted in the first bike census way back in 1923.

For this first attempt at a model however, I think we have our arms around the population of classic bikes in the countries explored. Doubtless, these initial findings will be refined, with the aim of gaining a clear idea where these historic vehicles are, and how many still exist. The answers to these simple questions will enable the caretakers of these vehicles to better conserve their charges, and obtain the necessary regulatory and political resources and priorities, to enable classic bikes to remain on the roads for another century.

The use of a much larger sample in New Zealand gave similarly consistent results for the major makes, as found in Australia. It was possible in New Zealand to compare the forecasts against some marque clubs estimates. The BSA estimate is consistent with expert assessments, as is the Indian estimate. The Vincent estimate was somewhat high compared to Vincent owners estimates there. As discussed above, this is what we would expect with smaller marques. Increasing sample size beyond a certain point, does not improve accuracy in these kinds of data. I think the Vincent numbers indicate both the small numbers of survivors, and the smaller numbers held by individual owners versus say BSA, where multiple bikes are normally held, and only one or two plated. If a rider only has one Vincent, he will want to ride it at least at rallies, and take the trouble to plate it. It's always worth it with a Vincent!

Other Classes of Classic Motor Cycles

Significant classes of classic motor cycles were omitted from my roadworthy bike survival analyses. Classic scooters and power cycles, whether roadworthy or basket cases were excluded, given that this book focuses on larger road-going and touring machines. I've nothing against mopeds and still daydream about finding and restoring my old Zundapp Combinette. Other classes of bikes normally not registrable such as classic racers and offroad bikes including motocross, trials and farm bikes etc, were also excluded. From the impressions gained in dissecting some of these classes out of the data presented, I guesstimate they'd inflate by some 5-10%, the total classic, vintage and veteran bikes covered in the survival model.

British Industry Exports to USA Market 1946-1974

In Table 11.1, is the composite production and export model that estimates the flow of classic British motorcycles exported to the USA, after WWII and up to the dissolution of the BSA Group. Despite the gaps in the data, it's possible to conclude that at best, approx 300,000 bikes were exported to the USA over the period. This compares with 7,000,000 Japanese bikes over a similar period, and 1,000,000 Harley-Davidsons produced. A minimax forecast of surviving USA classic British bikes is 30,000-60,000 bikes. As with such industry models, it includes census data, estimates, blanks, interpolations, provisions and data bridges.

Illus 11.4 Indians are all about in NZ and this fine example shows why.

Table 11.11   British Motorcycle Industry Export Sales to the USA 1946 - 1974

Year	Triumph Production	Triumph US Exports	Triumph USA Branch Sales West	Triumph USA Branch Sales East	Triumph USA Branch Sales	BSA Production ****	BSA US Exports ****	BSA Grp US Exports	Other UK US Exports	Total USA UK Imports	Japan US Exports **	USA Total Bike Market	Harley-D Production *	UK/US Exports (VMCC) % Variance	YMCC:Model Model / % Variance VMCC	Model Forecast	Total UK Prod. ***
1946	9,477	4,208	na	na	na	1,000	5,208	2,378	7,586	37,586	0	30,000	n/a	-	9,064	na	na
1947	10,000	5,400	na	na	na	3,000	8,400	5,073	13,473	43,473	0	30,000	11,260	-19.7	13,473	na	na
1948	11,841	7,933	na	na	na	3,000	10,933	2,000	12,933	42,933	0	30,000	8,178	-58.1	12,933	na	na
1949	11,877	7,542	na	na	na	3,000	10,542	2,000	12,542	42,542	0	30,000	4,267	-193.9	12,542	na	na
1950	14,306	9,442	na	na	na	4,000	13,442	2,000	15,442	45,442	0	30,000	8,582	-79.9	15,442	na	na
1951	5,065	3,277	na	na	na	4,000	7,277	2,000	9,277	39,277	0	30,000	8,195	-13.2	9,277	na	na
1952	7,000	4,200	na	na	na	4,000	8,200	2,000	10,200	40,200	0	30,000	na	na	10,200	na	na
1953	8,000	4,800	na	na	na	4,000	8,800	1,000	9,800	39,800	0	30,000	5,000	-96.0	9,800	na	na
1954	9,000	5,400	na	na	na	4,000	9,400	2,000	11,400	41,400	0	30,000	na	na	11,400	na	na
1955	9,000	5,400	na	na	na	4,000	9,400	2,000	11,400	41,400	0	30,000	na	na	11,400	na	na
1956	9,000	5,400	na	na	na	4,000	9,400	2,000	11,400	41,400	0	30,000	10,000	-14.0	11,400	na	na
1957	9,000	5,400	na	na	na	4,000	9,400	2,000	11,400	41,400	0	30,000	7,926	-43.8	11,400	na	na
1958	7,588	4,553	1,756	2,797	30,000	4,500	9,053	2,000	na	41,053	0	50,000	na	na	11,053	na	na
1959	9,542	5,725	2,458	3,267	30,000	4,500	10,225	2,000	na	62,225	0	50,000	na	na	12,225	na	na
1960	10,977	6,586	2,787	3,799	30,000	4,500	11,086	2,000	na	73,086	10,000	50,000	na	na	13,086	na	na
1961	4,145	2,487	1,009	1,478	30,000	4,500	6,987	1,500	na	78,987	20,000	50,000	na	na	8,987	na	na
1962	7,512	4,507	2,047	2,460	27,000	4,200	8,707	1,000	na	100,207	40,000	50,000	na	na	10,207	na	na
1963	12,788	7,673	3,378	4,295	26,000	4,050	11,723	1,000	na	142,723	80,000	50,000	na	na	12,723	na	na
1964	15,958	9,575	4,773	4,802	25,000	3,900	13,475	1,000	na	224,475	160,000	50,000	na	na	14,475	na	na
1965	25,563	15,338	6,531	8,807	24,000	3,750	19,088	1,000	na	390,088	320,000	50,000	na	na	20,088	na	na
1966	20,000	10,000	na	na	12,852	3,600	13,600	1,000	na	464,600	400,000	50,000	na	na	14,600	69,500	na
1967	19,000	10,450	na	na	43,436	5,971	23,302	1,000	na	574,302	500,000	50,000	na	na	24,302	na	na
1968	18,000	9,000	na	na	38,809	3,000	14,971	1,000	na	615,971	550,000	50,000	na	na	15,971	71,010	na
1969	17,000	8,500	na	na	20,000	2,550	11,500	1,000	na	662,500	600,000	50,000	na	na	12,500	64,521	na
1970	15,000	6,000	na	na	17,000	1,500	8,550	800	na	709,350	650,000	50,000	na	na	9,350	86,650	na
1971	10,000	4,000	na	na	10,000	1,050	5,500	800	na	756,300	700,000	50,000	na	na	6,300	48,832	na
1972	10,000	3,000	na	na	7,000	750	4,050	800	na	854,850	800,000	50,000	na	na	4,850	48,439	na
1973	7,000	1,750	na	na	5,000	100	2,500	800	na	1,453,300	1,400,000	50,000	na	na	3,300	40,000	na
1974	0	0	na	na	500	na	100	na	na	850,900	800,000	50,000	na	na	900	na	na
Total	323,639	177,546	na	na	na	na	288,270	46,951	na	8,555,221	7,030,000	1,190,000	na	na	335,221	na	na

Notes to Table 11.11

- Figures in bold are actual data , sourced from the VMCC, company and secondary records such as Tragatsch, Wilson etc. Remaining data are estimates.
- BSA Group Exports over 1946-1974 reached approximately 290,000 bikes
- Provision for 3-5000 other British exports over 1975-1979, mainly Nortons
- Provisionally approximately 300,000 net new UK bikes were exported to the USA between 1946 and 1974, allowing for returned goods.
- About 7 million Japanese bikes were exported to the USA over the same period.
- Harley-Davidson made approximately 1,000,000 bikes over the same period.
- The surviving UK bikes in the USA are estimated at 1 in 10 or approximately 30,000 bikes

*   *Estimates based on Harley-Davidson secondary sources*

**   *H Sucher, The Milwaukee Marvel, p188*

***   *Tragatsch (in 1974, with Triumph closed and BSA semi-closed, still 40,000 bikes were produced nationally)*

*****Steve Wilson, (BSA Motorcycles since 1950). 1966/67 was the peak production year*

Illus 11.5 A restored 1955 AJS Model 20 500cc twin sold in NZ

12 *The Bonnie Index*
The Consumer Price Index for Classic Bikes

"The price of error is not a slow lap but a short life. Get it wrong and a wall or a tree usually awaits." M. McDiarmid on the TT

The Bonnie Index is the first substantial economic analysis of classic motorcycle price movements covering the 1975-2006 period, with forecasts out to 2010. The Bonnie Index is designed to become the consumer price index for classic motorcycles. It is so called as it charts classic bike price movements using Triumph 650cc twin model prices as the guide. The prices are collected and formed into a collection of price series for six groups of different Triumph models. These six series are aggregated into a master price series from which the Bonnie Index is derived. In other words, the price series are in £ and the price indices in numbers.

Triumph twins were chosen for much the same reasons as the 'Big Mac Index' is used by economists when comparing the cost of living in different countries. Triumph twins were the most successful bikes exported by the British industry for decades, and went to more countries than any other make, save perhaps BSA. No other marque or model achieved the enduring international sales success of the Triumph twins that is so necessary for the formation of a consumer price index with international comparisons. The only other possibility, BSA twins survive at only about 50% to 60% of the Triumph rate – too few to form an index.

The Bonnie Index has been developed for both the UK and Australia. To make the Index more widely applicable than just to Triumph Bonnevilles, separate series and indices are provided for different Triumph models and measured over three Triumph design time periods. These design periods were chosen from the *Classic Bike 1993-1994 Buyers Guide* categories as best representing important model groups under the Triumph marque. They were also checked against Roy Bacon's published product group records. Only bikes manufactured up until 1980 were included to keep it consistent with other parts of this book's statistical modelling. The two model groups were firstly the Triumph Bonnevilles and secondly, the single carburettor variants of the Bonneville twins, the Thunderbirds, Trophys and Tigers. These two Triumph model groups were each broken down into three time periods, as described above. The structure of the Bonnie Index is shown in Table 12.1.

The Bonnie Index is aggregated from six price series developed for each of the Triumph product groups in Table 12.1. By developing a basket of price series, I expected to validate the price differences for these model years that had caused Classic Bike to devise these categories in the first place. Also making the Bonnie Index a broadly-based index would better represent the wider movements in classic British marque prices generally.

Table 12.1		The Bonnie Index Construction			
Bonneville Groups			**Tiger/Trophy/Thunderbird Groups**		
Group 1 **1959-1965**	**Group 2** **1966-1970**	**Group 3** **1971-1980**	**Group 4** **1954-1965**	**Group 5** **1966-1970**	**Group 6** **1971-1980**
T120	T120	T120	6T	TR6	TR6
		T120R	TR6	TR6SS	TR6R
		T120V	T110		TR6C
		T140			TR7
		T140V			

The British Bonnie Index

The Bonnie Index and associated price series for the UK are shown numerically in Table 12.2, which shows the price series in both current and 'real' price terms. Current prices are the actual prices paid in the years to which they relate. Real prices show prices after allowing for the effects of inflation and are discussed in greater depth below. Also shown are the annual percentage changes.

The index numbers on the right of the table show that prices have risen by approximately 650% since 1981 in current prices, an average annual compounded growth rate of 26%. After allowing for inflation the index has still risen by 231%, an average annual compound growth rate of 9.2%. While the index numbers above are useful, it can be tedious inspecting lists. The interesting findings are better shown in the charts, starting with the UK Price Series in Chart 12.1.

Table 12.2   UK Bonneville Index 1981 - 2006

(Index Base 1990=100)

Year	RPI	Price series Current Terms	Price Series Real Terms	Annual Change Real Terms	Bonnie Index Current Prices	Bonnie Index 1990 prices
1981	69.2	£687.00	£992.77	–	100	100
1982	73.8	£781.00	£1,058.27	6.6%	113.7	106.6
1983	77.3	£851.00	£1,100.91	4.0%	123.9	110.9
1984	80.2	£920.00	£1,147.13	4.2%	133.9	115.5
1985	84.2	£1,051.00	£1,248.22	8.8%	153.0	125.7
1986	86.4	£1,217.00	£1,408.56	12.8%	177.1	141.9
1987	89.6	£1,314.00	£1,466.52	4.1%	191.3	147.7
1988	93.7	£1,755.00	£1,873.00	27.7%	255.5	188.7
1989	99.0	£2,087.00	£2,108.08	12.6%	303.8	212.3
1990	106.7	£3,250.00	£3,045.92	44.5%	473.1	306.8
1991	114.4	£3,140.00	£2,744.76	-9.9%	457.1	276.5
1992	118.0	£2,995.00	£2,538.14	-7.5%	436.0	255.7
1993	121.4	£3,128.00	£2,576.61	1.5%	455.3	259.5
1994	123.9	£3,158.00	£2,548.83	-1.1%	459.7	256.7
1995	127.7	£3,110.00	£2,435.40	-4.5%	452.7	245.3
1996	131.2	£3,529.00	£2,689.79	10.4%	513.7	270.9
1997	134.3	£4,166.00	£3,102.01	15.3%	606.4	312.5
1998	136.9	£3,925.00	£2,867.06	-7.6%	571.3	288.8
1999	139.1	£4,307.00	£3,096.33	8.0%	626.9	311.9
2000	141.2	£4,325.00	£3,063.03	-1.1%	629.5	308.5
2001	143.2	£4,062.00	£2,836.59	-7.4%	591.3	285.7
2002	145.4	£4,419.00	£3,039.20	7.1%	643.2	306.1
2003	147.7	£4,488.00	£3,038.59	0.0%	653.3	306.1
2004	149.5	£4,528.00	£3,028.76	-0.3%	659.1	305.1
2005	152.3	£4,804.00	£3,154.30	4.1%	699.3	317.7
2006	156.0	£5,127.00	£3,286.54	4.2%	746.3	331.0

This first chart shows the annual changes in classic bike prices in the UK over 1981 to 2006. The Triumph twins that sold for an average price of about £500 in 1970, were fetching £687 by the start of the index period. Classic bikes then entered a sustained 'price boom' stretching from 1981, or even a bit earlier, throughout the 1980's decade, and accelerating towards a peak in 1990. UK riders will remember the 1987-1990 period as a frenetic one, the time when investors and speculators moved into the classic motorcycle industry, following the 1987 stock market crash. This pattern of capital flight from shares into assets and collectibles, is typical after stock-market booms and will probably happen again to the classic bike market. As in all bubble markets, a crash followed. By February 1991 *Classic Bike* was reporting dramatic falls in realised prices of 25%. Interestingly, much of this decline was reported as occurring the previous year i.e. 1990. Yet the price series reports 1990 as the peak year for boom prices. How can this be? Reading *The Classic Motor Cycle* of that year, it seems that auction sales were the main sales data source available to classic journalists - so they were used. These sales prices were generalised as if they also measured dealer and private sales. In fact they didn't, and those sales channels behaved differently to auctions.

The price crash sequence can now be traced. It started in auction houses during 1990, probably initially affecting the more premium priced bikes. Dealer sales prices, and certainly privately advertised prices remained at record levels during 1990. Price declines began to affect dealer and private prices during 1991 and

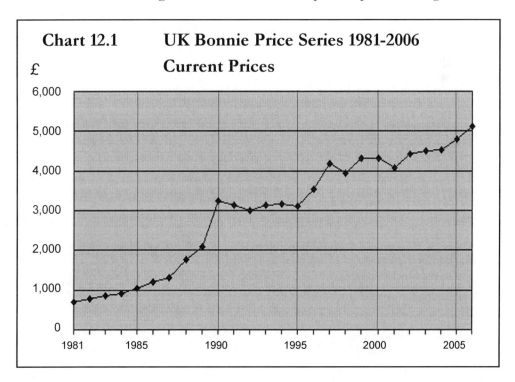

1992. The chronology of events is interesting, in that the falls in private and dealer sale prices lagged behind the auction results by up to a year. This sort of lead/lag situation is typical in economic time series. It's worth noting that future auctions should again provide an early warning of imminent shifts in general classic bike prices. In other words, classic motorcycle auction prices are a 'leading' economic indicator. Owners thinking of selling or buying around such times, may find this knowledge very useful in timing their sale and purchase.

While the thrust of the Bonnie Index is to represent classic bikes across the marques, it's composition enables us to look inside the market leader's product assortment, and examine how the various Triumph models reacted during that dramatic period of 1981 to 1997, and later. The 1981-2006 price series for the six model-group components of the Bonnie Index are shown in Charts 12.2a and 12.2b

The first point to note in these charts, is the same general path of the price series through the 1980s as shown in the main Bonnie Price Series itself. All Triumph models showed the same consistent, narrow advertised price range during the 1980's. However in 1987, this consistency ended with the Group 1 (pre-unit Bonnevilles 1959-1965) rocketing up in price from 1987 to 1990, leaving all other model groups behind. This class nearly tripled it's prices during those boom times. These models then experienced the severe price crash, wrongly if understandably, reported by *Classic Bike's* editor of the time as a general decline across market channels. It wasn't. The Group 1 Bonnevilles came out of their price trough only around 1997 and, after another price correction in 1998-1999, appreciated steadily to 2006 with a price of £7,000. In retrospect, their experience mirrors the other high-value marques such as Vincent, Brough and Velocette. Ongoing research into these smaller marques is expected to show similar price movements that will further cement the Bonnie Index as the benchmark price index for classic bikes.

In Chart 12.2a, the Group 2 (1966-1970) Bonnevilles also experienced significant price inflation during that wild ride over 1987-1990, and peaked in 1990, but with a lower rate of growth than their earlier brothers. They also fell back into a trough over the early 1990's and, after 1997, experienced steady growth in prices. Their price series reached £6,000 by 2006, but never quite closed the gap that had opened up with the early 1959-1965 Bonnies. The wet-frame or 'Late 1971-1974 Bonnies' by contrast, appear to have been hardly affected by the events above - only modest price rises and falls were recorded over the boom and bust periods. The price series for these models reached only £3,500 by 2006, and clearly diverges from the other Bonneville groups. The price positioning of the three Triumph Bonneville model groups in the market is now so separated, that they might be different marques altogether. This further supports the representativeness of the Bonnie Index.

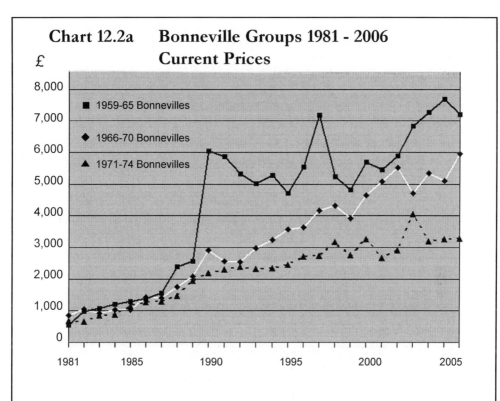

Chart 12.2a   Bonneville Groups 1981 - 2006
Current Prices

£

- ■ 1959-65 Bonnevilles
- ◆ 1966-70 Bonnevilles
- ▲ 1971-74 Bonnevilles

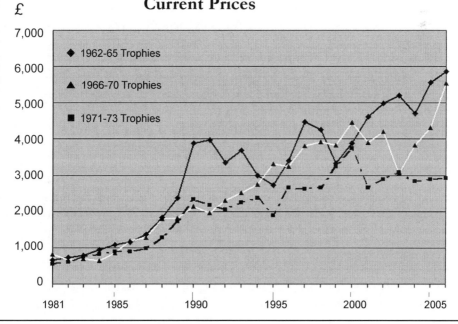

Chart 12.2b   Trophy and Tiger Groups 1981 - 2006
Current Prices

£

- ◆ 1962-65 Trophies
- ▲ 1966-70 Trophies
- ■ 1971-73 Trophies

The single carburettor Triumph models (Chart 12.2b) went through the same mill, and show echoes of the Bonneville experience. The Group 4 Triumphs (1954-1965 Tigers) rose along with their early Bonnie cousins from 1987, but to a lesser extent. They entered a shallower trough in the 1990s and after the 1998-99 hiccup, experienced steady price growth. Their price series reached £6,000 by 2006. Group 5 Tigers (1966-1970) reflect the muted responses of their Bonneville cousins above through the boom and bust period, with their steady appreciation reaching £5,500 by 2006. The Group 6 (1971-1980) Triumphs follow the same path as the wet-frame Bonnevilles, with little real price growth. Their price series reaches just £2,500 by 2006.

What conclusions can be drawn from this analysis to act as a guide during future market fluctuations? First, the classic bike market is a diverse product market. Brands, and even different models within the same brand, clearly react in different ways. Second, auction prices are not representative of market prices as a whole. Third, the market does experience cyclical changes, as do collectibles generally, and fourth, the price trend for classic British bikes is upward over the long term, is likely to remain so, and is likely to spike upward every few years.

That coherent, homogeneous Triumph 650cc twin product range of 1981, now spreads out to cover the spectrum of classic British bike prices. The pre-unit 1959-1965 Group Bonnies have overtaken both Velocettes and Comets and are rising in price towards Vincent twins. The 1966-1970 Group Bonnies and Early and Middle Tigers are also now up there with Velocettes and Comets. By contrast, the later wet-frame Bonnies and Tigers languish with their price series down in the £2,500-3,500 range.

It's also noteworthy, that the typical prices reported for Triumph twins in the *Classic Bike Price Guides* over 1993-1994, consistently overstated the actual advertised market prices as quantified in the Bonnie Index. If the variance were going the other way, one might doubt the Bonnie Index data suspecting bias from a gap between advertised and realised prices. However, it's hard to see owners advertising their bikes at prices consistently less than in the *Buyer's Guide*, and then somehow realising far higher prices. The derivation of the *Buyers Guide* was never detailed by the magazine, but judging from the composition of the figures and their monthly frequency, it is probable that they were mainly auction figures, and/or from proprietary market research data such as *Glass' Guides*. Auction figures can often overstate market prices, given their more selected product mix, not to mention the herd mentality that can overtake even rational classic buyers at auctions. They prove useful only as a leading price indicator and as a value guide for high-end bikes only.

The quantum shifts in bike prices over the 1981-1991 decade and beyond are best seen in the Real Terms Bonnie Price Series, Chart 12.3, which reflects prices after the effects of inflation have been removed. Stripping away inflation, we can see there is actually far more movement in the real prices of bikes. These real movements give a far better insight into the true 'value' of bikes rather than their 'prices'. Classic bike prices bottomed out by 1992, and stayed in a trough until 1995 when prices again rose quite sharply until 1997. During 1998 and 1999 prices fell again. In the new century, real classic bike prices entered a period of steady increase, ahead of inflation, until the present. 2005 and 2006 have seen steady growth, taking the series to a new peak of £3,287 (in real terms), and £5,127 (in current pounds).

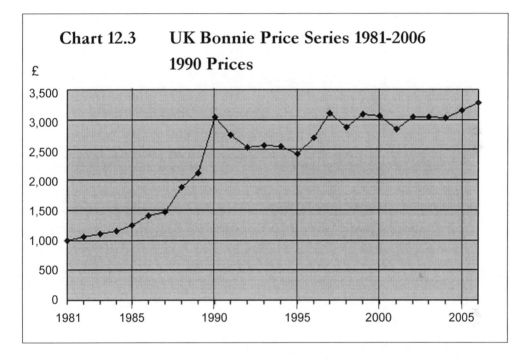

Chart 12.3   UK Bonnie Price Series 1981-2006   1990 Prices

Classic riders who proofread this chapter commented that they recalled some of the major changes it shows. The past that contains the roots of our passion is very interesting, but more important is the future of classic motorcycling. The time series from 1981 to 2006 show striking linearity, and this enables us to base forecasts on the Bonnie Index with some confidence.

In Charts 12.4 and 12.5 overleaf are price series forecasts for the UK classic bike market to 2010. Forecasts are made both in current prices and 1990 prices (i.e. real terms), to get a better feel of things. Regression forecasting in current prices indicates that the Bonnie Price Series will pass £6,000 by 2010. This is an annualised growth rate of approximately 5% over the period, and some 25% overall. In real 1990 pounds, the 2010 forecast is just on £4,000, with comparable real growth rates. To convert this to 2010 pound terms, and compare the twin forecasts, then simply multiply it by the estimated inflation for the 2007-2010 period. I'll leave that for interested readers to work out.

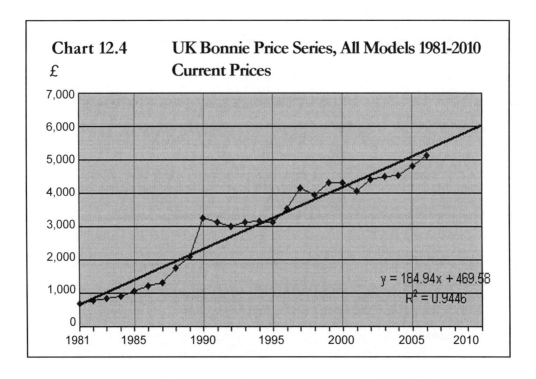

Chart 12.4   UK Bonnie Price Series, All Models 1981-2010
£   Current Prices

$y = 184.94x + 469.58$
$R^2 = 0.9446$

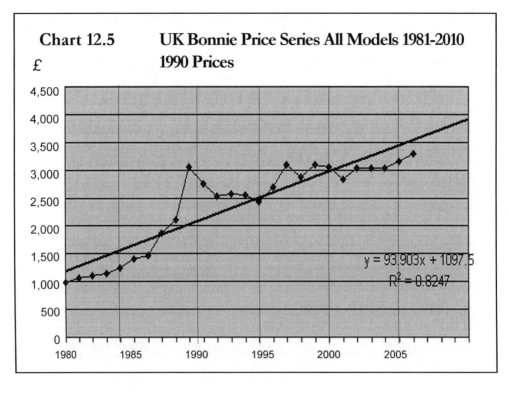

Chart 12.5   UK Bonnie Price Series All Models 1981-2010
£   1990 Prices

$y = 93.903x + 1097.5$
$R^2 = 0.8247$

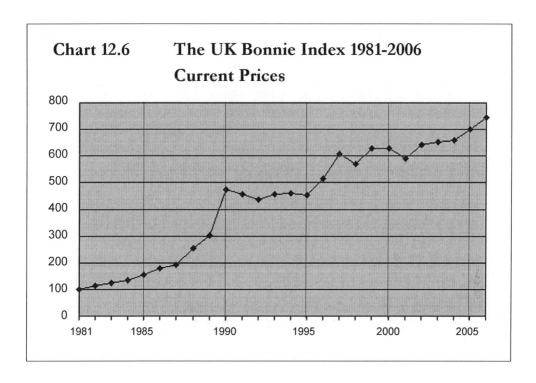

Chart 12.6   The UK Bonnie Index 1981-2006 Current Prices

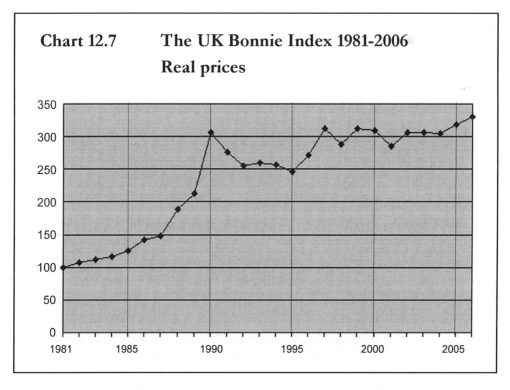

Chart 12.7   The UK Bonnie Index 1981-2006 Real prices

Charts 12.6 and 12.7 show the Bonnie Index itself in numbers. The Bonnie Index simply expresses all the changes in the various price series in a single percentage change each year. Each annual percentage change is related to the starting year i.e. 1981, so a clear grasp can be made of the changes in classic bike prices over the twenty-five year period. In chart 12.6 the Index reached 746 in 2006, nearly a 7% rise on 2005. This shows classic bikes in general have appreciated about 6.5 times in value over the past twenty-five years. This is remarkable appreciation for a collectible, or for that matter any investment. Those astute riders buying British bikes in the 1980s and holding them, have been well rewarded. In chart 12.7, in real terms, the index reached 331, a 4.2% real increase on 2005. After allowing for inflation, there has been a real growth in classic bike values of 2.3 times since 1981, again a striking capital gain in real terms.

Charts 12.8 and 12.9 show the Bonnie Index forecasts out to 2010, in both current and real terms. The Bonnie Index is predicted to reach 849 in current prices by 2010 and allowing for inflation, 385. This represents a 14% increase in current prices and a 16% lift in real terms. There is unusually strong linearity in both data series, and especially in the current price series. The coefficient values of 0.95 and 0.83 show the trend line is explaining 83%-95% of the annual price variations around the trend lines. This is quite sufficient to allow forecasting with reasonable confidence. However, no one number can possible stand for every make and model of classic motorcycle. These forecasts should be taken as a guide to likely future developments for classic and vintage bikes in general. For example, if BSA Bantams suddenly become fashionable and prices were to hike up, no index number could possibly account for this.

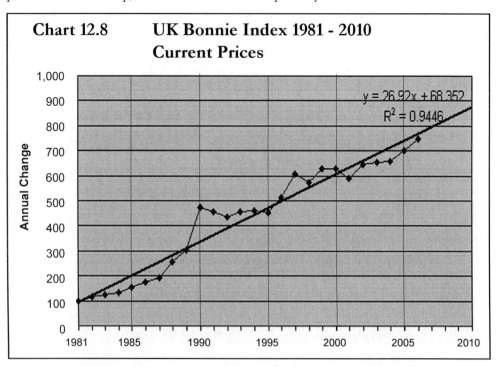

Chart 12.8   UK Bonnie Index 1981 - 2010
Current Prices

$y = 26.92x + 68.352$

$R^2 = 0.9446$

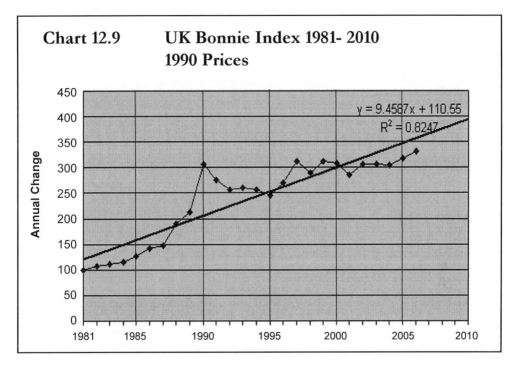

**Chart 12.9   UK Bonnie Index 1981- 2010
1990 Prices**

$y = 9.4587x + 110.55$
$R^2 = 0.8247$

A caveat on forecasting: a wise forecaster once said the only certainty in forecasting is that you'll be wrong. That dictum applies to the classic bike market, given the striking boom-bust changes in the 1980's and the smaller but similar changes in the 1990s. The latter changes probably reflect the impact of the inflation and interest rate changes of the time on the collectibles market, including classic bikes. Forecasts rarely predict the sort of dramatic boom seen in 1987, but we know these changes are cyclical and will reoccur. It would be a brave forecaster who forecast no sudden changes in bike prices over the next five years.

After reviewing the charts and tables of the Bonnie Index, this forecaster believes there are some trends that can trigger another boom in classic bike prices sometime over the next five years. These include for example, the mass of retirees from the post-WWII generation who rode classic British bikes in Commonwealth countries in the 1960s, and are now returning to riding; the inevitable price increase from supply-side restrictions that accompany classic bikery, and the possibility of international economic corrections before 2010. Events like these will probably lead to capital entering the classic bike market, as it did in the 1980s and 1990s. As and when that happens, the 1997-2006 period of stable prices may be seen in retrospect as an ideal time to buy classic motorcycles! And you read it here first.

Further to this, it's worth noting the latest price spike in the Bonnie Index for 2005-2006. This is also clear in the Current Price series and also in the Real Terms series, showing it isn't a background inflationary rise. It is a specific rise in classic bike prices, after eight years of plateaued prices in real terms. Given the demand factors discussed above, I chance my arm and predict we are heading into another boom period of rising bike prices, akin to the 1995-1997 period when the Bonnie Index rose a thousand pounds over two years. That sort of rush would put the Bonnie Index at the predicted 2010 level...as early as 2007-2008, when you may be reading this book, soon after it's launch. We have already eclipsed the peak market prices of 1990 and 1997, and are pushing through the next cycle of record classic prices. Doubtless prices will subside once more after we reach the latest peak, whether in 2008 or 2010.

The UK Bonnie Index seems to provide much useful information about classic bikes, whether looking into the past or the future. (The author hopes to publish regular updates to this index in future years.) To show the British Bonnie Index is no 'flash in the pan', I developed the companion Bonnie Index for Australia, on the same lines as the British Index.

The Australian Bonnie Index

(Please note the Australian dollar, A$, is used in this section: multiply the dollars by 0.4 to convert to British Pounds.) For Australia, the majority of sales data were harvested from the *Trading Post*, (akin to the *Old Bike Mart* in the UK), and which was (and still is) the primary interstate channel for used motor vehicle sales over this period. Key magazines including *Just Bikes* and *Motorcycle Trader* were also canvassed. The breadth of the Price Series and Index was determined by the product range of Triumph twins offered for sale around Australia over those twenty-five years. While there was a surfeit of 1971 and later Bonnevilles, there were less Bonnies from 1959-65 in the records. Earlier Tigers and Trophies were consistently offered for sale throughout the period. This reflects the Australian distributors' original choices of which bike models to import. It also reflects the trans-Pacific trade flows of the period for Triumph and BSA. It is widely recalled in Australia that many BSAs and I think, also Triumphs sold downunder were US specification bikes unsold from the previous season's promotional push in the US market. Whatever stock went unsold in the East Coast US market was trucked across to the crucial USA West Coast market. Unsold bikes from there were shipped across the Pacific to Australia and New Zealand. The Bonnie Index for Australia is shown numerically in Table 12.3.

Table 12.3			The Bonnie Index Australia 1981-2006					

Index Year	Bonnie Index Current Prices	CPI Index	Bonnie Index Real Prices	Annual Real Change	Annual Current Change	The Bonnie Index Current Prices	Bonnie Index Real Prices	
1981	$1,925	54.3	$3,545	n/a	n/a	100.0	100.0	
1982	$2,469	60.3	$4,095	15.5%	28.3%	128.3	115.5	
1983	$2,345	65.5	$3,580	-12.6%	-5.0%	121.8	101.0	
1984	$2,478	67.2	$3,688	3.0%	5.7%	128.7	104.0	
1985	$2,998	72.7	$4,123	11.8%	20.9%	155.7	116.3	
1986	$3,270	79.8	$4,097	-0.6%	9.1%	169.9	115.6	
1987	$3,885	85.5	$4,544	10.9%	18.8%	201.8	128.2	
1988	$4,217	92.0	$4,583	0.9%	8.5%	219.0	129.3	
1989	$4,099	99.2	$4,132	-9.9%	-2.8%	212.9	116.5	
1990	$4,376	106.0	$4,128	-0.1%	6.8%	227.3	116.4	
1991	$4,449	107.6	$4,135	0.2%	1.7%	231.1	116.6	
1992	$5,095	107.9	$4,722	14.2%	14.5%	264.7	133.2	
1993	$4,680	110.0	$4,255	-9.9%	-8.2%	243.1	120.0	
1994	$4,773	112.8	$4,231	-0.6%	2.0%	247.9	119.4	
1995	$5,300	118.5	$4,472	5.7%	11.0%	275.3	126.2	
1996	$4,351	120.3	$3,617	-19.1%	-17.9%	226.0	102.0	
1997	$5,501	120.0	$4,584	26.8%	26.4%	285.8	129.3	
1998	$5,854	121.9	$4,802	4.8%	6.4%	304.1	135.5	
1999	$5,350	124.1	$4,311	-10.2%	-8.6%	277.9	121.6	
2000	$5,802	131.3	$4,419	2.5%	8.4%	301.4	124.6	
2001	$5,948	135.4	$4,393	-0.6%	2.5%	309.0	123.9	
2002	$5,468	139.5	$3,920	-10.8%	-8.1%	284.1	110.6	
2003	$6,012	142.8	$4,210	7.4%	9.9%	312.3	118.8	
2004	$5,753	146.5	$3,927	-6.7%	-4.3%	298.8	110.8	
2005	$6,377	150.6	$4,234	7.8%	10.8%	331.3	119.4	
2006	$7,141	155.1	$4,604	8.7%	12.0%	371.0	130.0	

(Base 1990=100)

The Bonnie Index reached 371 in 2006 in current prices and 130 in real 1990 price terms. The Bonnie Indices for the UK and Australia are compared in Table 12.4 below.

Table 12.4	UK and Australian Bonnie Index at 2006			
Country	**Current Index**	**+/- %**	**Real Index**	**+/-%**
UK	746	+101%	331	+155%
Australia	371	-50%	130	-60%

The magnitude of the market differences is clearly shown in Table 12.4. During the last 25 years, the UK Bonnie Index has doubled the growth of the Australian Index in today's (current) prices. In real terms the gap is relatively greater, once again encouraging the repatriation of bikes to the UK. While the index numbers are extremely useful, the most interesting findings are better disclosed in the following charts.

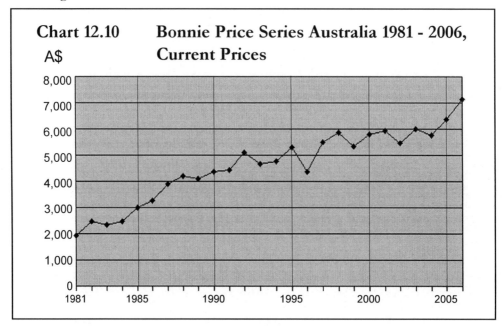

Chart 12.10   Bonnie Price Series Australia 1981 - 2006, A$ Current Prices

Chart 12.10 shows the annual changes in classic bike prices in Australia from 1981 to 2006, in current prices. The Triumph twins exchanged hands for an average price of A$1,925 by the start of the index period. In Australia, classic bikes prices trended upward from 1981, accelerating after 1984 and peaked in 1988, adding 70% in value over this latter period. This correlates with the UK Bonnie Index findings. Over 1988-1989 there was a sharp correction of 10% in real terms. This was triggered by the 1987 Black Monday stock market crash. It contrasts with the UK where the correction did not occur until 1991. The difference in timing probably reflects the speculative element in the UK that was self-perpetuating for a time, pushing the UK market into an overhang, plus some imperfect market knowledge amongst Australian owners. The chronology of events is again interesting, and may prompt UK buyers and sellers to monitor Australian market prices, as a leading indicator for UK classic price trends. By 1992 prices broached A$5,000, and after ups and downs reached A$6,000 in 2003. Over 2003-2005, prices grew in line with inflation, but from 2005 to 2006 double-digit price growth resumed with the series price reaching A$7,141 by 2006.

As in the UK, the major shifts in bike prices over the 1981-1991 decade are best seen in the 'Real Terms' Bonnie Price Series (Chart 12.11), where inflation is taken out of the bike prices.

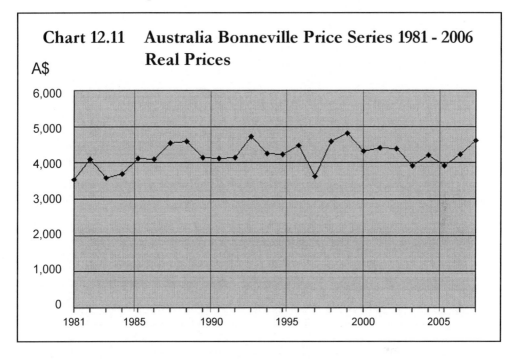

**Chart 12.11   Australia Bonneville Price Series 1981 - 2006
Real Prices**

In Chart 12.11, it can be seen how the declining prices bottomed out by 1990 then stabilised until 1996, when prices again dropped sharply, (perhaps cause by a rise in inflation and interest rates during 1995). Bike prices bounced back in 1997, again displaying the sensitivity of classic bike prices in Australia. From 1997 classic bike prices declined in real terms for five years until 2002. Since then prices have recovered and have grown by 17% in real terms between then and 2006. It's noteworthy that the 2005-2006 period sees the first back-to-back growth years in a decade.

Apart from the leads and lags between classic bike prices in the UK and Australia, discussed above and the long-term trend gap, there seems to be general agreement between the Bonnie Series turning points for both countries. This is reassuring. Like the UK data, the Australian series shows excellent linearity over the 1981-2006 period which enables confident price forecasting shown in Charts 12.12 and 12.13.

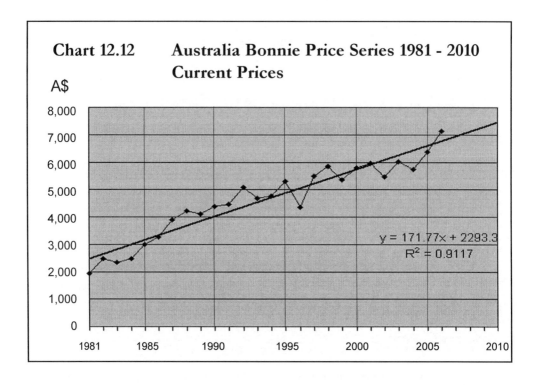

Chart 12.12   Australia Bonnie Price Series 1981 - 2010 Current Prices

A$

$$y = 171.77x + 2293.3$$
$$R^2 = 0.9117$$

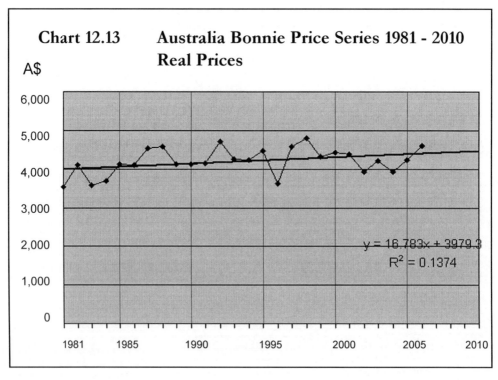

Chart 12.13   Australia Bonnie Price Series 1981 - 2010 Real Prices

A$

$$y = 16.783x + 3979.3$$
$$R^2 = 0.1374$$

In Chart 12.12, the 2010 forecasts, based upon the 1981-2006 period and current prices, indicate continued growth with prices forecast to reach A$7,500. In Chart 12.13, the 2010 forecast is A$4,500 in real terms. This indicates a slight decline in real terms compared with 2006 prices, though as discussed below there are international signs of resurgent prices in 2005-2006.

Chart 12.14 below is an example of one of the constituent index series, this time the 1966-1970 Single Carburetter Tiger models. As expected in a single group index, there is more variation in the data, but the series broadly follows the Bonnie Index, similar to the UK data.

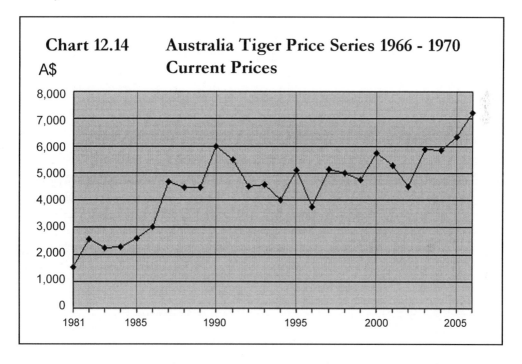

Chart 12.14   Australia Tiger Price Series 1966 - 1970
A$ Current Prices

Despite the relative flatness of the growth curves in Australia, all is not doom for collectors. Looking closely at both charts, it can be seen that recent growth over 2005-2006 mirrors that in the UK. The two year growth figures here are remarkable at 24% and 17% in real terms. In the UK they are 13% and 9%. I believe this recent UK and Australian growth shows both an Anglo-Australian linkage in prices, and an international boom beginning in classic bike prices. Looking at past classic motorcycle price cycles in these charts, it is possible to discern a six or seven year cycle. I would expect that by 2007 we will be half-way into another price cycle, with continued inflation of classic bike prices. At these price levels, the Australian Bonnie Index, is predicted to further decline relative to the UK Index by 2010 and should reach a value of less than half the British Index, allowing for exchange rate differences, as shown in Table 12.5.

Table 12.5 The UK and Australian Bonnie Index as at 2010

Country	Current Index	+/-%	Real Index	+/-%
UK	849	+125%	385	+205%
Australia	378	-55%	126	-67%

As this gap widens, we can expect speculators to enter the Australian and New Zealand markets, and once again ramp up bike exports to the UK. This will be accentuated if UK classic prices spike upward, just as US bike stocks are diminishing. This scenario would force up Australasian prices in a knock-on effect. One mechanism for this is the international trading facilities provided by EBay. These allow today's classic owners to become familiar with global bike prices, and to buy and sell internationally. It requires no forecasting ability to predict an international equilibration in classic bike movements and prices over the next decide.

In Australia as in the UK, the Real Terms or inflation-adjusted series shows the yearly shifts in used bike prices well. On the other hand, the Current Price series appears to provide a somewhat better base for forecasting, as in the UK. Now may be a good time to invest or speculate in classic bike futures, if there were a such a market! For those readers wishing to familiarise themselves with the workings of the Bonnie Index, or to devise an Index for their own country, I append detailed notes in the next section on the methodology. (Readers with less interest in statistics may choose to skip this section.)

Methodology Used In The Bonnie Index Model

For readers wishing to study how the Bonnie Index is devised, here are the details. The basic structure of the index is the same as that used for Consumer Price (CPI) or Retail Price Indices (RPI) in most countries. A group of products and their prices are tracked and tallied for some years. The price changes for a product group are collected from year to year as percentage changes e.g. say a 4% increase for petrol prices in 2007 over 2006. Next, one year out of the ten or twenty years being covered is selected as an 'anchor' or base year for the price index. Each year's prices are compared with that base year, and expressed as a percentage of it. The list or series of these percentage changes or 'first differences' forms the price index for that product group. Product groups are collected and the average percentage change in prices becomes the national CPI or RPI.

Once any country's national CPI or RPI is laid down, all sorts of individual products, including classic motorcycles prices can be similarly listed and compared with the CPI or RPI gross changes. This enables us to better understand the changes in bike prices over the long term. We can also use the national CPI or RPI to 'strip out' of our classic bike prices, the effects of general price inflation. The resulting list of bike prices, is expressed in so-called 'real terms'. They're called 'real terms' because we've taken out the effects of general inflation and can now see just the real bike values changing year by year, i.e. the changes in prices that are specific to the classic bike scene. These real percentage changes are compared directly and the changes year on year give us additional insight into classic bike prices, and especially their value. It's in fact these 'real percentage changes' that are collected for the six Triumph product groups that go to form the complete 'Bonnie Index'.

Technical Notes on The Bonnie Index

The Bonnie Index is a composite of six indices in order to better show general trends in classic motorcycle prices.

Index Data Collection

I collected price information and divided it into three Triumph design periods based upon the *Classic Bike 1993-1994 Buyers Guide*. I checked the bases of the three periods against Roy Bacon's design and production records in his book *Triumph Twins and Triples*. The 1981 start date was to give a buffer period following the collapse of the BSA group so as to let prices settle down. The Triumph Twins were divided into two model groups, Bonnevilles and 650cc non-Bonnevilles i.e. the single carburettor Thunderbirds, Trophys and Tigers.

Index Sampling

The UK price data were collected from a near complete collection of 1981-2006 issues of *Classic Bike*, as well as from issues of *Classic MotorCycle*, *Classic Bike Guide* and *Old Bike Mart*. Bonhams auctions provided the auction data. Thus the raw data covered the major advertising channels in the UK with the exception of the local press. EBay was not used due to it's newness. Once EBay has amassed say five or even ten years of back data, and assuming the data are made available, it becomes the logical choice from which to project a Bonnie Index, based upon all marque sales. In Australia the *Trading Post* was the obvious choice, and fortnightly issues for the past twenty-five years were physically scanned for every relevant bike advertisement. The Australian Index then, has a greater weighting towards private sales, than the UK Index.

The survey aim was to collect thirty or more bike prices annually for each model group shown in Table 12.1 and within the six model manufacturing periods. In the UK this was over-achieved, with often fourty or more entries for each model group. As in the Survival Model sampling, care was taken to avoid consecutive issues of all publications, to minimise the risk of counting the same bike twice. Even so, some bike ads persisted for months. Recognising and rejecting them was simple due to the differences in ad style and content, and thanks to the diligence of the readers who spent days in libraries qualifying and harvesting the bike prices. In Australia, the narrow range of Triumphs imported prevented the target thirty bikes per class being obtained in some classes at some times. Twenty bikes then became the target, to preserve the integrity of the Index. This wasn't a problem with Trophys and Tigers, but was noticeable for early Bonnevilles. I assume this is a consequence of Australia at times being second in line for exports after America, and forced to take whatever was left over from the West Coast sales push. After 1970, that was no longer an issue and quota filling for all Bonneville classes was easily achieved.

Index Formation

The annual data were summed by model group. The avaerage (mean) of the groups were found and these means themselves were averaged by year. These six group means per year were averaged and the resulting grand mean entered into the Bonnie Index as the price for that year. While averages are a very useful part of any price index, the variation of prices around that average is also important. This 'variance' is usually quoted in statistical work. In a motorcycling book, it would perahps detract from the main points. However, for those readers interested, I did measure the coefficients of variation for all index series. These showed that prices typically lay within 20-40% of the average for the models' groups. This indicated the expected variation in price data for the Bonnie Index, i.e. for bikes which were roadworthy but differed in completeness, originality and restoration, and thus also in asking price. No dragons there.

Index Prices and Real Values

We can use the national CPI or RPI to strip out the effects of price inflation from the classic bike price index. The resulting list of prices, is expressed in so-called 'real terms'. They're called 'real terms' because they are free from the effects of inflation from other sorts of goods and services in the economy, and the 'real' price changes year to year generated within the classic bike scene (i.e. those generated by the actions of buyers and sellers) can now be seen. These percentage changes give useful insight into classic bike price shifts. It's in fact these percentage changes that go to form the 'Bonnie Index'. Care should be taken in recalling that the indices are based upon advertised asking prices. These are rarely the same as realised prices, given the fondness for haggling when buying a bike! Therefore I suggest before citing the Bonnie Index in order to bargain the price down on the next classic purchase, that 10% or more be deducted from the Index price to allow for this margin. If selling a bike, this advice perhaps need not apply!

A General Bike Index

As with the Classic Survival Models in chapter 11, The Bonnie Index was developed for different countries, beginning with the UK and Australia. To make the Index more widely applicable than just to Triumph Bonnevilles, I formed separate indices for different Triumph models and measured these over three Triumph design periods. The resulting six-group sampling method proved to be a useful way of breaking out the more and less expensive Triumph models, and so better represent the mainstream of classic British bikes.

Forecasting

Given the shape of the data series, I undertook linear regression forecasting out to 2010. I initially tested non-linear models as well, but the linear forms better fitted the data. Coefficients of Determination are shown on all forecast charts, and show the regression model explained 85-95% of annual price variations, so enabling confident trend-fitting. The cyclical patterns in the price data series are evident, and could be further analysed.

Analysis of the periods contained in the data series gave valuable insight into how, why and when key events happened in the industry, particularly over the 1987-1991 period. The Bonnie Index model shows that the roots of the long-term price growth in classic British motorcycles lie in the recovery period of the early 1980's - after the closure of the bulk of the UK industry, and the rapid penetration of the Japanese motorcycle industry. That recovery accelerated into a boom, bust, and then recovery again at much-elevated prices, and then the long-term incremental growth in used bike prices that takes us to the present. What will the Index for the next decade show?

An Index for Other Marques?

The Bonnie Index works because of the long-term international sales success of Turner's Triumph Bonneville. No other British marque achieved such sales success for so long, in so many countries. Thus it is doubtful if such an approach is possible for other marques. BSA and Norton twins would perhaps be the only other possibilities in the UK. In the USA the Harley-Davidson Sportster would be a possibility, given its sales success over the past fifty years.

As the Triumph twins occupy positions across a wide range of British bike prices, this enables some forecasts to be made for different models in different price niches. In Table 12.6 below are projections of bike values expected by 2010 compared with their existing value.

Table 12.6   British Bike Values in 2010

Value Category	Value 2006	Value 2010
High Value Models	£7,000	£9,000
Medium Value Models	£6,000	£7,000
Lower Value Models	£3,000	£4,000

13 *Improving Perfection*
Projects For Any Classic

"The bike held me like a hand, caught me and took me with it so that the engine seemed to be my engine, the wheels my wheels. It was singular, visceral, unlike any other motorcycle I had ever ridden...All that from a collection of nuts and bolts and metal and paint but more, more than that..." G. Paulsen 1997.

Here is a selection of proven projects for any classic motorcycle. The projects assume no great mechanical expertise. They have all been developed, tested and used on my own bikes. Our fathers experienced a fairly spartan approach to motorcycling compared with today's riders. Onboard bike systems for classics were often basic. When looking back on one key determinant of classic motorcycle manufacture, designs were judged against how many pounds of metal they used at so many pence a pound - riders shouldn't be too judgmental. It's no surprise that many assemblies and systems can be upgraded at little cost or effort, and without sacrificing much originality. The projects in this chapter are designed for riders wishing to improve safety, riding comfort, bike performance and rider feedback. These are satisfying projects for just about every make and model of classic or vintage motorcycle. They are designed and written for people like me, i.e. the sons of engineers who missed out on inheriting their fathers' genes for mechanical aptitude!

WARNING: *I do not warrant these special projects will work on every make and model of classic motorcycle. As with all the advice given in the preceding chapters, you should use your own judgment in taking up any ideas or recommendations made in this book. If in doubt, consult a classic mechanic or engineer.*

Project 1. Theft: Protecting Classic Motorcycles From Villains.

Our fathers seemed to assume their motorcycles were always left in such law-abiding places that security was unimportant. Perhaps it was back in the 1950s and '60s? I can't remember, but we're told that's normal if you had a good time in the 1960s. Classic bike numbers are unexpectedly small. I estimate only 200-300,000 classic British bikes remain intact around the world. With scarcity comes rising value and the interest of villains. It's wise to secure these old bikes, just as riders of modern bikes do.

Classic bikes, especially those with simple magneto ignitions, had no key or ignition switch. Keys and switches on coil ignition bikes were often rudimentary and a screwdriver would act as a substitute for a lost key in many cases! Anyone could jump on any bike and start it. So one method to secure the bike is to simply install a concealed toggle switch under the fuel tank and run the ignition circuit to earth. This prevents the bike from being started. On a bike the author sold, the switch was so effective it prevented the next owner from starting the bike for weeks - until he found the secret switch. With later classic bike alternator systems this is still possible, but more complex wiring circuits make it hard to give a single best installation. I suggest referring to the bike wiring diagram and with a club Agony Aunt, work out a simple switch method for the bike model. If that's not possible, then one simple approach is to put a second switch, in series (in line) with the ignition switch, requiring both to be switched on for the system to activate. That way, if the villains hot-wire one they may miss the second. For this approach, it's prudent to check the circuit diagram to ensure any additional switches and wiring are correctly rated for the current they'll carry. The wide use of transistor ignitions like Boyer etc, also calls for care in this area lest the transistor box and/or coil be damaged by unwise switch installation. Boyer Bransden provide suggested kill-switch connections on request. For example, with positive to earth systems as on BSA Unit Singles, a momentary kill switch may be installed across the transistor box-ignition switch lead (white) and the transistor box-coil (black) wire. Boyer Bransden warns that leaving this circuit closed will overheat the coil and so is best not used as an immobilizer.

Deterrence is important as classic bike theft can be opportunistic and amazingly quick. It takes about 30 seconds for two people with a bike to vanish into a van. Unfortunately the modern riders' choice of brightly-coloured disc brake locks is impossible for classic drum brakes. Wheel-locking is a practical alternative, and a variety of chain, wire and hoop design locks are worth considering. One of the most cost-effective designs is a tough U-bolt or hoop lock, with a hardened bar and keylock (Illus. 13.1) which lock up the front wheel across the forks. They are plastic-coated so as not to scratch the mudguard paint and do double duty by adding a visual deterrent. Hardware and department stores are often a cheaper buy for these than specialist bike outlets.

Cabling or bolting the front wheel to a lamp post for example, will also stop a thief lifting a locked bike onto a trailer. Some chainlocks can be heavy and unsuitable to carry on social riding. I suggest selecting a cycle or outboard-motor cable or hoop lock that can be mounted on the bike, perhaps on the crashbars or frame. This saves carrying it and ensures it's always to hand. The types with a five tumbler lock and hardened steel design are preferable. The key lives in your jacket pocket so there's no panic at the next rest stop.

Illus. 13.1 (top) A typical hoop-lock fitted to a classic bike.

Smaller bicycle versions of the cable locks are ideal for securing a helmet when leaving the bike at a rally, club run, or in the event of a breakdown. Harley-Davidson make an excellent (and for Harley surprisingly cheap) helmet lock for clamping to frame or crashbars. They require the helmet to have a D-ring or similar fitting, so may not cater to some types of chin strap. Royal Enfield make a similar part.

Many insurance companies, especially in Australia, already require valuable bikes such as Harley-Davidsons to be garaged securely and chained down (Illus. 13.2). It's not a bad idea for other appreciating classics. To protect a most expensive or treasured bike in this way, one of the thicker cable-locks an inch or more in diameter works well. Chains, no matter how heavy, can be more easily ground, sawn or cut through than hardened steel cables which do not provide a good cutting surface for tools. The cable can be secured to a floor mount held into the garage floor slab with masonry anchors. The kind usually suggested are the DIY type of expanding bolt anchor, commonly termed Dyna-Bolts or RawlBolts.

Illsu 13.2 (bottom) A high security cable and floor mount installation

A 'chemical anchor' is worth trying. These are readily available, and are typically a polyester resin cartridge to insert in the hole, like a small mining rock anchor. A threaded stud is then drilled down into the mix. This is fast setting and gives a very secure fixing. It has the advantage that it can't be worked loose by a determined villain whacking the steel eye bolt with a lump hammer to loosen the bolt anchors by cracking the concrete around them, then making off with the bike, eye bolt, anchor and cable! Also, when riders change house, it's easier to grind off the studs level with the slab, after salvaging the floor-mount.

Project 2. Mudflaps, Oilflaps And Chainflaps

Why are mudflaps now as rare on contemporary bikes as... crashbars? Once nearly every motorcycle had both. Modern riders can be excused as their fairings count as one giant mudflap. Yet front and rear mudflaps are just as rare on classic bikes. The answer seems clear enough for Australian classic riders - they don't ride in the rain. Club runs downunder are often called off if it threatens to rain. Classic riders in wetter climes such as NZ or the UK may be incredulous but it's true. Aussies live in such a dry continent they don't get much practice riding in showers, let alone English or Kiwi rain, slush, fog and snow. If it rains on a club ride here, expect the ride-leader to pull over for coffee, fuel, or comfort.

As Australia is such a dry continent and if riders don't ride in the wet, why then are mudflaps needed at all? Just consider how many screws, nails, bolts and other artifacts are scattered along the roads. How often does something kick up under car mudguards? It happened to me just last week in Sydney. In heavy traffic, I rode over a large piece of metal that kicked up, deflected off my mudflap, and loudly clanged off my left crashbar, which protected my knee. Imagine a steel roofing screw kicking up into an alloy engine, or into a knee joint? At 55 mph, it's a bit like firing a nail gun into the knee. So that's the front mudflap then?

Now, let's say it: British bikes leak oil. They did when new and after fifty years they still do (although see the section below on breathers that explains how to cure this failing). Along the road out of sight, the slipstream is stripping off the oil leaks, and aerosolling them back over the rider's visor behind. Just a moment - the engine's in front of that rear wheel - so that oil aerosol must be passing over the rear wheel, en route to the other riders' visors? We could reduce this and help rear tyre grip by fitting an 'oilflap' at the front of the rear mudguard. The forward guard mounting bolts are ideally positioned to fix such an oilflap. It's surprising how much oil it collects, oil which used to coat the rear tread. Interestingly, new Harley Sportsters include one as standard even though they don't leak much oil these days.

Of course a mudflap at the back of the rear guard is still a good idea. Not only does it intercept more of that oil aerosol (useful in club-run convoys), but also bits and pieces from the road, as well as the odd raindrop in Australia. While at it, ever noticed that with a freshly oiled chain a lot of it flings back over the rear rim and tyre? Trevor of BSACNSW has the remedy: cut a small oilflap to extend the chainguard. Once more it's surprising how much oil it keeps off the tyre, as shown in the photo below.

Making Flaps

Making functional flaps is straightforward. The best material is a heavy rubber, of $1/8$" to $3/16$" and preferably a nitrile compound for the rear flaps to resist oil attack. Fabric-reinforced rubber is better for larger flaps as it maintains the desired shape. It's best to start with a paper template, roughly cut to a wide, cake-slice shape, for the front guard. Depending on the wheel and guard shape, ground clearance, and aesthetics, riders can scissor away to achieve a pleasing shape. It's worth resting the bike on the side stand, to get a better idea of how it will look out on the road when its carrying some weight. A one bolt fixing is fine, say through a drilling at the rear base of the guard. To help the flap follow the contour of the guard, and to stop the build-up of stones and dirt, use either a large mudguard washer or better, a strip of scrap metal on the inside of the rubber. I also pre-spray the guard with an anti-rust compound such as WD40 or fish oil, to prevent any rust behind the flap. Next cut the rubber and punch the hole. A stainless or brass bolt saves unsightly rust.

For the rear guard flaps, a similar approach is taken for the rear mudflap and chainguard flap. The rear flaps provide excellent sites for 'period items such as red reflectors and also for club badges, license labels etc. Authentic cats-eyes reflectors are still available new, in bicycle shops.

The forward rear guard oil flap fixing is less common and access and tolerances are tighter. This flap is shaped out in a similar way, ensuring it clears the chain on the left, especially when the bike is under load. It also needs to fit inside or outside the swing-arm. I prefer a position behind the swing arm if possible, so there's less chafing. It is usually fixed through existing guard mounting holes. Here it effectively rubber-mounts the guard, thus helping reduce secondary vibration. If the bike is blowing taillights regularly, and/or facing cracks in the rear guard,

Illus. 13.3 Rear mudflap and chain oilflap fixed to a BSA B44.

then it's worth carrying on and inserting rubber washers to the other guard mounting bolts. As mentioned above, taillight function should be checked as the earth return via the frame may no longer work. In this case an earth wire back to the frame is easily added. The new rear flaps also provide flexible mountings for loose items in the vicinity e.g. the battery vent pipe, and any oiltank or engine breathers that may be waving around nearby. A small saddle bolted into the oil flap keeps them tidy, and stabilises the flap as well.

Project 3. Improving Engine Breathing And The Bunn Breather

The breathing of classic motorcycle engines is a neglected subject. Consider the piston as it rushes up and down the barrel. As the piston descends there is a rush of air into the crankcase. This air has to compress and would surely blow out through gaskets or seals if the crankcase were closed and must also drag power from the engine. To avoid this British makers vented their engines with flapper valves and timed breathers. They designed crankcases to operate with a small vacuum, to control oil leaks. Some classic breathers didn't work when new, and fewer work now. It's easy to improve on the original breathers to help these engines work efficiently and to cut oil leaks. There's not much on breathing in the literature on classics, even Phil Irving has little to say. The best coverage is by Peter Williams, in his June 2005 *Classic Bike* article. He summarises the causes, problems, and answers for classic bike owners, as follows. *"Because of the high pressure a little of the hot gas above the piston leaks past it, into the crankcase... at several thousand revs per minute it does not take very long for a very high pressure to build up in the crankcase"* He identifies five problems arising from this pressure: gaskets and oil seals will rupture; even slight crankcase pressure drives oil out through the porous alloy engine casings; the oil pump will start pumping blow-by gas, and wet-sumping can follow. The blow-by swirling around the crankcase causes drag and power loss. Blow-by gas is *"Nasty, noxious and corrosive stuff, and it is best to have as little as possible in the crankcase"*. He argues that as high crankcase pressure damages gaskets and seals, causing oil leaks, then reducing crankcase pressure should reduce the problems. His solutions include engine breather tubes, non-return valves in breathers to reduce crankcase air pressure, and an effective scavenge pump.

Blow-By Hazards.

Coincidentally, for years I had been researching ways of reducing oil leaks on BSA and Triumph engines, rocker boxes, gearboxes and chaincases. What I learned worried me more than the oil leaks that had set me on this path. While external oil leaks are a sign of breathing problems, what was going on inside the engine is more serious. I began to recognise that blow-by gas isn't some benign, inert stuff. It's actually approximately 70% unburnt and flammable fuel, plus water, sulphur compounds, nitrogen oxides and soot. Oxides of nitrogen are formed under conditions of high temperatures and high pressure which clearly exist in high compression, air-cooled classic engines where cylinder temperatures reach 160C-

230C, whilst water-cooled car engines operate at just half that temperature. The hydrocarbons, nitrogen and sulphur compounds which exist in blow-by gas form a corrosive mixture - a concentrated acid rain falling inside the engine. Letting this stuff stay in the crankcase is like spraying acid inside and watching it rust. Blow-by causes more problems than those identified by Peter Williams. These include oil dilution and contamination, sludge formation, loss of the protective oil film from engine components, corrosion of ferrous components and bearings, crankcase fire risk and deterioration in rubber components. As Phil Irving noted, just 5% unburnt fuel in the sump causes a 25-30% loss of oil viscosity. That's a major concern these days with multigrade and synthetic oils. So is the approximately 50mls of water that can collect in classic sumps if breathing is neglected. Irving reckoned 1% water in the oil or about 25mls was the maximum!

Classic Breather Faults

Later British breather designs actually worsened blow-by problems, by venting breathers into the oil tank, rockerbox, timing chest and chaincase. This spread the corrosive acid mix over the points, Boyer unit, alternator, clutch and primary chain, and denatured the oil supply, as well as pressurising oil tanks. This problem afflicts later Triumphs, Nortons, BSA's Royal Enfields and Harleys. No wonder classic motorcycles have high-maintenance engines. Where tolerances are high, and engines are worn crankcase blow-by happens each time we start up. Engine breathing solutions must account for blow-by, as well as for crankcase pressure. Classic breathers need to flush this dangerous blow-by material out of the engine.

Turning to car engine breathing for answers, I found that the car PCV (Positive Crankcase Ventilation) breathers are closed systems. Car engines are also different being multi-cylinder engines, where the big wet sump and barrels act as a surge chamber, soaking up pressure changes. While there's lots of air turbulence, there is less air displacement in and out of a car crankcase compared with classic singles and twins. Car PCV valves are both non-return valves and metering devices. PCV valves have a specific flow rate for a make and model of car engine. It would be just luck if one matched a classic bike engine. Also routing flammable crankcase gas into an Amal air intake would open a flame path to the cases, inviting a crankcase fire in the event of a backfire. Re-feeding blow-by into the air inlet dilutes the intake charge, interferes with intake air pressure, fouls the carburettor and injects oxides of nitrogen, which impact on engine temperature and pressure at higher revs. All this leads to wear and power loss from classic engines. Car breathing systems, along with modern bike systems, were designed more in response to 1960s USA EPA demand for pollution-control than to assist engine operation and are clearly unsuitable for classic British bike engines. Fortunately, classic bikes are not bound by the emission control requirements of regulatory authorities.

Non-Return Valves.

Classic riders have tried an amazing variety of non-return valves in their efforts to relieve excessive crankcase pressure and cure oil leaks. These include automobile PCV valves, other car diaphragm valves, ball-valves, reed valves, umbrella valves, photocopier and even plumbing valves. Generally none of these work satisfactorily in classic motorcycle engines, especially on big singles or bikes with similar displacement issues such as Vincents and Harley-Davidsons. One of the few non-return valves that do work well on classic engines is provided in the Carlel BlowBye Kit designed by the author.

The BlowBye Breather Kit

This Kit uses one-way valves descended from the old flapper valve designs, but with today's technology to provide better performance at lower cost. The BlowBye Kit valves use special floating seals with low inertia and operating pressure range. This Kit is installed on hundreds of classic motorcycles around the world. The BlowBye Kit is simply installed via crankcases, rockerboxes, gearboxes or chaincases - indeed any engine compartment where pressure leads to oil leaks. The BlowBye Kit cuts oil leaks common on British classic bikes by restoring the reduced crankcase air pressure, originally designed in by the manufacturer; but does not purge the system of blow-by gases.

Genesis Of The Bunn Breather

There are several factors in any classic engine that can be exploited to improve breathing. Dry sump engines have an effective scavenge pump that handles air as well as oil. Most classics are singles or 360 degree twins, with considerable air pressure fluctuations compared with car engines (except VW and other boxer engines). Classic bikes are not bound by pollution control requirements and so do not need to re-feed blow-by into the intake tract. Lastly, there's a path linking the top and bottom of the engine via pushrod cavities and oil channels. Air has weight and inertia, and that can be exploited. The challenge was to invent a classic bike breathing system to evacuate blow-by, cut power losses, avoid crankcase pressurisation and run the cases below atmospheric pressure, whilst preventing the intake of contaminated external air via open breathers.

Of all conceivable breather systems, the ultimate classic bike breather would be a purpose-designed crankcase evacuation system, where filtered fresh air would be pumped through the crankcase to flush out blow-by. Air pressure would be reduced under the piston during the downstroke, and increased during the upstroke to maximise power development and reduce drag. Crankcase air pressure would never exceed 760mmHg (normal air pressure), and average pressures would be kept below this figure to reduce oil leaks. There would be no passage of blow-by to other compartments. There would be no recycling of blow-by. These became the principles of the 'Bunn Breather Philosophy'. One night, I woke up with the breather concept in mind. After a good deal of physics and engineering work, I bench-tested a prototype - and it worked. I installed it on three bikes and satisfactorily road-tested them all. The next steps were patents and developing a commercial kit. The Bunn Breather Kit is now available internationally for every classic rider.

The Bunn Breather Kit

This Kit employs twin breathers to form a blow-by extraction system. An Exhaust breather is connected via the crankcase. A filtered Inlet breather is connected through the rockerboxes, or sometimes the other way around. It's worth recalling the rockerbox is the hottest compartment on a classic bike, as it lies over the exhaust valve, which reaches approximately 600C, and it's a sealed box. By opening this box and flushing in cool air, the rockerbox can be cooled. The cool filtered air is pumped down to the sump thereby assisting the oil return which can be a problem with classics. Over successive strokes, blow-by is evacuated by the fresh air. The exhaust and inlet breather airflows are balanced to ensure the crankcase never becomes pressurised. The features and benefits of the Bunn Breather are summarised below

Table 13.1 Features and Benefits of the Bunn Breather Kit

Features	Benefits
Reduces peak crankcase pressure	Cuts oil leaks, restores crankcase air to designers build state
Reduces air pressure range	Reduces 'push-pull' strain on gaskets and seals, and so reduces oil leaks
Purges/flushes blow-by	Cuts wear and corrosion, to extend major engine maintenance
Flushes filtered air through rockerboxes	Cools rockerboxes and improves oil return and engine operation
Creates a unidirectional airflow	Reduces entrained oil and oil foaming in sump. Reduces oil blowing out breathers
Introduces fresh, filtered air	Cuts the intake of dirty air via seals, pores and gaskets.
Reduces oil drag	Power and torque increase shown by dyno trials Improved acceleration on dyno trials
Vacuum distills and purges sump-water	Bikes with poor breathing get sump-water. The Bunn distills this off, cleaning the engine and conserving oil viscosity and lubricity.

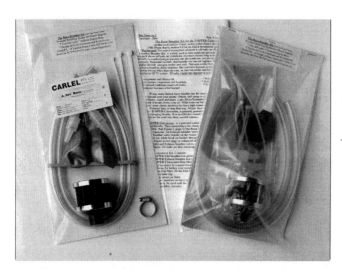

Illus 13.4 The Bunn Breather Kit, for all classic bikes.

NB There is a voucher at the back of this book which will give you 10% off the price of the Bunn Breather Kit designed by the author.

After I introduced the Bunn Breather, I stumbled over a prescient description of the 'perfect engine breather' by one Charles Falco on the internet. I was fascinated to see the Bunn Breather came surprisingly close to his ideal, The internet thread has closed and I've no idea who or where Falco is. I think he'd like the Bunn Breather.

> *"...an even 'more ideal' situation - albeit an unrealistic one to achieve - would be if it could somehow be arranged that atmos. pressure were in the cases during the upstroke, and... a ... vacuum were created under the piston only when it reached TDC. Otherwise the piston, which has a surface area of ~9 sq. in. in the case of a 500cc, would have to travel the entire length of its stroke against a force of ~130 pounds (9x14.7=132). Although, I hasten to add, since there would be no pumping losses for the air in the crankcase - since there wouldn't be any air in the crankcase - it would get all of this back on the downstroke. However, if our new 'more ideal' breather could somehow, without pumping losses, introduce atmos. pressure air into the crankcase for the upstroke, and suck it all out again for the downstroke, there would be another ~30 h.p. available at the crank of our 500cc engine at 5000 rpm. And, all without oil loss, since the crankcase never would be subjected to pressures above atmos. Although this magic breathing scheme would be impossible to achieve, it does illustrate the number of horsepower rattling around inside the engine unable to get out. Even if a timed breather achieves only 10% of this ideal of atmos. pressure for the trip toward TDC, and vacuum on the way back down, that's a very useful additional 3 h.p. available for free. Venting the crankcase straight to atmosphere is another way to keep the oil in, but it also keeps these extra h.p. in." Charles Falco 30/9/96*

Dyno tests show the Bunn Breather increases power by 3 bhp or some nine percent - it is releasing some of Falco's 30 horses from beneath our pistons. Riders report changes in exhaust note, engine braking and idle speed, consistent with reduced power losses

Project 4. Wet Sumping And Staying Dry Without Stripping The Engine

The oil tank is higher than the sump and over long periods gravity pushes oil down to the sump, assisted in part by gear driven oil pumps. The favourite fix of the manufacturers was to insert a ball and spring valve in the line. Unfortunately these valves are easily propped open by circulating oil debris and the spring loses its temper after years in hot oil. Not surprisingly, after a holiday we come home to find the oil tank empty and the dry sump wet.

If the bike can start, it feels as if it's a 'tight' engine. The oil won't compress as the piston goes down, and the pressure blows oil out the breather. Some riders claim to have blown their sump cover off, so it pays to fix it by pumping out the sump using the kickstarter, or walking the bike in gear. Another symptom is finding oil seals are leaking, and oil is holidaying on the floor. This needn't mean an engine strip-down. Once the oil level has dropped inside the engine, the leaks stop. If the oil level is down and the sump and floor are normal, it's worth checking the gearbox. The missing oil may have crept into the gearbox (in a unit conctruction engine) through the timing case, joints or shafts. It happened to me. There's headroom in the gearbox, which can hide a surprising amount of engine oil.

Illus. 13.5 Oil tap installed in the feed line.

The proper answer is to replace the ball and spring. However, to avoid the strip down there is an easier path. A mechanic friend reckons mechanics, like surgeons always leave a few scars. I avoid dissecting my geriatric engine, if there's a conservative option.

An Easy Wet Sump Solution

1. Head to a shop selling compressed air or plumbing equipment. Buy a ball valve. A chrome ball gives best sealing and service life. Next, two brass unions to screw into the valve - $^5/_{16}$ or $^3/_8$" ID unions will often fit.

2. Find a space to insert the valve into the oil feed line i.e. the line that carries oil from tank to engine. I prefer the valve to be in sight, so I remember to switch the oil 'on' before I start - the consequence of forgetting, is a seized engine. ***Be warned and follow Step 3***

3. An effective way of preventing rider forgetfulness is to fit an earthing switch with the oil tap. This ensures the bike won't start unless the tap is open, or it can be set to switch on a light on the handlebars or sound the horn etc. Details of such an electrical switch married to a valve are shown in Illus. 13.6.

4. Put a mark such as a red dot on the speedo glass, to remind you about the oil valve. Also, borrow a pilot's habit and make up a starting mnemonic to include the oil valve. Always turn on fuel and oil taps together.

NB. If riders ever forget the tap, the engine seizes. Do not attempt this modification unless you fit an earthing device as in step 3, a drawing for which is shown below. You have been warned!!

Wet sumping was a major problem for bike dealers in classic days. Below is an extract from a 1967 Triumph Service Note outlining their common causes of wet sumping.

In almost every case this (wet sumping) was caused by foreign material being lodged under the return oil pump check ball. The problem is also caused by:

1. *An air leak in the crankcase oil scavenge pipe.*
2. *An air leak in the oil pump to crankcase joint face.*
3. *A porous crankcase casting.*
4. *On B range models an air leak at the E4539 oil way plug.*
6. *Oil pump check ball cap leaking.*
7. *A partial blockage in the return oil line caused by misalignment of E3673 oil junction block gasket.*
8. *A stuck oil pressure release valve piston.*
9. *A blocked oil tank vent pipe.*
10. *Scavenge pipe too long - bottoming in sump plug or not pressed into the crankcase boss all the way, which can also cause an air leak.*
11. *Sump screen mesh too fine - original equipment on 1960 'C' range and 1968 on 'B' range.*

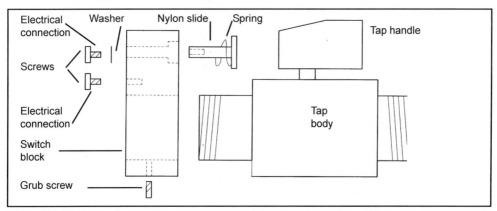

Illus 13.6 Drawing of a en electrical switch for the oil tap shown in Illus. 13.5

In the drawing of the switch for the oil tap (illus 13.6), the switch block should be made from brass or aluminium to avoid corrosion and can be made with a pillar drill. Drill a large hole to slide over one of the threaded ends of the tap. From a piece of plastic make a slide as illustrated, tapped to take a screw in order to secure the electrical connection and washer. The other connection mounts to the switch block. Wire the switch such that when the tap handle is turned to the off position current flows through the circuit and the ignition is grounded, or an alarm sounds. An alternative is to use a burglar alarm mini reed switch and a rare earth magnet attached to the tap handle.

Project 5. Electrical Shockers - Preventing Electrical Problems

Weather Proofing

Sometimes it's instructive to stand by a bike, and take a close look at it's electrical weatherproofing. An electrical system on a bike is like that in a car. Imagine the problems if a car's wiring hung outside it, exposed to sun and rain. Its staggering that the original designers of classic bikes, in a liquid environment like the UK, failed to waterproof electrical systems. Reading period magazines, electrical problems were commonplace. Most systems were by Lucas who earned the sobriquet 'Prince of Darkness'. In fairness the bike designers were perhaps as much to blame.

On my BSA B44, I peered under my saddle after a 1970 Australian road-tester complained the tank shape allowed rain to run down over the main ignition circuit. He was right. The answer is a rubber shield covering the tank-seat gap to deflect the rain. (What makes this design flaw doubly damning, is the ignition switch is badly placed: you give yourself a prostatic massage searching for it!) While the rubber sheet and hollow punches are out, it's worth looking under the speedo. If it's mounted at the usual angle any rain and insects are going to blow up inside the expensive Smiths speedo. A small piece of rubber deflects rain and bugs but allows air into the instrument to avoid condensation.

Earthing

Earthing is a common failing on classics. A plumbers view helps, seeing the bike as a household drainage system, with electricity (freshwater) flowing from the dynamo/alternator/battery, and the 'waste-water' draining back via the frame into the battery. If the drain blocks, everything stops. Earthing problems can be subtle. I once had a speedo light fail and expected the bulb to have unscrewed or blown from vibration. The bulb was in place and sound. The only unusual thing was the speedo cable nut, was a bit loose. The penny dropped. The speedo was rubber mounted and the cable was the earth path to the frame. When the nut loosened the circuit broke. I installed an earth wire from steering head to frame, and the problem never came back. This illustrates the tradeoff between earthing and vibration. Ideally, fittings are mounted in rubber to stop vibration blowing bulbs and loosening nuts. British makers accepted vibration, and relied on bolting fittings down hard to get current back to the battery via the frame. If the rear mudguard is mounted in rubber, helping a potential vibration fracture point, the tail light goes out as the circuit is broken. To fix this, as in chapter 9, an earthwire can be run from taillight to frame.

Fuses

The fuseholder, if there is one, is often next to the battery. They were originally metal holders, and it's worth preventing shorts by swapping this item for a plastic or rubber waterproof holder. Often there's only one fuse protecting the whole system. This wasn't a problem when systems were simple, but there are more accessories today. The fuse was often 35 amps, a size not popular these days. If a bike is blowing fuses, check what accessories are running. Classic alternators don't have spare capacity for airhorns, spotlights, handwarmers, and a radio.

Wiring Loom

If the wiring loom is old it's worth checking for corrosion, broken strands, dry joints and worn insulation and grommets. New technology wiring products that assist with fixing these faults include heatshrink tubing, loom tubes, spiral binding, self-amalgamating tape, thermotite heatshrink and liquid electrical tape. These save time and give a professional finish. All are available from the local electronics supplier e.g. Jaycar in Australasia. In the UK consider R.S.Components, Vehicle Wiring Products etc

New wiring looms are available and are cheap. They save many hours of repairs, and it's often cheaper to install a new one. It's worth labeling each wire for reference. Electronics suppliers have label printers that deliver tiny numbered self-adhesive labels. These show forever where each wire goes, regardless of which end is picked up. It's also useful to take an A3 size photocopy of the wiring diagram, and write the wire numbers on it, ticking off each wire as it's connected. It'll save head-scratching next time the wiring is looked at.

Project 6. Vibration - You Don't Have To Ride A Kango!

Compared to modern bikes, classic British bikes are noisy at both ends and suffer from intense vibration. Single cylinder bikes are often worse than twins. Even twins vibrate badly compared with say, a new Honda single. This reflects improvements in engine design and manufacture to reduce primary vibration, i.e. that generated by the engine internals. It also reflects success in dealing with secondary vibration due to the frame and other components vibrating in sympathy with the engine. This vibration science was well known in the early days and Phil Irving covered it in his seminal *Motorcycling Technicalities* in the 1930's. His conclusions apply to every classic bike today, and indeed every modern bike.

Vibration can be a problem for aging riders with arthritis in the wrists and hands. This can make riding painful and forces otherwise fit riders from the saddle.

Indeed, the last owner of one of my singles sold it for this reason. I've largely cured vibration in the same bike by using Irving's ideas and anti-vibration solutions from modern bikes.

While purists may object, I believe ideas borrowed from modern bike design can improve classic bikes. This improves rider safety and comfort without altering the classic appearance. A good place to start is a wrecker to examine how frame parts and assemblies are put together to reduce vibration. There are plenty of rubber mountings of the 'sleeve and grommet' type that can be recycled. Such fixings are usually out of sight on a classic.

Handlebars

Next note the narrow handlebars on many modern bikes. Irving found wider bars exaggerate secondary vibration. Many classic bikes coming in from the USA today wear 'cowhorn' bars, that intensify vibration. Narrow, Norton-type bars make a big difference. As a rule of thumb, bars wider than 29" vibrate more, but each bike is different. It's worth experimenting with bar mount positions for levers and switches. These have a surprising effect on vibration by altering the frequency at which the bar vibrates in sympathy with the engine. Also consider buying new rubber handlebar mounts. Similar rubber mounts for mirrors stop them vibrating. They're a standard fitting on modern bikes and classic riders also need a clear rear view. They also fit classic mirrors nicely.

Modern bikes often have bar weights on the handgrips. These are not just for show. They have a potent vibration-damping effect. The principle was known from the beginning. Irving recalls how Handley the early TT racer, filled his Velocette bars with lead to cure vibration. The modern bar weights don't fit easily with classic handgrips. A practical bar weight can be made using old masonry anchors. The common 'Loxin' sleeve anchors, or equivalent types in size $^3/_8$" are a nice fit inside the typical $^7/_8$" handlebar. They can be found at most Saturday markets for a few pence. They weigh about 80gms, which soaks up vibration on a 250cc single. On a 441cc single, the vibration frequencies differ, and 100gms is effective, achieved by adding extra nuts to a longer bolt through the anchor, (see photo). Twins may need up to 130gms. A 'weight vs

Illus 13.7 A 'Loxin' anchor, with heatshrink film, ready to install in the bar.

vibration' chart would be useful, but the technical data isn't about. Trial and error is best. The Loxin should be a snug fit inside the bar, if it's loose, tighten up the bolt and use a thread sealant. When the weight is right, screw up the anchor to hold it while road testing. Once happy with the weight, encase the Loxin in heat shrink tube, so it won't rattle or move, and tap it in. Lastly, replace the handgrip and the installation is invisible. As a bonus, the weights act as a steering damper - very useful if the bike doesn't have one.

Illus. 13.8 A spiral-wrapped racquet grip, over the throttle twist grip.

This is a very cost-effective solution to handlebar vibration. The BSA B44 is slated by road testers for extreme vibration. Thanks to handlebar weights I never suffer from wrist ache on mine, even after a days riding in the country. As a bonus, I no longer need to replace my taillight, speedo and parking bulbs after every long ride.

TIP: For further vibration proofing, buy two black tennis racket grips. Spiral-wrap these around the handgrips where they absorb impact stress. Increasing the handgrip diameter also gives improved control and comfort.

My father could have done with these back on Christmas Eve 1930 in another extract from his true story of...

The Desert Road

"The Desert Road at its best was a mass of loose pumice (volcanic ash), from side to side. That year it had been closed during the winter and hadn't really been fixed up when some heavy spring rains caused further road damage and closures. There was a grader working on the road near Waiouru, and as soon as I passed it, I ran into trouble. The road had dried out and cracked into brick-sized pieces which I rode through. There were large wheel ruts and many places where cars and even trucks had been bogged down. These places were often around washouts and the road was littered with old tyres, logs, sacks, posts, rocks and other debris as big as half the side of a big house left over by drivers filling up large potholes: anything to avoid getting stuck. The ride was wild and woolly and at one point I found myself with the engine roaring in low gear and the bike stationary. My footrests had grounded on either side of a big rut, and the back wheel was spinning up dust for yards behind me, as if I were on a speedway track!" A.C. Bunn, Christmas 1930.

Engine Mountings

Now let's move down from the bars and examine the engine mountings. As vibration starts in the engine and spreads through the frame, these connections mediate the worst handlebar and mudguard vibration. BSA state in their workshop manuals that an astonishing 90% of all vibration complaints to the factory were due to problems with engine mounts. The alloy engine mounts wear against the steel frame plates when bolts loosen over time. Don't be satisfied if the mount looks tight. Further in where it can't be seen, the engine may be flogging around on its bolt which has worn inside the alloy engine mount. Frames flex at high speeds and this opens up gaps invisible at rest. If very worn, the experts advise welded repair.

However ther is a simpler solution. Select a new bolt or better a stud (a bolt with threads at each end), that's a snug fit inside the frame plates. Sometimes switching to the nearest metric up-size will snugly fit the worn hole. Have the threaded section short enough, so the engine and frame plate rests on the unthreaded shank, rather than the thread. In other words find a bolt or stud with just enough thread, so it can be tightened. Washers and spacers achieve the right fit. This gives a tight engine mount, minimising vibration. When measuring for the new bolts, it's good to pack out any gaps between frame and engine. Such gaps may indicate a missing engine spacer. If the frame was ever fitted with more than one engine, or served two model series, it's a fair bet spacers were used. Sometimes the technical writers forgot to draw them into parts books so it is worth checking the number of spacers shown on the text page, adjacent to the exploded diagram. The missing spacer is sometimes counted, even if there's no drawing.

Another telltale for missing engine spacers is the bike leaning when on it's centre stand. This doesn't always mean a past accident, but can indicate a local warping due to over tightened engine mounts. Where spacers are absent and washers can't be inserted, consider E-clips. These pack the gap with the stud in situ. Purists may scoff, but they do work. There's more than one way to flense a feline! Even a small reduction in frame distortion can help correct annoying misalignment of the secondary chain and exhaust pipe fouling around the gearbox. Finally, it's worth using a Nyloc nut or locknut on the new mount bolt.

Rubber Washers

Smaller gains from secondary vibration can be achieved by using rubber washers wherever possible around the bike. They're easy to make from rubber sheet and hole punches. These can be used on speedo, speedo light, headlight, taillight, crashbars, seat, guards, tinware etc.

Project 7. Engine Feedback: Adding Sensors To Your Engine

When stepping out of the car and back onto a classic motorcycle, the absence of dials and gauges is obvious. Where are the fuel, temperature, oil pressure and charging lights to scan whilst driving? All there is, is a speedo (often unreliable) and a highbeam light - pretty meagre stuff. Riders wouldn't drive a car like this: why tolerate it on the bike, where the first symptom of an engine problem can be a seized engine? What would riders give to avoid this? Help is now available. Riders can choose from a range of low-cost, digital instruments, and install them in five minutes, without tools. Call by the nearest electronics store. In Australia and New Zealand, Jaycar is the choice for classic motorcyclists, in the UK Vehicle Wiring Products do a fair range of instruments for 12v negative earth systems. A first step is to fit a temperature gauge. This will warn if the engine is running hot and heading for a seizure, just as the car temperature gauge does. I used to sell a Kit for this, but for about £8 an Atech digital sensor is a good choice. This can be mounted discreetly on a fork top nut, beside the speedo then run it's sensor wire back to the engine casings, oil lines, oil filter or oil tank. Taping it to the oil filter, with some foam rubber, ensures the oil temperature is measured as it leaves the engine.

In this position the gauge monitors several variables. Firstly, 'engine temperature' is monitored via oil temperature. It's surprising how engine temperature varies on a ride, and not just as speed changes. I'd never realised how sensitive air-cooled engines are to changes in ambient temperature, until fitting the gauge. Variations of up to 30% are common when riding through different patches of air. Riders quickly learn an engine's typical temperatures and automatically relate these to conditions.

Secondly, 'abnormal changes' in engine temperature are signaled. For example, if the gauge starts trending up outside it's normal range, say after adjusting the carburettor settings, a lean mixture might be considered and action taken before the bike overheats and seizes, or holes a piston.

Thirdly, and most importantly the gauge tells riders the oil pump is working within 60 seconds of startup. If the oil pump has failed, then riders have time to switch off before the engine seizes. As cold oil enters the filter from the sump, the gauge first drops for a short time, (as the oil displaces warmer ambient air). Next, the gauge reverses as warm oil starts flowing into the filter, and readings climb progressively until reaching normal operating temperature. For riders who worry about that 30-40 year old oil pump, this is a relief. Riders never have to take the oil tank cap off again to check the pump is pumping.

The sensor also switches to show air temperature - useful if you were wondering why it's so hot inside the helmet. These sensors can also switch to show the time, reminding riders to stop for a safety break. They are removable, and rated to 70^{0}C, with $^+/_1$^{0}C accuracy. There's an expanding range of such sensors and they now include models which are illuminated, show and store minimax temperatures, measure humidity, monitor battery voltage, allow timing and lap counting, and even give an ice warning. If interested in such digital devices, drop by a bicycle store and pick up a new digital speedo. They work well on classic motorcycles using a wheel rotation sensor, and are a lot cheaper than repairing an old analogue speedo: they are also very useful for off-road bikes. The gauges are so small, they can be concealed for example down by the forks, behind the headlight etc and they are removable so riders can still win that concours trophy, pop back the gauge, and drive home with confidence. So why ride blindly any more?

Illus 13.9 Oil temperature gauge installed on a BSA.

14 *Some Thoughts For The Road*

"Once you have ridden, you can't not ride..." Darrell Eastlake, Australian Sports Broadcaster

It's proving quite a ride through the twenty-first century on a classic motorcycle. An author is also a reader and has to wait till the book is finished so he can read it. Like the curate's egg, I found this one good in parts. I guess if there are enough 'good parts' to meet readers' various expectations, a book earns its place on riders' bookshelves. Helping this book stand up is the original research, especially the latter three chapters. Chapters eleven and twelve are wholly original, and should uniquely assist any classic rider to see the pursuit in new ways.

Classic bike ownership rarely stops at one. If a rider has one classic bike and is completely fulfilled with it, that's great. We can after all, only ride one at a time. Somewhere however, an opportunity pops up to buy a second classic bike, even if not looked for. Many riders end up with more than one - it is a kind of life cycle. A rider stumbles over that first classic: he spends one or two years restoring it, and maybe another one or two years riding it. Perhaps he becomes progressively bored, as there's nothing more to do to it. He starts tinkering, adding redundant accessories, upgrading sound but worn parts. Finally he sees that garage-time with the bike is nearly as good a feeling as road-time. At that point, the preference shifts in favour of a second bike. For some riders the process extends till their family says enough, or they run out of space. It's like collecting anything - stamps, books, or antiques. Collectors structure their collecting and focus it into a theme or a period perhaps around a country of origin, a marque or an engine design. Marque singles was my fate, after coming across an older rider's collection of bikes that complemented my first bike. It took nine months of negotiations to settle. Riders often make reluctant vendors.

With multiple classics, riders can cosset the first bike and prolong its restored build state, perhaps indefinitely. Some riders only take the best bike out on trailers to rallies. There's a logic to this, two bikes can be ridden twice the miles for a given maintenance input. There's always one roadworthy bike. Parts can be swapped for comparative tests. There's twice the chance of finding bargains at swapmeets.... it just gets better!

Index

Readers will find a useful 'search engine' in the comprehensive *Contents List* at the start of the book. The *Contents List* is unusually detailed in this book and designed to assist readers zero in on the required topic.

AA and international membership, 54-55
Accident risk, 66,94-100,106
Advertising channels, 10,255
AJS, 8,84,88,205-215
Anderson, Hugh, v-viii
Ariel, 8,12,26,62,88,100,190,205-215
Asia, 1,75,126,153
Assessing a bike, 34-42,35
Auctions, 10,27-30,70-771,205,218,
223-7,239-242
Australia, 8,46,80-85,208-210,248-254
Autojumbles/Swap-meets, 31-2,71-73,79,142,196
Availability, 7-8
BABs and COBBERs, 4,54,59,100,104,112,173
Back braces and prostheses, 133-134
Bacon, Roy, 20,41,236,
Basket cases, 11,31,78,183,207,216,
218-221,227,232
Big-Mac index, 236
Blow-by, 154,168,263-6
BlowBye Kit, 265
BMW, 205-215
Bonding with bikes, 57-69
Bonnie Index, 236-257
    UK Bonnie Index, 237-248
    Australia Bonnie Index, 248-254
    Modelling, 255-257
Boots, 13,129,132-133
Brakes and braking, 17,37,102,52,120,187,259
Breakdowns, 7,54,59,139,170-173,180-182
BSA, 2,5,8-9,17,26,77,83,88-93,
146-147,153, 164,177,205-215,217,
222,232-235,264,270,274
Bunn Breather, 263-266
Bunn Breather Kit Voucher, 280
Cables, 37-38,144,158-159,165-166,
170,173
Carburettors, 75,77,142,154-161,264,276,
    Concentric, 158
    Monobloc, 158
    Tuning, 155,159-161
Case Study, Triumph, 39,40-42
Chain-flaps, 261
Change blindness, 115-116

Classic period, v, 7,13,16,33,61,220
Classic retail outlets, 24,80-91
Clothing, 2,9,26,27,44,106,119,120-133,
Clubs, 2,15,20,27,32,43,45-47,54,93,
180-181,186-190
Clutch, 36,42,52,76,94,97,141,144,
148-151,165-166,177-178
Completeness, 19,154-159,172-173
Concentric, *see Carburettors*
Concours, 28,59-61,68,94,111,
183-185,276,
Conservation, bike, 61,70,94,99,137,153,163,
213-220
Conspicuity, 104-106,115
Cornering lines, 65,102-103
Costs and budgeting, 8,10,48,50,54,71,79,99
Cramps, 101,113,133-134
Crankcase breathing, 263-267
Crashbars, 106,113,260,261,275
Csikszentmihalyi, Mihaly, 60-68
Defining a classic bike, 33
Dehydration, 113-114,123,134
Demographics, 1-2,30,93-99,186,218,220,229
Distributors, 7,12,24,59,74,78-80,137,
153-154,158,178,248
Documentation, 34,55-56
Dyno tests, 266-267
Earthing, 171,269-270
EBay, 10,20,29-30,70,255
Electrical system, 20,71,128,155,171,270-271
Engine feedback, 275-276
Engine mounts, 164,274-275
Engine sounds, 174-178
Ergonomics, 12-14,113-115
Escapism, 60,68
Etiquette, swap-meet, 72-74
Falco, Charles, 267
Feedback, 271,275
FIFO, 106,201
Filters (fuel, air & oil), 161-163,169
First aid, 110,114,116-119
'Five-Four-Five' breathing, 67
Flow, 57-70
Forecasts, price, 3,122,216,218,222,226,231-236,
243-247,251,253

Fossicking, 30-31,218
Fuel, 1,4,22,34,37,47,146,161-164,
169-172,177,182,201,263-264,
269,275
Fuel additives, 161
Fuel system, 172
Fuses, 144,271
Garage, 7,12,19,34,138-139,169,184,260
Gloves, 128
Greases, 167
Growth, market, 1,205-235,236-257
HALE, 221
Hand signals, 101,103,105,128
Handlebar weights, 272-273
Harley-Davidson, 4-5,12-15,83,85,89,93,
101-102,204,208-209,259-260,
Sportster, 5,20,57,61,198,202,205-215,257,261,
Helmets, 2,9,44,106-111,118,130-132,260,
Hinckley Triumph, 6
HOG, 20,54,98,201
Holmes and Smith, 3,7
Honda, 8-9,14,85-86,178,205-215,271
Image and style, 15
Injuries, 106-107,116-118,130-133
Insurance, 1,2,9,45-46,53-55,98,134,230,260
International licensing, 55
International riding, 202-204
Irving, Phil, 5,263-264,271-272
Jackets, 9,27,121,127-128
Kick starting, 21-22,114,132
KUFO, 106
Lambretta, 4
Leather, types, 23,135-136
Leathers, 126
Leggings and chaps, 121
Licensing, rider and bike, 1-2,16,49-55,215-216,
226-227,230
Long distance riding, 126,199-201
Magazines, 7,10,26-27,125,137,188,205,
223-227,248
Maintenance, 38,58-61,71,118,137,145-170
Cables, 165-166
Chains, 152-154
Clutch, 148-151
Oils & greases, 167-170
Tappets, 145-147
Tyres, 167,173
Wheel alignment, 151-152
Marques, 7,8,33,
Marwick, Arthur, 2
Matchless, 8,84,88,205-215
Mechanical breakdowns, 170-174
Membership, club, 32,54-55

Methodology, 225,255
Mnemonics, 21-22,43,53,112,116,169,269
Monobloc, *see carburettors*
Mud-flaps, 261
Museums, 7,213
Near misses, 111-113
Negotiation, 38,43-44,277
Newspapers, 25-26
Noise, exhaust, 49,105-106,164
Non-return valves, 265
North America, 1,5,90-91
Norton, 8,16,20,33,151,155,163,198,200,
205-215,225,257,264,272
NOS parts, 1,74-75,81
Nuts and bolts, 140,164
Offroad riding, 90,107,186-190
Oils, 167
Oil-flaps, 261
Originality, 18-19,38,59
Overpants, 122
Parts, 2,74-81
Pop-culture, 2
Prostheses, 133
Projections, validation, 230-232
Projects, 258-277
Theft, 259-261
Mud, chain and oil flaps, 261-262
Crankcase breathing, 263-267
Wet sumping, 268-270
Electrical improvements, 270-271
Vibration, 272-274
Engine feedback, 275-276
Purchasing, 7,24-44,58,70
Racing, 33,49,62,65,102,111,121,124,
126,132,190-199,212
Rainwear, 132
Rallies, 15,122,181-182
Reasons for buying, 58-61
Reasons for riding, 60-61,67-69
Recency, 8
Recognition, 19
Registration,
UK, 45
USA, 46
Australia, 46
NZ, 47
Reliability, 20
Resources, 70-91
Restoration, 9,11,25,61
Rider profile, 93
Rides,types of, 15
Road and traffic conditions, 16,103
Road craft, 116

Royal Enfield, 2,4-6,61,83,87,207,218,260,264
Salvage, 20,53-54,172,201
Scooters, 4,210,228,231-232
Scrappage, 31,213-218,221-223,232
Seat heights, 13-14
Security, 19,37
Selye, Hans, 65-67
Sensors, 275-276
Services clothing, 121
Shipping bikes overseas, 29,55-56,204
Shopping channels, 25,31,78,80,124-125,
127,128,262
Shops, 24,81
Signalling, 103-105
Solo riding, 181-182
Sportster, *see Harley-Davidson*
Spouses, 3,11,60,73
Starting, 15,20-23,53,269
Stress, 65-69,99
Style, 15
Suspension, 17,35,47
Survival, classic bike, 205-219
    UK, 205-208
    Australia, 208-210
    New Zealand, 210-215
    World, 215-219
    Modelling, 223-233
    Exports to USA, 233-235
Survival, rider, 104-106,110,130
Swap-Meets, *see Autojumbles*
Tappets, 47,145-148,174
Tasks, bike, 145
Test, passing riding licence, 50-52,
Theft, 259-261
Throttle friction, 101
Time travel, 16,204

Tips for riders, 34,51-53,104-106,108,139,148
Toolkit, 38,138-144
Top dead centre, 21
Training, 49-53,94-98,100-104,116,118
Tricks of the trade, 78-80
Triumph, 2,6,8,11,16,25,40,83,88,148,
152,155,177,205-215,231,
234,236-257,263,269
Triumph, case study, *see Case study*
Troubleshooting, 71,143-144,160,170-174
Trousers, 129
Trout fishing, 116
Tuning, Carburettor, *see Carburettor*
Tyres, 167,173
Ulysses Club, 7,32,93,98,181,201,221,
USA, exports to, 233-234
Used parts, 74
Valves and valve noise, 36,146-148
Valves, breather, 263-264
Valve lifter, 21
Valve seat recession, 161
Velocette, 7,8,83,169,191,205-215,229,
240,242,272
Vespa, 4
Vibration, 176-178,270,271-275
Vincent, 7-8,14,83,85,89,91,180,190,
205-215,221,228-229,232,
240,242,265
Vintage period, 33
VMX, 186-189
Waders, 120,129
Weights and bike selection, 12
Wet sumping, 169,268-270
Wheels, 17,23,35,42,151-2
Zeitgeist, 2